Between the
CRACKS OF HISTORY

Essays on Teaching and Illustrating Folklore

Publications of the Texas Folklore Society LV

Between the
CRACKS OF HISTORY

Essays on Teaching and Illustrating Folklore

Publications of the Texas Folklore Society LV

Francis Edward Abernethy, Editor
Carolyn Fiedler Satterwhite, Assistant Editor
Illustrations by Cynthia Fisher

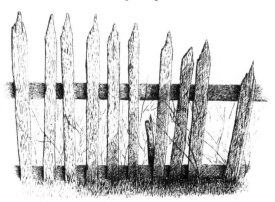

University of North Texas Press
Denton, Texas

5 4 3 2 1

Requests for permission to reproduce materials
from this book should be directed to

Permissions

University of North Texas Press

PO Box 311336

Denton, TX 76203-1336

The paper used in this book meets the minimum requirements
of the American National Standard for Permanence of Paper for
Printed Library Materials, z39.48.1984. Binding materials have
been chosen for durability.

Library of Congress Cataloging-in-Publication Data

Between the cracks of history : essays on teaching and illustrating
folklore / edited by Francis Edward Abernethy.
    p.   cm. — (Publications of the Texas Folklore Society ; 55)
        Includes bibliographical references and index.
            ISBN 1-57441-036-9 (alk. paper)
    1. Folklore—Texas. 2. Folklore. 3. Folklore—Study and teaching.
        I. Abernethy, Francis Edward. II. Series.
            GR110.T5B47 1997
        398'.09764—dc21   97-17598
                                    CIP

Cover and interior design by Accent Design and Communications

Contents

Between the Cracks of History

I wonder if folklorists follow historians like gleaners—or cotton strippers in west Texas—and collect the leavings from academic historians, all the tales and songs and traditions that the historians allow to fall between the cracks? Or that historians sweep under the rug? Or drop? Or choose to ignore?

Historians research, document, and file the facts of a happening. They are supposed to get the details right, but sometimes in following the letter of the investigation, they lose the spirit—which falls between the cracks of history where it is pounced on by the ever-lurking folklorist, who scarfs it up like a hog on a mushmelon.

Maybe its not just historians who let pouncable things fall between the cracks. Maybe folklorists follow doctors around for their droppin's and leavin's, and find out that urine relieves bull nettle burn and that tobacco eases the pain of a yellow-jacket sting and that chicken soup is as good for the flu as anything doctors prescribe. And maybe folklorists follow wildlife biologists and conclude that if they hear an owl hoot in the daytime, that owl is watching a buck walking. I hold firmly to that latter belief, by the way, and when the owl hoots I can see vividly in my mind's eye a big, old mossy-horned buck easing his way through a pine thicket.

On the other hand—

On the other hand, maybe historians followed folklorists at some dimly remembered past time to see what fell between the cracks as the folk passed along myths, legends, and folktales. Tell me, what history did not begin with the leavin's of folklore, the oral traditions that went back to the myths of the creation of the world and Eden, the legends of the great kings and warriors of Camelot, and the folktales that grew out of all these hand-me-downs and became the *Iliad*?

What science did *not* begin as folklore? Modern scientific meteorology was preceded by Zeuses and Thors and Jehovahs who rumbled their presence with bolts of lightning and volcanic eruptions and with floods that drowned the world. The folk were using levers, screws, and inclined planes as part of their inherited artifacts before physics became an acknowledged science. A student could easily learn his valence tables when chemistry was in one of its folkloric stages, when all matter was made of various combinations of earth, air, fire, and water. In geology, that science and the whole universe was simpler when folks thought that the earth was flat and was twice as long as it was wide and that it was surrounded by the great river Ocean and that it was created in 4004 B.C. —and that it was created for man who was unique and it sole inheritor. And the manipulation of holy numbers by the Mayans and Aztecs to understand the peregrinations of the sun and the moon and the seasons made mathematics a religious exercise long before it was an academic discipline.

Singing and dancing, making music on drums and with flutes, painting on walls and sculpting gods and gargoyles: all these things began with the folk before the academic fine arts were ever envisioned.

So, folklore might be that which falls between the cracks of history (or biology or sociology, *ad infinitum*) but students and teachers must not forget that long before these leavin's fell through the cracks from the anointed hands of academia, folklore was the beginning, the Alpha, and most probably will be the Omega.

All of which is a garrulous prelude to an introduction for this volume's contents. *Between the Cracks of History* is partially pedagogical. The introductory essays, which were spawned at the Fort Worth meeting in 1995, are concerned with defining, explaining, and teaching folklore. Some of us have been immersed in folklore for so long that we assume that everybody defines and understands folklore the same way as we do. That is not necessarily the case, however, and it behooves the Society to pause periodically to examine basic premises.

The essays which follow illustrate the definitions and, with luck and latitude, illustrate the title of the book, *Between the Cracks of History*. Gideon Lincecum did not completely fall through the cracks of history, but when one encounters his name in Texas history books, he will not find much about Gideon as a fiddler. Chapters on west Texas history will discuss rodeos as one part of that area's social fabric but will probably neglect the machinations of the Bluebird Mare. East Texas histories will spend a long chapter on the East Texas oil boom of the 1930s but will leave out Mattie's Palm Isle and the other oilfield honkytonks of that exciting time. Burial rituals, oil camp customs, and railroad yarns—all are parts of the history of their times; but when historians tell us about handgun violence or an oilfield opening up or a train wreck, some of the personal remembrances, the folklore, falls between the cracks. Some of these leavin's lie around for years before a wandering folklorist picks them up, scratches through the grime on the surface and realizes he has found gold.

I tell my students, and anybody who will listen, that if they wish to study the world and mankind in all of their dimensions of time and space, then folklore is the teacher to whom they must turn.

For the sixteenth time, I thank this volume's contributors for the time and energy they spent writing and correcting and doing all the things one has to do to get a manuscript ready for publication. The Society has a strong and loyal and involved membership, if you haven't noticed.

The Texas Folklore Society thanks English Department head Patricia Russell and Liberal Arts Dean James Speer of Stephen F. Austin State University for their support. The Texas Folklore Society would not be here on the campus without the generous assistance provided by President Dan Angel and his administration. The Society has been on the SFA campus for twenty-six years, and several presidents have come and gone during that time. But all of this university's presidents have supported the Society generously and personally, and we hope that we have responded in kind. The Society cannot exist without the full commitment of its university host, which provides space, time, office expenses, and intangibles too numerous to mention. We appreciate the hospitality of our host.

And this editor and this Society thank Assistant Editor Carolyn Satterwhite for her work on this fifty-fifth volume of the Publications of the Texas Folklore Society—and for all her work as the Society's Secretary and Treasurer.

Francis Edward Abernethy
Stephen F. Austin State University
Nacogdoches, Texas
February 17, 1997

Essays on Teaching Folklore

Classroom Definitions of Folklore

F. E. Abernethy

Myself when young did eagerly frequent
Doctor and saint, and heard great argument
About it and about: but evermore
Came out by the same door where in I went.

Rubaiyat XXVII of Omar Khayyam

[The following panel of folklorists came together at the seventy-ninth annual meeting of the Texas Folklore Society. We met at the Green Oaks Inn in Fort Worth, and we discussed Texas folklore, both generally and specifically. Your Secretary-Editor was the chairman of a pedagogical section on defining folklore, and the following papers were a result of that session.]

This program on folklore pedagogy comes to you by popular demand. Members really have asked what folklore is, and it *is* difficult to define. We did this defining exercise at a TFS meeting twenty-five years ago, and after all the academic verbiage that generation of pedants flung about, Martha Emmons rose up in her tutorial majesty. She disgustedly looked at the members and the complicated mountain we had made out of a simple mole hill and said, "Folklore is what the word *says* it is! *Folk* is the people and *lore* is the learning. It is the learning of the people." And that is pretty close. The "folk" is the common denominator among a particular social group, and the "lore" is the traditional learning which the group passes along within itself. As a consequence, I went back to my class notes and boiled my definition down to "Folklore is the traditional knowledge of a culture." And I still use that definition.

Of course, when you make a university degree program out of folklore (as they did at Penn, Indiana, and UT), you cannot define it as simply as Martha did. Or if you are simply teaching a course—or talking to a reporter—you need something more impressive.

When I began teaching folklore around 1960 there were no texts, to speak of. Russell & Reaver would send you their mimeographed text and Kenneth and Mary Clarke had a paperback called *Introducing Folklore*, but both were incomplete and unsatisfactory. It was not until 1968 when Jan Brunvand published his *The Study of American Folklore* that English-teachers-turned-folklorists had a college-level folklore textbook with definitions and illustrations to help them in their exploration of that academic wilderness.

I have since written my own folklore textbook, and I have been working over Brunvand's definition for twenty years, and what I tell my students when I am defining folklore is essentially my simplified definition ("Folklore is the traditional knowledge of a culture") and Jan Brunvand's definition through characteristics. And I use John Minton's mnemonic guide to remember the characteristics: "The O̲ld T̲estament v̲erifies A̲dam's f̲all." That is, folklore is o̲ral—t̲raditional—v̲ariational—a̲nonymous—and f̲ormularized.

Characteristics of Folklore
(after Jan Brunvand's *The Study of American Folklore*, I)

Folklore is the traditional knowledge of a culture.

1. *Oral*: Folklore is informal; that is, it is transmitted customarily by word of mouth, by demonstration, or by a combination of both. Tales and songs are passed on by word of mouth. Cooking or quilting instructions are frequently passed along by both oral transmission and demonstration. Dance steps are usually taught by demonstration.

2. *Traditional*: Folklore is passed on in a fairly set form from one generation or group to another. Wedding customs are traditional. The virgin bride wears white and something borrowed and something blue; rice is thrown to insure fertility; and the man carries the woman across his threshold. Traditional American celebrations are the Fourth of July, Halloween, Easter. Folk groups— kickers, hippies, yuppies—adhere to similar dress styles agreed on and passed on among themselves.

3. *Variable*: Folklore is continually being changed by those who use it, and the same story, song, custom, or belief can therefore be found in many forms and variants. The eighteenth century (or earlier) Anglo-Irish ballad that came to be called "The Unfortunate Rake" was the story of a young soldier dying of a venereal disease. A hundred years later cowboys in Texas were singing about a dying cowboy on "The Streets of Laredo." "The Ocean Burial" evolved through many singings and many miles of travel

to "Bury Me Not on the Lone Prairie." And Saint Nicholas becomes Santa Claus.

4. *Anonymous*: Because folklore is passed on by folk who are continually remaking it to suit their own personal moods and needs, authorship is lost in transmission. The name of the scop who first sang the tale of Beowulf is lost to history, as are the names of the author of "Greensleeves" and the creator of the froe.

5. *Formularized*: Folklore is one expression of man's genetic need for order. Therefore, much of it is in traditional formulas and set patterns. The pattern of threes is widespread and we read about "The Three Bears," "The Three Little Pigs," and the Indian Trinity of Brahma, Vishnu, and Shiva. Seven is also a traditional formulaic number as illustrated by the Seven Sisters, the days of the week, and Snow White's dwarfs. Other recurring patterns are the medieval ballad stanza, to which "Barbara Allen" is sung; the youngest-best theme found in "Cinderella;" the once-upon-a-time story beginning; and similar folk clichés and stereotypes.

That is the traditional definition and characteristics that I require that my students know by heart. When I get serious and really let the hammer down (during the second week of class), I define and present folklore in what I consider to be the universal approach to understanding folklore and to understanding life generally, the ethological approach, the study of animal behavior. I define folklore as "the ultimate cultural response to man's genetic, instinctual drives of sociality, dominance, territoriality, and sexuality."

SOCIALITY is that drive which causes animals to cling together in groups for protection and propagation. For man, this herding instinct has multiplied his teeth and nails and has allowed a poorly armored and punily armed animal to survive. Most folklore has as its purpose the solidifying of the group in response to the sociality drive. In an instinctive reaction against the unfamiliar, folklore establishes familiar patterns of action—religion and ritual, customs and traditions—that bond a group together. Folk poetry, music, and dancing strengthen the social bond as the people chant, sing, and dance in a psychological response to a need for togetherness. A people dress and talk alike, they all know the same songs and stories, and they all worship the same god in the same way, and the social bond is glued a little stronger, and the group's chances of survival are a little greater.

DOMINANCE is the drive to establish a pecking order in a social group, an order that is necessary for survival. It assures the group of protection and leadership and of the continuation of the best of its genes, because the dominant males attract the dominant females. In folklore, dominance legends are the "test" stories of the struggles of such heroes as Hercules, Jason, Arthur, Horatio Alger in their climb toward the room at the top. "Cinderella" stories are compensations ("There'll be pie in the sky by and by."), wishful thoughts that the dominance pattern can be upset or broken with the help of fairy godmothers and other supernatural agents. Robin Hoods and Jesse James types rob from the rich and give to the poor in a satisfying (to the poor) upset of the dominance pattern. Religious pantheons and other Great Chains of Being, however, are the ultimate folkloric establishments of the order of dominance.

TERRITORIALITY comes in two sizes. Individual territoriality is that hypothetical space bubble which surrounds an animal and which is a sense of distance, both literal and figurative, that the animal wants to keep between itself and others. Territoriality more generally defined is that sense of space which an animal has which gives him a feeling of belonging to a particular piece of land that will support him and his group. A dominant male will mark his territory by signs, scents, and sounds. Folklore that is used to protect the individual in his personal space consists of customs and manners which evolve to insure the maintenance of a proper *figurative* distance among people. The never ending struggle to gain and defend territory generally is best seen in games: king of the mountain, capture the flag, musical chairs, monopoly and chess, football and hockey. Most games—chess, bridge, and dominos included—are sublimations of the territorial and dominance drives and are battles for space and hierarchy.

SEXUALITY is the reproductive drive. In the animal world the males' energies are directed toward acquiring status and territory, thus maintaining a stable social order. The energies of the female are directed toward the continuation of the species by obtaining a male of the highest status and best possible territory. Dominant females get the dominant males, and the species is guaranteed the continuation of the best of genes. In folklore the world-wide and traditional acceptance of the double standard is probably not so much a result of man's culture and conditioning as it is the result of his vague knowledge that the female actually *is* responsible for all sexual consummation, excluding rape. This knowledge is an aggravation to the male ego, for which he compensates by his fictions and folksongs in which the male, always in charge, sweeps the female off her feet—and in his mythologies, in which the female is cast as the corrupter of the world. Eve and Lilith, Pandora and Barbara Allen are females in folklore whose stories indicate that the male is well aware of the sexual power of the female and is embarrassed by it.

My conclusion, after defining folklore from the ethological approach, is that behind every move that man makes is a genetically wired-in behavior pattern which man holds in common with his animal kinsmen. This means that man has little control over *what* he does, only in *how* he does it. The "how" is his folk-lore, his culture, his way of life.

Joyce Roach

Defining Folklore for My Students

I teach a course at TCU in Fort Worth entitled "Folklore in American Life and Literature." The students are predominantly juniors and seniors and haven't a clue about what folklore is—just the kind I like to get—and I can, as the scripture advises, bring them up in the way I want them to go.

The course has never been offered before, and it may not ever be offered again. I don't know. The closest the university ever came to a folklore class was Mabel Major's Southwest Literature course which was taught from the Thirties to the Fifties— and, yes indeed, I was one of her students. The English department knew that TFS was going to meet in Fort Worth (I told them often enough) and the chair, Dr. Neil

Daniel, asked me if I wouldn't like to teach a folklore course. I jumped at the chance, and I do mean jumped—as in up and down, off the walls and ceiling.

I found no satisfactory text because I wanted to teach folklore from an American Studies perspective, but F. E. Abernethy's *Introduction to Folklore* (1983), which he put together for a course at SFA, came close. Richard Dorson's and Jan Brunvand's books supplemented Abernethy's text, and publications of the Texas Folklore Society fully illustrated all the different kinds of folklore. Tests consisted of formal papers using a different approach for each genre, such as cultural anthropology (folktales reveal a culture), folk music and song, regional collecting, ethnic collecting, literary criticism, and personal family saga.

Defining folklore is an on-going process. It is hard to give a short definition without using someone else's. "All that falls between the cracks of history" is one. "A bunch of stuff about dead people in the olden days" is Jim Lee's favorite. If that is so then perhaps popular culture might be defined as a bunch of new stuff about live people now. A dictionary definition speaks of the beliefs, customs, and habits passed down through oral tradition. A definition from M. H. Abrams *Glossary of Literary Terms* says:

Folklore . . . has been the collective name applied to traditional verbal materials and social rituals that have been handed down solely, or at least primarily, by word of mouth and by example rather than in written form. Folklore developed and continues to flourish best in communities where few if any people can read or write. It includes, among other things, legends, superstitions, songs, tales, proverbs, riddles, spells, nursery rhymes; pseudo-scientific lore about the weather, plants, and animals; customary activities at births, marriages, and deaths; and traditional dances and forms of drama which are performed on holidays or at communal gatherings. Elements of folklore have at all times entered into sophisticated written literature (Abrams 63).

Folktales, folk drama and folk music are considered "of special importance for written literature" (63).

My own personal definition is this: "Folklore is the ways and means committee—all the ways a culture has of accomplishing its life (folk-make, folk-do, folk-think-believe, folk-speak, folk-be) and the means used to accomplish that life." Every aspect of folklore falls under that definition without my having to name any of the categories already addressed. I don't have to hit you over the head for you to be able to divvy up the other namings under my categories.

Further, I believe that folklore exists on two levels: one, on that level I have just described; and two, historical myth. Myths— those stories which often explain a culture's conception and birth and of the heroes and heroines who accomplished the deeds to bring it about—fall under the category of folk-think-believe. There is that kind of larger myth which results in ideologies—speculative and visionary philosophy embraced as the gospel truth by some—which characterize regions, cultures, and ethnic groups. These myths, or set of generally prescribed-to beliefs or assumptions, account for the ideas of the American Dream, the Southern Myth, and especially the Frontier Myth containing sub-myths such as the Code of the West. Along with the ideologies, there are stereotypes who carry out the workings of ideologies. Both myths and accomplishers are detailed in literature, and often folklore of the first definition supports and reveals the ideologies at work.

Since the course aims at both life and literature, making the connection with literature is important, and I make sure that the works read illustrate folklore on both levels. Novels used to illustrate my points are Dorothy Scarborough's *The Wind* (use of folksong to foreshadow, ways and means of West Texas ranch country, juxtaposing Southern Myth and Frontier Myth, stereotypical women of the range); Elmer Kelton's *The Wolf and the Buffalo* (ways and means of Comanche culture as well as cavalry organization, juxtaposing slave/Civil War/black with Plains perspectives); Victor Villasenor's *Rain of Gold* (ways and means of border culture, the Black Legend ideology, juxtaposing Anglo and Mexican/Chicano viewpoint). Yes, I am guilty of focusing on Texas and Southwest materials. So, shoot me. It is, as they told me, my course.

For non-fiction treatments which make my points, I use the works of C. L. Sonnichsen, and yes, they too are about Texas and the Southwest. *Tularosa, Judge Roy Bean: Law West of the Pecos, Colonel Greene and the Copper Sky Rocket, Billy King's Tombstone* and essays in *From Hopalong to Hud* cover ways and means, stereotypes and myths/ideologies. It was Sonnichsen who first introduced me to J. Frank Dobie's phrase, "suitable to time and place." Sonnichsen adapted the phrase to "appropriate to time and place" and he put it to more sophisticated use than Dobie. He first made the application to Indians and the U.S. Cavalry. He said to remember that when the Indians massacred, burned, pillaged, raped and destroyed, they probably did not do it out of a sense of wrong-doing, but because they knew that it was right and meet to do so. Likewise, the cavalry representing the settler and the law, responded in the very same way and for the very same reasons. Added to the idea was that we have no right to impose twentieth-century Anglo notions about right and wrong on nineteenth-century conditions or other cultures.

And if all that has been said is my definition of folklore, then what is a folklorist? I found a definition that satisfies me in the words of Sut Lovingood from George Washington Harris' *Tales*

Spun By A Nat'ral Durned Fool. He says of the Widow Yardley that, "She war a great noticer of littil things that nobody else ever seed." Sut, of course, implied that the Widow was nosey and furthermore she speculated about what she saw according to her own understanding of it. For better or worse, that's what I do and I think many of you do, too.

I try hard to teach my students a little of everything I've mentioned, and I'm sure I try to cover too much ground. But I am reminded of the words of that old gospel hymn, "Work for the night is coming when man works no more." I may never get a chance again to teach folklore to university students and so I must dump the whole load. Tucked in among a hundred other ideas is that one ought to learn to look for signs—that is, if they want to. I see signs and symbols occasionally, but now and then, one ups and hits me between the eyes as it did when I arrived at this year's meeting place. As we were gathering to prepare for this 1995 meeting registration in Fort Worth and making a dozen trips in and out of the building, I looked out the large, picture windows of the hotel onto the garden walk and pond. There, equally busy and darting to and fro, was our totem, the roadrunner, in a place totally out of keeping with his natural habitat. He was fat, in fine health and form, and obviously at home in somebody else's territory. The chaparral cock, in a place he had no right to be, had adapted and adjusted—an outsider who had made himself at home in whatever circumstances and surroundings he occupied. Just like the membership of the Texas Folklore Society, he gathered and garnered pursuant to his own interests, went his own way even among others of his kind in the midst of a maddeningly modern world. Yes, I believe in signs and interpreting them according to my own understanding.

Works Cited

Abrams, M. H. *A Glossary of Literary Terms*. New York: Holt, Rinehart and Winston, Inc. 1941, 1957, 1971, Third edition.

Folklore and Cinema

Jim Harris

Note: The idea for this paper was prompted by a session at the 1995 Texas Folklore Society meeting in Fort Worth, a session full of definitions. I know there was some moaning in the audience over the number and length of the definitions, but I liked the abstract nature of the discussion. I decided that in addition to the fine papers that show the results of field work and collecting, the excellent personal remembrances, and informative humorous talks, perhaps the TFS ought to have a designated generalist. As drinkers should have a designated driver, perhaps the TFS should have at least one designated writer of the abstract.

Think of the sun. Think of any folk group. Think of the sun as a folk group, and the planets that orbit it as other groups or institutions that may take from and influence the particular traditions, customs, and practices of the folk group at the center.

In the nearest orbit are other folk groups who might absorb, influence, or give back an individual tradition. In the second orbit envision art and media, such as literature or newspapers or television. A little farther removed, in the third orbit, find study groups, such as academic departments in universities and organizations like the Texas Folklore Society. In the fourth orbit, see such things as the economy of a country. In the fifth orbit, find politics. And at farther orbits find other institutions.

In this model, the closer the group or institution, the more likely there will be exchanges or influences. In this model, politics, for instance, is less likely to have a profound impact on a particular tradition within a group than is art and certainly less likely than another folk group.

My subjects are folklore and cinema, subjects that on the surface seem light years from each other—the first the traditions, customs and practices of a given group of people, the second the technologically sophisticated visual creations of a collaborating group of people, ostensibly under the artistic control of one individual, the director.

On closer examination, however, the two do share similarities, at least as they relate to the production of an artifact—such as, for example, the ghostly hitchhiker urban legend or Ron Howard's film *Apollo 13*. The folk tale changes with each oral version told within a community. In its production a movie changes with each contribution of such people as grips, costume designers, photographers, actors and editors, no matter how static the screenplay remains.

It might be said that the final products are similar in that the true folk tale is various within the minds of different tellers and listeners, just as the real movie is the one that exists in the mind of a single viewer and at the same time exists independently in the minds of other viewers.

In addition, could the sitting with many other people in a darkened theater, could the cinema experience be similar to a folk celebration? If, for instance, Lubbock forms a community, where else do the diverse elements (as they relate to ethnicity, education, social and economic status, religion) of the city come together in one location for the sharing of one experience?

But more than how folklore and cinema are alike and more than how they are different, I am interested here in functional and dynamic relationships. These are the questions I would like to ask about the two subjects: 1. What relationships do exist between them? 2. What have those relationships been in the past? and 3. Can we speculate as to what those relationships will be like in the future?

I must begin with a personal note. These are two subjects I have loved for many years. The 1996 Easter conference was my twenty-third consecutive year to meet with the Texas Folklore Society, and cinema has been an important part of my life since I was a kid growing up in Dallas in the 1950s. I do not think I would be able to write about any part of all my personal experiences without acknowledging some impact from my folklore studies and cinema. I include such subjects as religion and philosophy, career and hobbies, family and friendships, and on and on. Folklore and cinema's impacts have been that strong. And I believe I am not unique in this influence that cinema has had; I believe I am typical of millions of Americans and other peoples who watch movies regularly and have for most of their lives.

Most everyone today will admit that the potential for impact from cinema is great. Witness the debate in conservative America over the influence of media violence on young people. Many folks believe film and television violence have helped make America the most violent nation on the earth.

After Oliver Stone's film *Nixon* was released in December, former Secretary of State Henry Kissinger wrote in the *Los Angeles Times* that the movie was a triumph of technique over truth, but we live "in an age when far more people gain their understanding of the past from movies and television than from the written word." (Kissinger D1).

I have a friend who married a Colombian woman in the 1960s and moved to her small, rural home town of Fusagasuga, sixty miles from Bogota. After living there five years, he moved back to the States and did not return to Columbia for fifteen years. When he went back for a visit, he found something in Fusagasuga that had not been there before. In an area with no people of African ancestry, he found prejudice against African-Americans. It took only a little time for him to see from where the attitudes came. Since he had been there, U.S. movies and U.S. television had come to the community.

It is my friend's belief, and mine too, that the racism and prejudice that is a part of American life is reflected in the popular culture of this country as it would be in the popular culture of any country. Furthermore, countries that import American culture through cinema and television adopt U.S. values, the bad along with the good. Being aware that his conclusions were not the results of scientific research my friend still believes the attitudes toward African-Americans found in the people of his wife's home town came from the movies, whether or not those films were intentionally racist or prejudicial.

But before I totally lose control of this subject, let me stop to offer brief definitions of a couple of terms.

By "cinema" I mean feature-length motion pictures made to be seen on a motion picture screen; I do not mean video games, video music, television programs, the internet or any other form of artistic or utilitarian communication. These may be subjects worthy of consideration as they are influenced by folklore or as they influence folklore, but I am interested here only in commercial cinema—that produced by directors such as Steven Speilberg, Francis Ford Coppola, or other creators of widely distributed flicks intended for the movie screen.

By "folklore" I mean simply the traditions, customs, and practices of any group of people who share and who are united by at least one trait.

That is a simple definition that works for me, but I do not think people defining it in the future will be able to be that simple or that specific. As communication technology advances and our potential ability to talk to each other across communities increases, it will be necessary to call for broader definitions. The formula might be as follows: as the world gets smaller through communication technology, the adequate and comprehensive definition of folklore gets broader. Or as barriers fall between groups, larger groups are formed and broader definitions are needed.

In his introduction to the 1976 TFS publication, *What's Going On In Modern Texas Folklore,* F. E. Abernethy wrote in response to my all-time favorite banquet speech, the 1975 C. L. Sonnichsen talk "The Poor Wayfaring Scholar." Abernethy used these words: "There is freedom in the discipline of folklore. . . . It is a part of every phase of our lives and every field of study . . . we know that we are ever in the midst of it—and it us (viii). . . . So it doesn't make much difference what you call it . . . you are into this field as soon as you start thinking about any subject that has anything to do with folk" (xi).

One initial way to deal with the subject of folklore and cinema is to relate examples of how folklore and folklife contribute to cinema. This approach would mimic the methods of literary scholars who detail the uses of folk materials by poets, novelists and playwrights. As Melville used the lore of whalers in creating *Moby Dick*, so Robert Redford used the customs of fly fishermen in making *A River Runs Through It*. Redford's movie, of course, originated as a short, autobiographical novel by Norman Maclean. Or it is easy to see the influence of legends in Francis Ford Coppola's *Dracula*, or the myth of the cowboy in Sam Peckinpah's *The Wild Bunch* or Clint Eastwood's *Unforgiven* or the folk humor used in Tommie Lee Jones' *The Good Old Boys*. (Tommie Lee Jones' *The Good Old Boys*? That doesn't sound right, since long-time TFS contributor Elmer Kelton wrote the novel on which Jones' movie was based.)

This approach suggests that cinema is a means of distributing folk ways, much like the dime novel or the literary novel might have done in the latter quarter of the nineteenth century. I wonder how many cowboys in the past had their customary life altered by dime novels or how many cowboys today have been changed by images of themselves in western movies? Here is how Wallace Stegner wrote of it: "Plenty of authentic ranch hands have read pulp Westerns in the shade of the bunkhouse and got up walking, talking, and thinking like Buck Duane or Hopalong Cassidy" (Stegner 102). In other words, today in our visually-oriented society, cinema takes the place occupied by popular literature one hundred years ago.

It is important, I think, to remember that cinema came into existence in the 1890s, a century ago when America was said to have settled what had been left of the frontier, when we did not have any more new territories to conquer, when we did not have any more West to settle up. It was as if we created an inexpensive means by which we could vicariously occupy new territory, as if it were very important for us to possess an inexpensive theater so the masses could stay displaced, rootless, and on the road.

But if the end of the nineteenth century signaled the end of America's frontiering and the end of one road, the end of the twentieth century seems to signal another profound change on the highways of our lives—and I hesitate to use the expression—the opening up of the information superhighway in which we can communicate with individuals around the world, can easily access minds in other communities, with the results being fewer and fewer barriers between cultures, fewer and fewer groups with which to label "the folk."

In January 1996, after a preliminary introduction to modern folklore in my Southwest literature class and after references to this tearing down of borders, I had a bright and articulate student ask if we will have any folklore in the future.

It is a good question, but the more appropriate question is, of course, who will be the folk of the future? What will folklorists study when Cajuns in south Louisiana are watching the same films on their VCRs that sailors on the Maine coast are watching? What happens to community life when Acoma Native Americans in New Mexico are viewing the same cinema as African-Americans in South Dallas?

Out of necessity, post-modern folklore will be defined differently from what it is today. One of the most important characteristics of American folklore will be the rate at which the mixing of the traditions of different groups will increase.

In a 1990 issue of the *Journal of American Culture*, Gene Bluestein writes that the redefining has already begun. Bluestein feels the old definitions just do not work, and he suggests a broader definition is in order. He offers "folklore as the ordinary mode of human creativity" (Bluestein 27), and estimates that "folklore and the folk process reveal the ordinary and basic modes of creativity" (24). That's a pretty broad definition. And when he writes of the "special circumstances defining the nature of the folk in the United States," he acknowledges the central place of popular culture—which includes cinema—as sources for folk ways (27).

Another way of saying this is to note that the different cultures in America have tremendous transference. At the 1995 TFS meeting, Joe Graham spoke of elite, popular, and folk cultures (see "Toward a Definition of Folk Culture," p. 27 in this volume). Cinema initiates transference between these cultures. It acts as a catalyst for adoptions of one community's folk life by another community. It is not beyond the realm of possibility to find music from Beethoven (the elite) played by a German orchestra on a Hollywood soundtrack for a film (the popular) and from there influencing the music played by local musicians (the folk) along the Texas-Mexican border. And while it acts as a catalyst, it may function to give us a sense of community. I understand that some three billion people around the world watched the 1996 academy awards presentations.

For two years (1994–95) I wrote a weekly movie review and commentary for the *Hobbs Daily News-Sun*, and it would not be right to write about cinema without a list of the best films for those years. Here are four movies from my 1995 Top Ten List and a suggestion about the folklore in each. *My Family (Mi Familia)*: look at the folkways of rural Mexican immigrants moving to Southern California's urban hell. The Oscar winner for best picture *Braveheart*: watch Mel Gibson recreate some of the legends about Celtic hero William Wallace. Those two are the easy ones. The movie *Seven*: Morgan Freeman plays a detective in a film noir detailing the grisly tales of a psychopathic killer intent on becoming legendary in his urban nightmare. Finally, the movie I thought was the best of the year is Martin Scorsese's *Casino*, which meticulously details the traditions of Mafia organizations in Las Vegas in the 1970s—Mafia traditions which moviegoers first learned about in abundant detail in Coppola's first *Godfather* movie.

Scorsese has developed the ways of the Mafia in three films: *Mean Streets*, *Goodfellas*, and *Casino*. Here is how critic Gavin Smith describes the three movies in the influential magazine *Film Comment*: "*Mean Streets* is about territory, *Goodfellas* about tribe, and *Casino* about a sacred place, or religion" (Smith 59). That sentence by Smith sounds to me more like the stuff of folklore studies than it does a movie review.

I cannot get away from the subject of best films without mentioning one of my favorites from 1995. It was *The Good Old Boys* that I noted earlier. It was not made for theater release, but what an excellent rendering of Kelton's great novel. Tommie Lee Jones is not only one of the great film actors of today, but he is also a fine director. My Southwest literature students not only read *The Good Old Boys*, but they saw the movie version of it.

Earlier in this paper I wrote that we are celebrating in the 1990s one hundred years of cinema. In only twelve years Texans will be celebrating another centennial, that of the Texas Folklore Society. It is not too far in the future to be speculating about the subjects for folklore meetings then. Who will the folk be? How much will we have changed? Do the changes in communication technology really signal dramatic changes in the next few years, or is all of the internet talk a commercial that allows Bill Gates to sell more computers? What traditions will be part of our lives in 2009? What customs will we celebrate? What practices will be common among us? Again, who will the folk be? How will we define folklore?

I do not know the answers to these questions, but I do feel something new is on the horizon. I do not think it will be coming from the internet, but from the sheer numbers of people who will be added to the population and will have to be somewhere doing something. What catalysts will accelerate that change that is coming? Will our Texas and Southwestern rootlessness be more of a factor?

Perhaps it is time for another *What's Going On? (In Modern Texas Folklore)*, TFS Publications #40, or one about *What Will be Going on in Postmodern Texas Folklore*. That which binds the young people of the future, it seems to me, will be very different from that which bound the folk of the 1909 world of George Lyman Kittredge, John Avery Lomax and Leonidas Warren Payne, Jr., the founders of the TFS.

Before ending, I feel a need to write something about the commercial side of the cinema experience. Making films, after all, is a business, a big business with the average film costing $20–40 million and extravagant ones like 1995's *Waterworld* costing four or five times that amount.

Customers purchase tickets as they buy other experiences and commodities. But in paying for a seat, sitting in a room full of diverse peoples in our communities, we share something with that group, and with the best of films we walk away knowing how the members of the audience are alike, how we share certain traits as human or inhuman citizens of the world, a nation, a state or a town.

Not only is viewing a movie an economic experience, it is also a bread we break and share. I do not think it is an exaggeration to say that it has the potential to connect us with our gods or let us know who we are. It is an act of consumption that lets us, in a sense, actualize ourselves.

I began this essay by using the analogy of a solar system to show influences on a folk group and the group's traditions. Any folk group might be seen as the sun about which orbit groups and institutions. In the center find what poet Wendell Berry calls "placed" people, folks rooted in a geography or a world wide web, and orbiting about them are other groups and institutions that have the ability to share, transfer and alter traditions, customs and practices. In the center, for instance, see Mexican villagers living in Paso Lajitas just across the Rio Bravo, folks who cross it in a row boat, but whose real bridge is a television set with a VCR. These are the folks who drive to Alpine for dinner, for shopping at Wal Mart, and for a movie at the Alpine theater, a cinema experience being had in El Paso, Big Spring, Dallas, and Texarkana.

In some ways, I think you can say watching a film is closer to being a folk experience than attending certain "folklorized" events such as those phony folk festivals created and designed by chambers of commerce to revitalize the local economy.

The universe I described at the beginning of this talk is one that is not expanding, but it is one contracting; its bodies are moving toward each other at increasing rates, and cinema is just one of the catalysts for this rapid change.

Thus, by mixing metaphors, I offer this definition: Folklore is a bright comet shooting across the sky.

WORKS CITED

Abernethy, Francis Edward. *What's Going On? (In Modern Texas Folklore)*. Austin: The Encino Press, 1976.

Bluestein, Gene. "Folk and Pop in American Culture," *The Journal of American Culture*. Vol. 13, No. 2, 1990, pp. 21–29.

Kissinger, Henry. "Nixon triumph of technique over truth." *The Los Angeles Times* and reprinted in *The Albuquerque Journal*, January 21, 1996.

Smith, Gavin. "Two Thousand Light Years From Home," *Film Comment*. January–February, 1996, pp. 59–63.

Stegner, Wallace. *Where The Bluebird Sings to the Lemonade Springs*. New York: Wings Books, 1992.

Toward a Definition of Folk Culture

Joe S. Graham

Folklore has long been of great interest to many academicians as well as non-academicians. The Texas Folklore Society has a very long history and has preserved much of the traditional culture in this state, as has the American Folklore Society for the United States. However, there has been some confusion as to exactly what the term folklore means. The definition I present below is the approach I use in all of my classes which deal with culture.

From an anthropological perspective, culture is the human-made part of our environment, as opposed to nature. Humans use their culture to organize their world and make it more liveable. There are many different ways of looking at and organizing the concepts associated with culture. For example, we use the term material culture to denote the physical objects made and used by humans, passed down over generations of time. Non-material culture includes that vast component of culture which consists of the values, behavioral rules, verbal expressions, language, gestures, attitudes, and whatever humans learn as they grow up in any given cultural group. Clearly, different groups have different cultural expressions and values, as well as languages. A number of folklorists have used a classification system to help define the concept of folklore and distinguish it from other types of culture (e.g., Bronner 3–46; Brunvand; Graham, *Hecho* 1–47). While these categories of culture sometimes overlap, the classification system is particularly useful in defining what we mean by folk culture. The three classifications of culture used in this system are elite culture, popular culture, and folk culture. All classifications are human-made, and to be meaningful, they must be based on a practical and consistent set of criteria. The classification system of culture—elite culture, popular culture, and folk culture—is based on the *process* through which the culture is transmitted.

Elite culture is defined as that culture which is transmitted through the formal institutions of society—schools, churches, governments, etc. It is called elite culture because it is often associated with the social (often the wealthier group) in any given culture. Often it represents "official" culture, or that culture recognized by and supported by law and government, as well as by other institutions.

Popular culture, on the other hand, is that culture transmitted through mass media and through participation in mass culture in our society—eating at McDonalds or shopping at Wal Mart. We are exposed to popular culture through television, radio, newspapers, magazines, etc. These are shared with the masses, and anyone with a television set or radio is exposed to much the same types of culture.

Folk culture, unlike elite culture or popular culture, is usually passed on in face-to-face interactions in informal situations. Even the social elite have their folk traditions. For example, an Aggie joke told by a highly educated, successful university graduate is still a part of folk culture. It is true that some Aggie jokes have been printed in small booklets and sold in various types of stores, becoming a part of popular culture. A significant part of folk culture includes folk aesthetics, a system of values transmitted through face-to-face interactions, as opposed to the aesthetics of elite culture, which is most often taught in classrooms and other formal teaching situations.

We shall explore the differences between folk, popular, and elite culture by examining five areas of culture: music, food, religion, occupations, and medicine. While most of us are exposed to all three of these types of culture, one may become more important to some folks than another.

The primary type of music associated with elite culture tends to be classical music. This music and its aesthetics are usually learned through instruction in society's educational institutions. To learn to play (or to appreciate) classical music usually involves taking courses in the subject and learning the aesthetics associated with this type of music. One can go to Julliard's School of Music to learn to perform this type of music. If one listens to a performance of Handel's *Messiah* or some other classical piece performed by a symphony orchestra, the same set of aesthetic standards apply whether the performance is in Germany, Finland, the U.S., Mexico, or elsewhere. Individuals from many different ethnic groups and even those of different social classes can learn to perform and appreciate this kind of music. In the Corpus Christi, Texas, area, there is only one FM radio station which plays classical music (no AM stations play this type of music), an indication of the relatively small number of people in the region who understand and enjoy this type of music.

Popular music, on the other hand, may be heard over many AM and FM radio stations in the area. This includes country and western music, rock and roll music, *tejano* music, and many other popular forms of music. One does not study these forms of music at the university, or even in the public schools, as one does classical music. Many people enjoy this music at dances and other events, or they simply buy tapes and records from the local store and play them at home. One doesn't learn to play this music through formal classes at such institutions as the university. One can learn on one's own or by learning from another how to play certain instruments, and then one learns to play new songs by listening to records or tapes or from printed copies of the music. While this music is very popular among many groups, this is not the type of music the wealthier classes listen to and enjoy. Very much of it is most popular among working-class folks and even middle-class folks.

Folk music has been greatly impacted by popular music, now so available via radio, records, and cassette tapes. Much of the folk music has moved into popular music through this process. As Dr. Americo Paredes (1958) has shown, around the turn of this century, folk music was very important to the Mexican Americans in South Texas (and elsewhere). The *corrido* (ballad) was still very popular, and one could hear this traditional form of music in homes, at parties, in cantinas, at weddings, and in many other places. Likewise, *conjunto* music developed as a folk music form in the early part of this century (Peña). This music is and has been considered working-class music since its earliest development, and those in the middle and upper classes looked down upon those who listened to this form of music. Their popular music was the *orchestra tipica*, played at dances and other celebrations. *Conjunto* music evolved into popular music when during the 1950s Mexican Americans began recording music and selling it in music stores. One can still hear the old vaqueros on ranches in South Texas sing old *corridos*, but this form of music has practically disappeared among townspeople. A similar pattern has occurred among Anglos and African Americans, among whom popular music has replaced, to a great extent, the traditional folk music. Peter, Paul, and Mary recorded a number of Anglo folk ballads, and these helped move the folk tradition into the popular culture tradition.

Another aspect of culture which gives us good insights into the different types of culture is foodways. When we look at foodways which are a part of elite culture, we find an extensive borrowing of terms from French. Such terms as *cuisine, chef*, and an extensive number of terms for different foods (for example, *escargot*) comes from the French language. The chef is trained through formal instruction in a school for chefs. Once their training is completed, they tend to work in fancy restaurants or for wealthy families. Most in the working class or even the middle class seldom if ever eat food prepared by a chef trained in such a school.

Popular culture food is generally found in places like MacDonalds or other popular restaurants for the working and middle class folks. Those who prepare this food are not trained in formal schools, but rather learn on the job. Too, if one goes to a supermarket, he or she will find extensive examples of popular culture foods available. Some are microwave dinners and others may take a number of different forms. One may be exposed to a variety of different ethnic foods in these eating places, but they are usually not made like they would be in the home. In one Elderhostel class I taught here at Texas A & M University-Kingsville, we discussed traditional foods of different ethnic groups, and I asked the students (all were older, middle-class Anglos) how often they believed that Mexican Americans eat tamales at home. The common answer was that Mexican Americans eat tamales about once or twice a week, when in reality, most Mexican Americans eat tamales at home once or twice a year. They may eat tamales at restaurants more often than this, but not at home.

Foods that are a part of folk culture are generally learned at home. A young girl (or young man) will learn how to cook by helping mother prepare food for the family, not through formal instruction. Foods at the folk culture level are usually clear boundary markers among folk groups. If one goes into a home of a Mexican American and an Anglo in South Texas, he will see very different types of foods served. While some Anglos have become lovers of Mexican foods, they still recognize them as Mexican foods.

Since most Mexican Americans in South Texas have been relatively poor or working class, they have relied on foods that Anglos often find not acceptable. A very popular dish among South Texas Mexican Americans is *tripitas*, a dish made of the intestines (tripe) of cattle. Working-class Mexican Americans often have a party (*pachanga*) called a *tripada*, in which the main dish is *tripitas*. In San Diego, Texas, for example, at the Pan de Campo celebration in August, the main dish is *tripitas*, served with *pan de campo*, or camp bread. Some Anglos have a bit of trouble adjusting to this type of food. Another popular dish among Mexican Americans is *gorditas*, a dish made of the internal parts of a kid goat which has been butchered to make another popular dish in this culture, *cabrito*. *Gorditas* are made of the heart, liver, lungs, and other edible internal parts, which Anglos might be prone to throw away. These are chopped up and wrapped in the *tela* (the internal visceral lining of the goat's stomach). A *tripita* (intestine) is wrapped several times around this to keep it together, and the dish is cooked either *al horno* (in the oven) or *a la parrilla* (on a grille). This same dish, which is very popular in West Texas, is called *buriñate* or *buruñate* there and is called *burrañate* in New Mexico (Graham, "Mexican-American Traditional Foodways" 1–29).

Working-class Mexican Americans in rural areas, when they kill an animal to eat, feel obligated to use every edible part, wasting nothing. I have observed that when in West Texas these Mexican Americans butcher a hog, they eat everything but the squeal. They collect the blood from the animal when they slit its throat and make a dish from this blood. They mix spices with it, wash out the pig's stomach, and put the mixture into the pig's stomach, tie the two ends tight, and bake it in the oven. The dish is called *morcilla*, and many townspeople (who don't butcher hogs) don't like this dish, though the rural folks think that it is wonderful. There are many other similar folk foods among Mexican Americans, many of which have become popular among Anglos.

One popular dish which moved into popular culture is *fajitas* (which Mexican Americans in West Texas did not eat). The term *fajitas* comes from the Spanish word *fajas*, meaning skirt steak, a lean strip of meat on the side of the animal. Anglos usually fed this to the dogs or may have included it in the ground meat, but they did not have a dish made of this cut of meat. *Fajitas* are heavily spiced (lime juice, garlic powder, lemon pepper, etc.) and are very delicious. Anglos like them, and the price in local stores has jumped from about forty cents a pound to over two dollars a pound. When it moved into popular culture (restaurants), a new type of *fajitas* developed, which has nothing to do with skirt steak. For example, one can buy chicken *fajitas* and even shrimp *fajitas* in some restaurants, and the restaurant cooks prepare the chicken and shrimp with the same spices and cook it the same way they do regular *fajitas*. They have no idea that the term *fajitas* comes from the term *faja*, or skirt steak. Clearly, it would be remarkable to find a chicken large enough to have skirt steak, or how would one like to jump into a pool of water with a shrimp large enough to have *fajas*? This dish has spread through much of the United States through popular culture restaurants. For example, one can now buy *fajita pitas* at most Jack-in-the-Box restaurants.

Anglos working on ranches often eat foods which horrify city folks. For example, while I was a youth living on a ranch near Marfa, Texas, we would have tourists come and watch us during roundup season. Sometimes they would be invited to eat with us at the chuck wagon. One of the foods often prepared during this time was mountain oysters (the testicles of the calves which had been castrated). One time, one of the visitors had eaten about half a mountain oyster, noting how delicious it was. He asked what it was made of, and when he was told, he threw up.

African Americans also have a significant number of folk foods, which they also made from whatever was available. Like the working-class Mexican Americans, when they butchered a hog, they ate everything but the squeal. We even have the term in American English, "eat high on the hog." This means, of course, eating things like pork chops, etc. Again, folk foods are a clear boundary marker among ethnic as well as other folk groups.

When we look at the different forms of culture in the area of religion, they are fairly clear. To illustrate elite culture, in the Roman Catholic church, to become a priest and represent the church, one has to attend seminary for several years, until the officials of the church decide that this person knows the doctrines, rituals, and other practices well enough to go out and represent the church. Then he is ordained a priest and sent forth to serve the church. If he violates the rules of the church, and the church officials feel that he is hurting the church and will not change his ways, he may be defrocked or even excommunicated.

On the popular level, the Roman Catholic church has radio stations and even television programs or channels. It reaches many people via these media. Perhaps a better example of popular religion are the television programs which featured such folks as Jim Baker, Jimmy Swaggart, and other television preachers. Their popularity is what kept them on television, not their doctrines or their rituals. So long as they were popular, they remained on television. Once they lose their popularity (as did Baker and Swaggart), they disappear from television. Billy Graham, for example, has remained a very popular figure on television for many years.

Folk religion is the part of the religious beliefs and practices passed down through families which do not necessarily fit into the official doctrine of the church. For example, in early South Texas, the priests visited the families on the ranches of this region only once or twice a year. These people lived too far from town to travel in wagons or carts to attend church on Sunday. Thus, a number of folk beliefs and practices developed among Mexican Americans (and Mexicans from Mexico) over the years since the first Spaniards brought the Catholic religion into the region. These are not necessarily shared by other ethnic groups in the Catholic church. One can find home altars in many Mexican-American homes in South Texas. Altars, of course, are the point of communication between man and God. Women on ranches were the spiritual leaders in these homes, and they created home altars to help them worship God and to help them teach their families to do likewise. One can see this practice documented well in Rudy Anaya's novel *Bless Me, Ultima*. Every time there was a crisis or something great happening in the family, Tony's mother would bring the whole family into the *sala* and they would kneel before the home altar and pray.

Other folk traditions (rites of passage) among South Texas Mexican-American Catholics include the *compadrazgo* (ritual co-parenthood), which develops when a child is baptized, the *quinceañera* (fifteenth birthday ritual and celebration for young women), which was a rite of passage moving the person from childhood to adulthood during the early ranching period of this region, the Mexican-American wedding ceremony and funeral ceremony. Roadside crosses erected when a member of the family is killed in a car accident or some other way are another important family religious tradition. This tradition helps the family cope with the loss of a loved one, and it dates to the earliest arrival of the Spanish into this region (Graham, "Descansos" 153–64; Barrera 278–92). Each of these rites of passage is distinctly Mexican American, and they are not part of Anglo or non-Catholic celebrations. When an Irish Catholic priest is trained at Notre Dame, is ordained a priest, and sent to Zapata, Texas, for example, he must learn these traditions to be able to fit in well with his parishioners.

Another significant area of any culture is the various occupations its members can choose from. Elite culture is becoming more and more important in the selection of occupations by citizens. For example, to become a college professor, a schoolteacher, a medical doctor, a pharmacist, a lawyer, a judge, or many other professional positions, one must be trained in the formal educational systems of our country. In some instances, one receives a license to practice, or a diploma. This makes the bearer an "official" practitioner, recognized by the government and by its institutions. One cannot practice law without a law degree or medicine without a medical license. To do so could subject the person to severe repercussions with the state law enforcement groups.

Occupations associated with popular culture are not necessarily learned through popular culture, though some are. To become a popular newscaster, weatherman, or other television personality, one needs to learn how to perform effectively before the camera. One is not required to have a college degree or a license from a government agency to perform such activities. The same is true for radio programs, for newspaper people, for magazine writers, etc.

A number of folk occupations continue into modern times. These are not learned through the formal institutions of society nor through watching television. The work skills are learned through one-on-one guidance and instruction, not through taking classes or watching television. For example, migrant workers learn their skills from family and friends. Perhaps one of the oldest and most well-known folk occupations is that of the *vaquero*, or cowboy, a tradition almost a thousand years old (Graham, *El Rancho*). The cowboy learns all of his skills from family or friends, not from college classes or the mass media. While modern transportation and good roads on the ranch have made major changes in the cowboy's life, the basic cowboy skills are still learned from family and friends. While many truck drivers also learned to be truck drivers through this method, there are now truck-driving schools which provide formal training. Many other occupations are learned through folk traditions, even though we are moving toward a more modern and technological world. Sometimes, one receives training through both folk and elite culture. For example, the *partera* (lay midwife) learns her skills from apprenticeship to another *partera*, but may now also receive formal training in medical practices. They become licensed midwives, once they complete their formal training.

When we examine the discipline of medical practice, we can see very clear distinctions among the three levels of training—folk, popular, and elite culture. In order to practice medicine in the United States, one must have a license to do so. Otherwise, one is liable to be arrested and fined. One gets a medical license by graduating from high school, attending college, and then attending medical school. After he passes the required exams, he does an internship, and when that is completed, he receives his license to practice medicine. A similar process is necessary for a pharmacist or a nurse. Formal training is essential to these occupations.

In popular culture one can, however, go down to the local grocery store and buy a huge selection of "medicines" which require no prescription. Such modern popular drugs as aspirin, Pepto Bismol, cough drops and a wide variety of cold medicines may be bought and used with no professional training. There is a wide variety of such over-the-counter drugs available in many stores. One learns of these drugs most often through popular culture—through radio, television, advertisements in newspapers and magazines. One has only to recall the television ad for Pepto Bismol, to see how the drug works. These explanations are not always 100% accurate. The television Pepto Bismol ad shows a pink fluid flowing into a glass stomach and coating the sides. Those who know how it works know that it does not coat the stomach as the ad shows. Likewise, many of us know very well that aspirin works, but we do not know how it works to reduce fever and pain. We simply take it because it is a part of our culture and we have had experiences with it that convinces us that it works.

Folk medicine is that medicine which is passed down over the generations through the process of face-to-face interaction, usually with our parents at home. In many cultures, herbal remedies are one of the central parts of folk medicine. In a recent study done by myself and several graduate students (funded by the National Institutes of Health), we surveyed 10% of the Mexican Americans living in seven communities in South Texas. The results showed that about 90% of these folks continue to rely on herbal remedies for major as well as minor illnesses. They provided the names and uses of about 100 different herbs in this region (Graham, "Mexican-American Herbal Remedies" 34–36). While some people are critical of this use of herbs because "they don't know how the herbs work," the same can be said about most of us who use elite culture medicine and popular culture medicine. I tease my students that if they ever get constipated, I have some herbs in my office which will unstop a drain impervious to a double dose of Drano, and they don't need to know how it works. They will find out that it does work, and that is what counts.

One woman in San Diego, Texas, gave me a remedy for pulmonia (pneumonia), which consisted of five different herbs. I had these herbs scientifically classified by a botanist at our university. I then used the NAPRALERT system (a computerized database of over 100,000 journal articles, books, etc., which have focused on the study of herbs, many of which are chemical analyses of these herbs) to determine which of these herbs might indeed be useful for treating a disease. To my joy, I found that all five herbs have been scientifically proven to have anti-bacterial, anti-fungal, anti-viral properties, and/or analgesic properties. One of these herbs is used in thirty-two different countries for the same illness (Graham, "Folk Medicine" 104–30).

The folk medical system among South Texas Mexican Americans can be divided into three levels: *remedios caseros* (household remedies), *barrio* (neighborhood) healers, and *curandero(a)s*, the healers par excellence in the culture. The *remedios caseros* are those remedies which are passed down from generation to generation, usually within families. Many of these are herbal remedies, though some healings involve minor rituals of one kind or another. These remedies are very well known in the area, and our research indicates that many of them apparently work. Dr. Eliseo Torres has also done extensive research in the herbal remedies of this region, including a major museum exhibit on them (Torres). Those in the elite culture have done some fairly extensive studies of folk remedies in some parts of the world. For example, researchers from Harvard University have done fairly extensive studies among the Mayan Indians in Mexico in recent years.

In summary, culture is that part of our world that is made by humans or part of nature that is adapted by humans for their use. Elite culture is that culture which is passed through time and space through the formal institutions of society, and it often becomes "official" culture. Popular culture is that culture which is transmitted through the mass media, including radio, television, newspapers, magazines, etc., as well as through participation in mass culture in our society. Most people in the United States are greatly affected by popular culture. Folk culture is that culture that is passed on through face-to-face interactions in informal situations, either in one-on-one relationships or in small groups. Folk culture exists in every group, regardless of its socioeconomic status, though it is clearly of greater importance among the poorer and lesser educated groups. Some cultures in the world continue to rely almost totally on folk culture. The Texas Folklore Society has done much to document and preserve the folk culture of Texas over the past century. We owe a great debt to those who have taken a strong interest in this facet of our culture here in the Lone Star State.

Works Cited

Anaya, Rudolfo A. *Bless Me, Ultima.* Berkeley, CA: Quinto Sol Publications, Inc., 1972.

Barrera, Alberto. "Mexican-American Roadside Crosses in Starr County." *Hecho en Tejas: Texas-Mexican Folk Arts and Crafts.* Vol. L of the Publications of the Texas Folklore Society. Ed. Joe S. Graham. Denton: University of North Texas Press, 1991. 278–92.

Bronner, Simon J. "The Idea of the Folk Artifact," *American Material Culture and Folklife.* Ed. Simon J. Bronner. Ann Arbor: UMI Research, 1985. 3–46.

Brunvand, Jan Harold. *The Study of American Folklore: An Introduction,* 2nd Ed. New York: W.W. Norton & Company, Inc., 1978.

Graham, Joe S. *El Rancho in South Texas: Continuity and Change Since 1750.* Denton: University of North Texas Press, 1994.

Graham, Joe S. "Mexican-American Herbal Remedies: An Evaluation," *Herbalgram* (Journal of the American Botanical Council) 31 (1994):31: 34–36.

Graham, Joe S. "The Effectiveness of Traditional Folk Medicine." *South Texas Studies*. Ed. Joseph Sekul and Richard Walker. Victoria: The Victoria College Press, 1994. 104–30.

Graham, Joe S. "Hecho a mano en Tejas." *Hecho en Tejas: Texas-Mexican Folk Arts and Crafts*. Vol. L of the Publications of the Texas Folklore Society. Ed. Joe S. Graham. Denton: University of North Texas Press, 1991. 1–47.

Graham, Joe S. "Descansos (Roadside Crosses): Folk Art and Ritual in Remembrance of the Deceased." *Out Near Phantom Hill*. Eds. Darrin Cozzens and Reed Harp. Stillwater, OK, and Bowling Green, OH: Southwest and Texas Popular Culture Association, 1990. 153–64.

Graham, Joe S. "Mexican-American Traditional Foodways in La Junta." *Journal of Big Bend Studies* 2 (1990): 1–29.

Paredes, Americo. *"With His Pistol in His Hand": A Border Ballad and Its Hero*. Austin: University of Texas Press, 1958.

Peña, Manuel. *The Texas-Mexican Conjunto: A History of a Working-Class Music*. Austin: University of Texas Press, 1985.

Torres, Eliseo. *Green Medicine*. Kingsville: Nieves Press, 1983.

Jan Roush

Folklore Fieldwork on the Internet:

Some Ethical and Practical Considerations

For the past decade traffic on the Internet has increased dramatically, connecting most of the modern world and allowing participants to transact business and share ideas about art, literature, and science, all in a relatively few minutes. Originally conceived in the United States during the 1960s by people in the field of computers who experimented with linking computers to each other and to people through telephone hook-ups, by the close of the 1970s such links had been extended to other countries, tying the world together in a web-like computer environment. In the 1980s this network, now known as the Internet, expanded at a phenomenal rate, a rate that in the 1990s has become exponential; some estimates now measure the increased volume of messages sent through the "Net" at over twenty percent a month. In less than three decades the Internet has quickly become an indispensable tool for people in diverse professions as well as an invaluable research resource and opinion market for students and lay persons. Many people now turn to it for answers to questions they might have, for information to enhance their knowledge, even to build new communities. It is within such communities that one finds new and innovative possibilities for doing fieldwork in folklore.

These new communities are only accessible through a keyboard; instead of being approached by a system of paved highways or dirt roads, they are entered via wires and optical fibers. That does not, however, make them any less real, for these cyberspace communities are as vibrant as any community found on the globe. Connected by an ever-growing collection of databases, this web reaches out to areas as remote as Siberia and Zimbabwe, populated by real people sitting behind their monitors who are defined more by common interests and computer related purposes than by their ethnicity or geography. Using new digital media developed expressly for the Net, these people talk, fall in love, and even get married after meeting in a cyberspace that transcends national and state boundaries. As the twentieth century draws to a close, the image of a community gathering around the cracker barrel in a general store has changed. Stories, traditions, beliefs—folklore—are still being exchanged, but the walls of the general store have expanded to encompass hundreds, even thousands of miles.

How has this new technology altered the concept of fieldwork in folklore? In two recent folklore classes I have taught: a *Folklore and Gender* class and the *Myths, Legends, and Folktales* class, I decided to find out. Using archival sources such as sites on the World Wide Web and Gopherspace, students collected information on their chosen topics; using Listserv and Usenet technology, they reached out to identify and interview informants who would ordinarily be well beyond their reach. The problems they encountered and the practical and ethical issues raised are both intriguing and far-reaching in their implications on the very nature of conducting fieldwork in folklore.

When I first decided to introduce the students in my folklore classes to the Internet, I did so for a variety of reasons. In addition to teaching folklore, I also have taught a number of electronic text production classes and serve as the English Department's technology liaison for the faculty. I was already aware of many resources available on the Internet and was coming to understand the impact the Net would have on all kinds of communication since it is my responsibility to serve on computer technology-related committees within both the college and the university at large, monitoring technological resources and keeping abreast of new advances in both computer software and hardware. Probably my foremost responsibility, however, is to facilitate a seamless transition between the technology itself and its users, be they students or faculty. So my first reason for incorporating computer technology into a folklore class was because I felt that students in all types of classes should have the opportunity to become acquainted with a technology that is destined to have a major impact on their personal and professional lives. My second major reason concerns the homogeneity of the students at Utah State University where I teach. Most of them come from a generally rural and conservative environment. My hope was that the Internet would expose them to a greater variety of people and their belief systems than could be had by collecting only from their local environment. Admittedly, the fact that they would be focusing, for example, on beliefs about gender had a great deal to do with my decision to incorporate this technology because their conclusions from their fieldwork would necessarily be enhanced by the larger informant pool.

What emerged from this first-time effort to incorporate the Internet into a folklore class went far beyond anything either the students or I could have predicted. As the students navigated the Net and applied what they were learning in class to what they were finding in this broader arena, a number of concerns connected with this larger concept of folklore fieldwork evolved. These concerns, which can be summarized in the following questions, ultimately will need to be considered if folklore fieldwork is to be conducted through the medium of the Internet. Does fieldwork, for instance, have to be conducted in face-to-face interviews in order to be defined as fieldwork, or is any interactive medium sufficient? Closely related to that question is yet another: How does an effaced interview conducted through electronic mail or real-time Chat groups alter the performance, the context of the collecting? Further, since Internet access is for now limited to a privileged few participants, how representative of vernacular culture is this type of fieldwork? Still other questions relate to the material once it is collected, like what assurance does the collector have that the informants are actually who they say they are, an issue particularly crucial in collecting certain types of lore like gender lore? Then there are practical issues that hinge on legality. How does the collector obtain valid consent forms? Further, if consent forms are transmitted through, say, the medium of e-mail, can this collected information legally be archived? Combine these issues with the tremendous learning curve that students—who are often only marginally computer literate—have to go through just to begin doing such research and one has to ask: Does the experience of doing fieldwork on the Internet substantially enhance the nature of a folklore class? After having students use the Internet now in several of my folklore classes, I submit that there are no easy answers to these questions as the following experiences of my students indicate.

The *Folklore and Gender* class I teach is a combination upper division/graduate class, so one would expect the students to have both some knowledge of computer technology as well as a grounding in the basic concepts of folklore. Reality did not bear that out. About one-third of the twenty students in the class had some experience in one, but not necessarily both, of these areas. So I began with an overview of folklore as an expression of everyday, vernacular culture, narrowing to gender issues, at the same time that I introduced them to Internet technology. To provide as painless and effective access to the technology as possible, I conducted the first several classes in the computer classroom where I invited several "technets" to guest lecture on such tools as e-mail, listservs, Gopher, news groups, and Netscape to reach the World Wide Web. Because of limited time available in a quarter system, we did not specifically address such interactive "live" media as Internet Relay Chat (IRC) or multi-user virtual reality environments like MUDs, MOOs, MUSHes, or MUSEs, although several students went on to discover and use these. As an important first step in introducing students to the Internet environment and its potential, I had them log on the very first class to the Folklore Listserv and begin to follow the various threads presented there. Also, in the interest of time efficiency, I urged students from the beginning of the quarter to start narrowing their research interests in gender for their final collecting projects so that they could use their individual preferences as a focus while they were exploring the Net.

One of the earliest hurdles I had to help my students overcome was a general phobia toward the Net itself, a fear of getting lost in its technology. I had presented an optimistic overview of what some of the Net's far-reaching benefits could be, how the students could use the Internet to "stay in touch with friends, relatives, and colleagues around the world at a fraction of the cost of phone calls or even air mail; discuss everything from archaeology to zoology with people in several different languages; tap into thousands of information databases and libraries worldwide; retrieve any of thousands of documents, journals, books, and computer programs; stay up to date with wire-service news and sports and with official weather reports; [or] play live, 'real time' games with dozens of other people at once" as Adam Gaffin outlined in *EFF's Extended Guide to the Internet* (Gaffin, html#SEC7)—all grand, wonderful concepts until students actually tried to accomplish these.

Unfortunately the Internet has grown, and still is growing, so quickly and is adding so many new connections constantly that written documentation or instructions for navigating the Net, especially those suited for a lay person, have not been able to keep up; hence students were frequently on their own while surfing. What I tried to relate to them was how navigation on the Net is itself a form of folklore, achieved largely through an oral tradition with old users helping new users, and that all they had to do was ask for help wherever they were surfing. That technique was okay once they began to assimilate what they were learning in the computer orientation classes, but unfortunately the time frame for this assimilation was highly idiosyncratic. Hence throughout the first part of the quarter, students varied tremendously in their ability to use computer resources. Until they began to feel comfortable in moving around on the Internet, students frequently were frustrated and fearful. As one student said, "The hardest part about [logging onto the Folklore Listserv] was getting over my own fear that I would do it wrong and thus send some very stupid messages all over the world that could be traced back to me."

Students felt that this initial process involved a great deal of time to become acclimated. Away from the computer classroom, they felt they were often left to the whims of lab consultants who themselves were not very knowledgeable about these resources, which delayed their learning process even further. They had difficulty overcoming the idea that "every little error counts," feeling that the amount of information they encountered was itself overwhelming and hard to focus so that it was very easy to become distracted. Not all of them were inhibited, however, for one student remarked that "instead of just wasting time, which is actually fun, you learn shortcuts after getting lost" and another noted that "Trial and Error [his caps], along with logical connections" were his main approaches to searching. Overall, however, the most difficult perception I had to counter during this initial period was the pervasive perception among the students that, because so much information was so readily available, it was somehow "cheating" to use it, which brings up some interesting speculations concerning what we are teaching our students about the nature of research!

As perplexing as some of these initial problems were, it is those problems encountered once students were fully involved in their research and collecting efforts, and the insights gained from them, that potentially will have the greatest impact on collecting folklore via the Internet. These can be classified into three broad categories, following the general collecting process itself: problems relating to accessing the technology; problems relating to performance or context; and problems relating to legal and ethical issues in citing and archiving lore once the collecting process is completed.

Problems relating to access:

Creators of the Internet have noted that "the new forums atop computer networks" (like Gopher, e-mail, listservs, or the Web) are, in their words, "the great levelers and reducers of organizational hierarchy. Each user has, at least in theory, access to every other user, and an equal chance to be heard. . . . [They] create a sense that the voice of the individual . . . really matters. . . . [Hence] decision-making processes can be far more inclusive and participatory. Given these characteristics, [such] networks hold tremendous potential to enrich our collective cultural, political, and social lives and enhance democratic values everywhere." (Kapor, html#SEC5). Yet even the creators insert a cautionary note as they discuss the infrastructure necessary to achieve such worthy goals, positing questions like "Who is to have access to these services, and at what cost?. . . [A]re we laying the seeds for a new information underclass, unable to compete with those fortunate enough to have the money and skills needed to manipulate new communications channels? Who, in fact, decides who has access to what?" (Kapor, html#SEC5).

Unaware of such questions, my students offered observations based on their own Internet collecting experiences that reflect these same concerns. One student said, "I am worried that the only people the collector will have access to are people who have Internet access and use that access." Another echoes that sentiment as she says, "Many of the . . . kinds of people researchers may want to reach probably don't even have access to the Internet. [For instance,] someone trying to interview senior citizens who are terrified of technology would probably get nowhere."

Problems of access related not just to the informants but to the collectors as well. Students frequently noted their own limitations connected to a lack of available hardware. Few had personal computer systems capable of allowing them to connect to the sophisticated forums they wanted to utilize in their research, so they were mostly limited to university computer labs. Said one, "It was very irritating to set aside time in my schedule to spend in the computer lab only to find all computers in use by other students anxious to be part of the technology boom. Then, all too often, when I was fortunate enough to find a machine available, I was delayed because the system I wanted to access (e.g., Lexus Nexus) was busy." Further, she said, "It was possible to find an available machine, have the system accept a request for an entry, and encounter another roadblock [based on the system not recognizing the keywords being used in the search]." Therefore, she said, "I often felt that my time was not being wisely spent."

Problems relating to performance context:

Assuming, however, that collectors do gain access to their folk groups, students noted they still are faced with a number of important difficulties. For one thing, there is the sheer volume of information they are exposed to. As one student noted, "There is so much information available through the Internet that one of the dangers of using it for collecting is being overwhelmed [by the sheer volume of material] . . . and not being able to sufficiently analyze it." More important than that, though, is the nature of the collecting arena, a concern many students had. One student described this new arena as "reduc[ing] the warmth and 'connection' associated with a personal contact in the collecting process." He continues, "Often the 'wholeness' of the information gathered from an informant is strengthened by the look in the eye, the intonation and expression of the voice, and the body language accompanying the telling. These body signals are missed as the message is sent through the cold, hard wires of the machinery." Another student noted that "you really have no idea what kind of people you're dealing with. Important details such as social and ethnic background, family situation, education, religion, etc., may not be accessible, or offered. [If offered,] information . . . may be intentionally incorrect," a particularly distressing problem in collecting gender lore.

Along with these difficulties come problems of following up on the information that is presented. While noting a frustration with the noninteractive nature of collecting on the Internet, one student asked, "Are we losing all the human contact?" She goes on to discuss the immediate impact this has had on her fieldwork, stating, "I am currently collecting survey answers and find it somewhat frustrating that I cannot receive answers to questions immediately. And, I begin to notice additional questions I should have asked in the original survey. In a normal [face-to-face] interview situation, I would have the opportunity to rephrase or probe further. On the other hand," she continues, "[this] format forces you to think more concisely and thoroughly in how you phrase requests. Additionally, I find it an exciting way of getting many viewpoints from many areas (geographically, mentally, academically). I've had responses from Kansas, Louisiana, Texas, and North Carolina—all areas that I would not have otherwise had access to."

Problems related to citing and archiving:

The final area of concern the students had was how to deal with the information they did collect over the Internet, issues that hinge on both ethical and legal concerns. They asked, "How do you obtain release forms? How do you know that the information is truthful? If you read something by mistake [say, through Usenet, or IRC, or a Listserv thread], can it be used? Is it part of public domain just because it is available electronically?" One student said, "I have received one response that the author withheld her name. Her responses were candid and an obvious source of personal distress. Is it ethical to use her anonymous response?" Ultimately, the student decided simply to be as candid as possible in her collecting efforts, making her informants aware that the responses they gave her would be used in her collecting project and submitting release forms through e-mail for them to "sign" and return electronically. The anonymous response was used only in formulating general conclusions, not as a specific citation, although other students in the class argued that "if an individual is willing to put the information out on the Internet, a very public media, they are, by default, giving permission for its use." Everyone agreed, however, that all information collected on the Internet should be properly cited and that some form of release should be signed by the informants, even though no criteria for archiving such collections has yet been established.

I have tried to outline here some of the difficulties that face folklorists today as they increasingly incorporate the technology of the Internet into the fieldwork either they, or their students, conduct. Granted, some of these at the moment seem insurmountable due to the lack of information we presently have to solve the practical, ethical, and legal issues outlined above. That should not deter us, however, in exploring the unique advantages that such a community offers, a sentiment ably expressed by one of the students who attempted doing folklore fieldwork on the Internet:

> Personally . . . I think that [the Internet] is an incredible resource for finding all kinds of information and will be an especially useful tool for folklorists because of the discussion groups where people from all over the world discuss nearly every topic imaginable. I think that the ethics questions will all be resolved in the near future . . . simply because the Internet is such a great resource and so many people use it and will want to use it. The Internet itself, the cyberspace in which it exists, has its own developing culture, even its own etiquette. It is a culture made up of people from many different cultures, with many diverse and many common interests and it would be a great shame to let it go to waste simply because we could not decide whether or not it could be cited appropriately.

So speak these folklorists of the future, being trained—as we once ourselves were—in methodology and theory that stand on the very edge of new frontiers in collecting vernacular culture.

Though we perhaps do not now have all the answers to their questions, I suggest we listen, then move forward.

WORKS CITED

Gaffin, Adam. *EFF's (Extended) Guide to the Internet: A Round Trip through Global Networks, Life in Cyberspace, and Everything.* Textinfo Edition 2.3, September 1994. http://sunsite.nus.sg/pub/eegtti/eegtti_6.html#SEC7 (18 March 1997).

Kapor, Mitchell. Foreword. *EFF's (Extended) Guide to the Internet: A Round Trip through Global Networks, Life in Cyberspace, and Everything.* Textinfo Edition 2.3, September 1994. http://sunsite.nus.sg/pub/eegtti/eegtti_4.html#SEC5 (18 March 1997).

Rhett Rushing

Beginning Within:

Teaching Folklore the Easy Way

Conjuring up images of rural folk gathered around a washpot, cookstove, hog killing, horse trade, fish net, or quilting bee means folklore to many casual observers—and they're usually right. Folklore is a simple thing to understand when you consider that "lore" can be just about anything important enough to the "folk" to be shared and passed down within the group. Whether it be basket-weaving techniques, a family sausage recipe, a special catfish bait, a song from the old days, a hunting story, a family quilt or tablecloth, or a carved wooden chain, folklore exists only if it is deemed important enough to be passed along to others.

In any attempt to define folklore, one must begin with the folk group. It can be a church choir, a construction crew, a boy scout troop, two farmers on opposite sides of a strong fence, or retirees gathering for breakfast at a local restaurant. Anytime you find two or more people with anything at all in common, then you've found a folk group. It's more a consideration of shared experiences and desires than any archaic, rural, uneducated gathering of the ancients at the whittlers' bench. The engineers at NASA on their lunch break, discussing their toughest college course, is as much a folk group as the women of a family in Laredo making tamales for Christmas.

I prefer to define folklore by examples found in my own backyard and not by distanced, far-stretched academic efforts grabbing at inclusiveness. Looking over the family photo album at Christmas with my grandmother, or wondering how academic parking spaces are assigned, simple questions bring forth innumerable stories and anecdotes and beliefs that they, the performers, feel important enough to express.

Understanding that some tales will be forgotten or judged inappropriate for telling at the time, those bits of lore that do get passed are the seeds for the next generation to handle and judge. With each telling the lore is embellished or underscored depending upon the teller, and those choices define what lore filters through. The performer, whether potter or planter, passes along what he or she feels is appropriate and necessary, and this sort of folk-editing or rebuilding occurs with each performance. With a working, personalized awareness of what folklore is, anyone can seek out a group and pick up on its lore by observation and inclusion.

Each and every baggage handler at each and every airport in the country has a "big tip" story. Certainly they all don't tell the same tale, but the fact that each has that type of story in his or her repertoire can only indicate folklore. Just as every pot isn't thrown the same way, or every batch of peach preserves doesn't taste exactly as the one before indicates that folklore, no matter how traditional, must have some variations.

From another angle, sometimes elements of traditional behavior will remain unchanged because the next generation doesn't understand the reasons for the behavior. For example, consider the cook who cut the drumsticks off the Thanksgiving turkey and laid them beside the bird before putting it into the oven for baking. She did this because that is the way her mother did it and for no other reason. Eventually she learned that her mother's oven was too small to cook a big bird intact, therefore the drumstick re-arrangement.

Traditional learned behavior can be hard to break or even amend; consider the Iroquois historian that must memorize a hundred generations of history and be able to recount it orally at festivals and family gatherings. On a smaller scale, many moderns will not step on a sidewalk crack, walk under a ladder, or be the third on a match. Quantitative research of such learned behavior is often irrelevant, because no matter how many times the phenomenon occurs, certain elements of the subject resist change. That, too, is the nature of folklore.

Putting Folklore to Use

In order to define folklore for my grade-school students, I designed a small take-home project for each Thanksgiving through Christmas vacation. Each student was required to interview family members and get examples of five types of folklore. By requiring students to study their own families (and therefore themselves), folklore is demystified from the realm of "them," and immediately opened within the category of "us." No longer just the property of remote snaggle-toothed hillbillies or ancient crones in rocking chairs, folklore can now be openly addressed as something shared and vibrant and on-hand, not something to be feared or mocked.

Granted, the mission statements of most folklore societies still cling to a rhetoric of "saving" or "salvaging" folklore before it fades into obscurity, but I try to guide my students toward preserving the performer as an entity and creator instead of just his or her leavings. It is a question of context—of all the factors surrounding, motivating, and guiding the expression—and without an understanding of the context, all one has is a shell.

After years of trying to teach folklore to students from sixth grade to graduate school, I have found it far easier to introduce the novices to examples of folklore than to bombard them with clinical definitions. I realize that this is a backdoor approach, but the retention and realization rate is markedly higher. The trick is to find that common ground that they all share—to illuminate their status as a folk group—and then to open up their shared beliefs and study them.

My first attempt at teaching Introductory Folklore to undergraduates found me sitting in the third row of my own class. The clock ticked and the students arrived, and we waited. No one knew that I wasn't a student (a part of their own folk group), and five minutes after class was supposed to start I stood and asked, "How long do we have to wait for this guy?"

Several others responded with a strict folk schedule of completely believed times.

"If the instructor is a full professor, we have to wait twenty minutes," declared one student.

"If he's an associate, we only have to hang here for ten minutes," piped in another.

"And if the guy's a grad student?" I posed innocently.

"Then we're outta here," came the general response.

"Where does it say that in the student handbook?" I asked feigning innocence.

No one knew. No one even knew where they had heard this arbitrary timetable either, but they were more than willing to

stick to it. They felt completely in the right according to something they'd learned "unofficially," and they were growing collec-
tively adamant in their shared belief. Eventually I introduced
myself as "that grad student" they were willing to abandon, and
we then discussed just how this "How long we gotta wait?" hierarchy came to be.

The important thing was to find that common ground. The
students learned first that they were a group with beliefs and
traditions of their own. Then, and only then, did we move to any
sort of breakdown (genres and definitions), and finally we discussed just why such beliefs might exist. It is very important to
ask the "why" and "how" questions in folklore, but the answer in
no way determines if something is folklore or not. More often
than not an informant does not recognize his or her actions or
beliefs as folklore. After all, to the uninitiated the term retains a
rural, uneducated connotation, and many folks will try to avoid
that if at all possible. For a person to discover suddenly that he
is somehow part of the "folk" can unnerve him, so it's best to do
it gently.

Once you have demonstrated to your students that everyone
belongs to folk groups and shares certain beliefs, then it is fun
to pick a few items and analyze them. Using the previous example, I asked one student why she said that a grad student
instructor gets a five-minute grace period, while another student allowed no room for grad student tardiness. Obviously they
both were firm believers that some schedule of waiting times
was out there somewhere, but the simple fact that their stories
diverged indicated variation within an item of folklore.

Where did they hear it? From a friend, maybe a friend of a
friend? Was it written into official policy anywhere? Sure, but
they didn't know just where. And finally, I asked, "What if the
grad student instructor showed up fifteen minutes late and then
took roll and docked everybody that left a letter grade for atten-

dance?" Murmur, half-spoken rebuttals, and then nothing. So I took roll.

Folklore is a process, ongoing and ever changing. There are genres or categories that many elements of folklore can be stuffed into, and by studying and exploring these, one can trace a clearer path to understanding folklore as a discipline. Find a group and listen and watch them. Don't be afraid of what you learn. Sometimes the material gathered may be tough to handle, especially if it hits close to home. Remember, though, if it is important enough to keep and eventually pass along, then it is important enough to be folklore.

For the remainder of this effort, I will keep trying to demonstrate by example. If any theory sneaks into the mix, it's probably your own. First I offer a collection project designed for junior and senior high school students that gently introduces them to a few typical genres of their own family folklore. Then I offer some guidelines toward a larger project for those wishing to preserve a somewhat thicker slice of themselves.

Example 1: Grade-school Family Folklore Project
How Did I Get to be Me?
Collect at least one example of each of the following types of folklore from your families, then tie them all together answering the question, "How did I get to be me?"

1. *Immigration Story*—Since none of us are truly native Americans (even the "Native Americans" crossed the Bering Land bridge between ten and fifty thousand years ago), then each family must have come from somewhere else. For some students this was a difficult step because family interest in genealogy fluctuates, but I asked that they go back as far as they could. Simply answer the question "How did I get here?"

2. *Family Heirloom*—Not every family has a set of pewter candlesticks that some relative brought over on the *Mayflower*,

but every family does have something from someone in their past. If the artifact is important enough to keep, then obviously it has a story that makes it worth keeping.

3. *Family Gatherings*—Whether calendar celebrations or surprise visits, each family has stories and remembrances of get-togethers. Not all of them are pleasant, but even the disastrous ones have a predictable dynamic to them. At meals, who does the cooking? Who sits where at the table? Who carves the bird or opens the wine? What family member is associated with which food item? All of this is traditional, passed down from one performer to the next generation, and deemed important enough to preserve in memory or story or photograph.

4. *Near-Miss Story*—Every family that I know of has a tale or anecdote dealing with some member that almost got killed, almost got rich, almost met the president, almost missed meeting his wife, almost made a huge mistake, etc. As before, the stories themselves will differ with each family and even with each teller within the family, but the fact is that every family has one of these types of stories. Knowing that some broad categories (or genres) exist in the family folklore saga, the folklore student can aim in these directions and generally score well.

5. *How I Fit In*—The teacher in me is seeking synthesis and closure here, but the underlying dynamic is learned. Translated: even if a student is telling you his or her version of how they fit into their family ("I've got Dad's eyes," " I've got Aunt Jane's sense of humor," "I've got Granny Anne's love of quilting.") what you're getting is the compounded opinions of all family members who have made this assessment before and drilled it into the student with repetition. Tell someone often enough, with enough inflection and influence in the voice, and that someone will eventually understand it as truth.

Example 2: The Family Folklore/Oral History Project

It began one night as I listened to my wife's grandfather tell story after story about his life as a minister. At the time, my wife and I were expecting our son, and I began to wonder if Zane would ever know much of his great-grandfather. My own grandfather passed away when I was ten years old, and though I had some wonderful times with him and many great memories, there are enormous gaps that I may never get filled. This project is designed to jump-start anyone interested in gathering and preserving parts of themselves and their families for future generations.

Equipment

Note-taking is the most natural way for many of us to get information down, but for a project of this importance, *it is imperative that a tape recorder be brought into play.* Almost everyone reading this has access to one nowadays, and the expense isn't prohibitive. Any make or model will get the job done as long as there is a microphone either built in or attached. Tape recorders pick up every word so that nothing is missed or overlooked. All you, the fieldworker, need to worry about is getting the tape recorder to do its job properly.

As for tapes, I suggest high quality cassettes of no more than sixty minutes in length (thirty minutes per side). Longer tapes are more convenient in the interview process, but they tend to stretch or "bleed through" over time. Shorter tapes require more frequent changing, and this can interrupt the interview unnecessarily.

Practice, practice, practice. Before you ever take a tape recorder into the field to record a conversation or interview, you absolutely must know what levels, numbers, or buttons to set or push. I like to set mine up on a table and write down whatever volume level number it is set for. Then I'll sit near the microphone and begin speaking: "I'm recording my own voice at level five. I'm two feet away from the microphone." Then I'll get up and move around, talking all the time about the distance I might be from the microphone. If I change levels, then I've got to note it on the practice tape.

When it is time for me to go do an interview, I know (or considering my memory, have written down on a notecard) just what level to set the recording volume depending upon what distance my informant and I are from the microphone. This may sound tedious, but *after* a two-hour interview is not the time to discover that the volume was too low for you to hear a single word spoken.

Camera: This is the simplest method ever invented of documenting physical facts. Use only black and white film, and try to use 35mm whenever possible. Take pictures of your informants, but also try to include those things surrounding your informants that make them unique or identify them. Does Aunt Gertrude have a quilt from before the Great War? Did Granny just finish putting up twenty quarts of peach preserves? Document not only the informant, but try to include a part of their life in the photo.

The camera can also be helpful in recording documents if you have a macro lens. Focus on the words of birth or marriage certificates, and position yourself so that you can read the whole page clearly through the viewfinder. Photos of documents are rarely substitutes for photocopies, but in case of a disaster, these pictures may be the only surviving record.

Paper and pen or pencils are a must. Though you may not want to distract your informant with your scribbling, many times you can jot down possible interview questions as they arise. You may also wish to note facial expressions or gestures during the interview for future reference. Sometimes a sketch of an item is required, or perhaps you need to record unmentioned details that will assist you in the transcription, such as noting that there are three Uncle Franks in the family. You don't want to abandon eye contact with your informant, but from time to time the notepad is a vital tool.

The Interview

Start with yourself! If you've got questions about your family folklore or history, ask them of yourself first. Use your responses as your first guide. What do you know, what do you want to know? Who's the best informant for each topic? Who was there? Starting with yourself gives you direction and background, because after all, you are a member of the family.

It is imperative that you work out family politics and personalities before you ask anyone a question. Use your own common sense as a sounding board. Are there any sensitive topics? Are there gender specific topics? Are there certain family members who will or won't give you certain kinds of information? Figure this out at home, before you take your tape recorder on the road.

Be aware of terms or nicknames that might get confusing in the long run. You may know Uncle Charlie (who may not really be an uncle, but a high school friend of your mother's) but your great-grandchildren will be totally confused. Clarify kinship terms on tape with your informants as soon as they are mentioned. It saves major headaches later on.

Look for natural family gathering contexts. Holidays, family dinners, weddings, funerals, births, etc., are all excellent places for you to collect information. Look for natural storytelling situations too, like card games after the children are put to bed, or domino games late at night. Meal preparations are usually excellent possibilities for recording family folklore, and you will often be surprised by what you get on tape! Reminder: choose your interview context carefully. Shoot for one informant at a time because two or more are a transcription nightmare. Plus, one person is usually a more dominant personality, and you will wind up with sixty minutes of them and nothing from your other informant.

Here are some rough guidelines for formulating interview questions and things to consider as you do:

1. *Plan your questions well ahead of time.* Each question should elicit a lengthy response, nothing that can be answered with a "yes" or "no." Begin by asking informants about things you know that they know, because a familiar story is often a great ice-breaker.

2. *Be a great listener.* Keep up the dialogue flow, but let your informant do the work. Try never to argue or correct informants; it shuts them up.

3. *Don't worry if your informant strays off the topic,* in fact, you may want to encourage it. The farther the informant runs, the more avenues you have to pursue. Be careful of cutting your informant off or trying to return to the topic, for you risk "correcting" them and intimidating them in the process. As with disagreements, if you have to correct them, they perceive that they've done something wrong. Be super careful. There will be plenty of time later to ask the question again. Also consider why the informant strayed on the question asked. Was there a plethora of related information he/she was trying to get out, or was the question as you worded it too clouded or sensitive to answer? Still waters run mighty deep, but egos run deeper.

4. *Realize from the start that there is just some information that you will never get.* You may never ask the right question, or you may be the wrong age or gender to elicit the response you're hoping for. Knowing this ahead of time saves you tons of worry, and actually signals you to bring in another interviewer if necessary. Great Grandma is just not likely to discuss honeymoon nights or childbirth details with a male relative sixty years her

junior. It's a fact, and you're only going to make things difficult if you pursue avenues uncomfortable for your informants.

5. *Don't be shy about using family photo albums or quilts or any kind of prop to help instigate an interview.* As long as you describe the item on tape (and hopefully document it in photos) there's no reason not to use anything that might help. Momentos, curios and knick-knacks often bring on strong memories, so don't hesitate to look around the room during a lull in the interview.

6. *Please keep your informants in mind at all times.* Octogenarians don't usually hold up well to four-hour interviews without bathroom breaks or glasses of water. Using sixty minute tapes is a plus here, because there is a natural half-hour break as you flip the cassette, and an hour interview deserves a stretch and a break for everyone involved. Encourage your informant to take a short walk or break away from the room. It allows you to check the tape you've recorded for any errors or ideas, and gives you time to prep for the next round.

7. *Keep the interview context in mind.* Are you taking the informant's time right before she normally prepares dinner? Are you keeping him up way past his bedtime? Is this session keeping them from church or any social engagements? Is the informant sitting on an uncomfortable chair? Are you in their favorite chair because they offered it to you as their guest?

What room did you choose for the interview? In most cases you will have a choice, and any room that is isolated tends to get good focus. On the other hand, a "busy" room tends to get the informant talking about a greater variety of topics. Find a comfortable middle ground. Guest bedrooms are quiet, but kitchens are productive.

8. *Never ever forget that you hold a great deal of power as the interviewer.* Not only are you validating the very life experiences of your informants, but you are probably switching roles with them too—you the interviewer in control, and they the agreeable

helper. Many times I've had informants say, "Oh, you don't wanna hear about that ol' stuff." That ol' stuff is precisely what you want to record, and by requesting it, you just placed great significance on the life and times of your informant.

You will notice a changed relationship with your informant, and you had better be prepared to react to the change. From the first interview on, you will be treated differently by your family members, and the topics of conversation you will be privy to will blossom. You will become known as the "family historian" and you will get late night phone calls every time Aunt Gertie remembers another anecdote. Your mailbox will fill and your phone bills will skyrocket. People will seek you out at any gathering, and your free time will diminish greatly. You will also find yourself laden with pictures and documents and momentos left to you in wills because you may well have been the only person besides the owner to show any concern for them. First born sons get the land, daughters get the jewelry, and you get the velvet Elvis paintings and Civil War letters. *C'est la vie.*

Keep your goal in mind at all times. The most mundane details of soap-making or hog butchering that your grandmother may remember will utterly fascinate your grandchildren. Never lose sight of the potential significance of any detail or story. You are providing a valuable service to your family, and you will be remembered as the one that "saved" the family.

Interview Question Suggestions

1. *Family origin stories?* Where did you come from? Old country? Surnames? Immigration stories? Traditional naming practices? Name changes? What do you know about your ancestors? Their childhoods, educations, occupations, marriages, religions, recreations?

2. *Famous or infamous characters?* How did their fame affect your family? How are their stories told in your family? Are they

hushed up or bragged about? Why?

3. *Won and lost fortunes?* Any near-misses with glory or wealth?

4. *Homes?* Where did the ancestors live? Any memories, pictures, etc.? Are there any stories of their first homes? Did any of them build their own? Of what? How? When? Where? What style: Dog run, saltbox, Victorian, Colonial? Are any of them still standing? Can you draw a floorplan from memory?

5. *Heirlooms?* What kind of possessions were passed down? Anything of great monetary or sentimental value? What about christening gowns, jewelry, quilts, etc. How have these been passed down? From whom and to whom? Are there any stories associated with the artifact? Where were the objects made? How did they get here?

6. *Occupations/Hobbies?* What were the lifelong jobs, tasks, daily chores, accidents, happenstance occurrences? Even the most mundane chore can produce a good story, for example, the time Granny Jo was attacked by the rooster while feeding the chickens. Also consider vices and habits. Who chewed tobacco or smoked a pipe? Did granny have a "toothbrush" for her snuff? Did anyone hold office or receive special recognition? Were there any societies or clubs? Was there military service (a huge potential for information), or a particular sideline? Did anyone play a particular sport? How about any "almost" or "always" stories: Uncle Fred always wanted to . . . .

7. *Religion?* This is a huge category that can elicit many memories. Have informants recall first communion or baptism. Were there stories or anecdotes about conversions, baptisms, communions, Sunday School, revivals, foot washings, prayer meetings, dinners on the ground, etc.? And the biggest one is the family Bible. Does one exist? Where is it? What is in it?

8. *Marriages and courtships?* Are there any extraordinary (and don't forget the ordinary—try for details) practices, superstitions,

costumes, locations? When and where were they married? What did they do next? Shivaree? Honeymoon? My grandmother loves to tell about the buggy she was married by. Anytime I ask about her wedding, that is her primary memory. Obviously that is important to her and should be recorded as such. Let your informants guide you. Don't bring a ton of baggage to the interview and expect to have it unloaded.

9. *Births?* Are there any family stories concerning awkward or unusual places or times of birth? Anything "usual" that you can get? Home births? First baby born in a hospital? What was the birth experience like? What did the doctor do? Were there any attempts at sex predetermination (suspended pencil or Drano tests)? Any folk beliefs or practices that came into play? Any predictions that came true?

10. *Deaths?* Are there any traditions associated with funerals, wakes, sitting up with the body, burial plots, grave markers (rubbings), prayers, feasts? Are there any unusual stories that have accompanied deaths in the family? Premonitions, accidents, tragedies, longevity, brevity? Who cries the most/loudest at funerals? Who behaved strangely? Any readings of the will that surprised anyone? Use caution here! Emotionally charged narratives can be double-edged swords. I find it best to get several tellings from family members and treat each narrative as a valid document, even if one is significantly different from another telling or another person's telling.

11. *Foods?* This category is immense! Consider family foods and food events by occasion, season, holiday (food as response to situation, or food as instigator of situation). What foods are served when, and why? Who makes these foods and why? Are there any family recipes or cookbooks? How have they been passed down? Who has them now? Are there any special names for foods, tools, measurements or techniques in the kitchen?

Are there any times when multiple family members are involved in a food event? What is the ranking system or pecking order?

Are there any favorite dishes? Truly horrible dishes that keep showing up? Really bad food experiences or substitutions? Are there foods that evoke specific memories, good or bad? Any "first time in the kitchen" stories, or "first meal as a married couple" stories?

Where are certain foods or meals always eaten? Not just in which room, but at whose house? Who sits where at the table? Any memorable meal experiences (the time the cat ate the turkey or the time little Roger threw potatoes and hit Granny)?

12. *Music?* Can you remember any songs from your youth? What kinds of music did you listen to? What songs did you (or were you allowed to) sing? Did you dance? Are there any singers or musicians in the family? Who played what instrument? Were they known for their musical abilities? Did anyone make instruments? Did anyone attend music school or classes (Stamps Baxter shape note singing classes?) Church choir or gospel groups? When and where was music played?

13. *Holidays/Celebrations?* Which holidays does your family celebrate? Rank them if possible. Are there any stories tied to certain holidays? (Uncle Bob passed away Christmas Eve or cousin Jimmy setting the jack-o-lantern on fire?) In addition, consider family gatherings, reunions, celebrations, and rites of passage (bar mitzvah, *quinceria*, etc.). Are there any traditions associated with each holiday? Who carves the turkey? Who reads the Bible on Christmas Eve? Who told little Jenny about Santa Claus and set her to crying for ten days? Don't forget high school proms and homecomings.

14. *Other entertainments?* What did you do for fun as a kid? Did anyone play sports, games of chance, or skill? What toys were there? How were they made and who made them? What

games did you play as a child? What were the rules to those games? Who were your playmates? Movies? Who was your favorite actor? Favorite film? Were there church socials?

Hunting and fishing stories alone can fill more tape than you may bring at one time, but once you get an old hunter or fisherman wound up, it's tough to get them slowed down. For fun, ask the *spouse* of the hunter or fisherman about the stories told to you!

15. *World Events?* The interviewer can usually trigger a flood of memories by simply mentioning the Great Depression or a World War. Any major event or even disaster (Hurricane Carla or Camille, the Dustbowl, the Texas City explosion, etc.) can bring about gobs of stories.

Politics are usually a bit more personal, but you might try asking about certain elections or candidates. Has anyone in the family ever met anyone famous? Has anyone ever held/run for office?

16. *Certain pets or possessions often trigger great responses.* Ask your informant about automobiles in their life. First car? Best hunting dog or roping horse? Favorite doll or dress? First time in a tuxedo? What pets have they had? Favorite guns, knives, tools, etc.

17. *Mapping.* Ask your informant to draw a map of her neighborhood when she was a child. Identify all the houses and stores that she can. Or perhaps take a "virtual stroll" down the street, county road, etc., and have her describe everything she "sees." Perhaps she might remember a particular store? Describe everything on the shelves, the clothing the sales clerks wore, the cars parked outside. Try asking about certain smells she might remember—the creosote plant, the sawmill, the bakery or dairy.

There are millions of approaches and even more responses, and this tiny sampling is only a patch. What is important is that you explore the possibilities and follow the paths where your informants lead you. If things slow down, try a different subject or branch off from the last big flurry of information. The material is truly endless.

A Few Publication Warnings

• *Before publishing anything, be aware of current copyright laws! If it is written or spoken, it belongs to the writer or speaker.* Plain and simple, you have to have a permission slip stating your intentions and directions with the material collected. Don't assume that "Aunt Grace" won't sue if you print that story of her night in Dallas in 1921. Cover your bases. (See sample permission form below). If there are any doubts or questions, write the government for more information: Copyright Office, Library of Congress, Washington, D.C. 20560.

• *Due to the personal nature of the information you are collecting, some relatives may not share your enthusiasm or see eye to eye with you on your presentation.* There are as many sides to a family topic as there are family members, so be careful. Never make promises you cannot or do not intend to keep.

• *You are going to be "taking" from your informants without really giving anything back.* Understand this ahead of time and prepare some kind of offering for those that helped you. Whether a transcript of their tapes or a completed family folklore project report, they need to feel a part of the process and the fieldworker is obligated to include them. Sometimes flowers, sometimes pictures, but always remember to "repay" your informants for their gifts.

• *Make the final product accessible.* Everyone that participated either needs a copy or needs to know where a copy is housed. If you build a "Legacy Trunk" and fill it with your findings, keep relatives aware that you have it, or just bring it out at holiday gatherings. Bringing out the trunk every Thanksgiving or Christmas may become a family tradition that carries on long after you're gone.

You may also wish to consider donating copies of certain materials to the local library or historical society. Make certain that the intended recipient institution is capable of handling your materials, both technically and professionally, and write a solid cover letter for their index.

- *Never record secretly. Never, ever record secretly.*

Sample Permission Form

In consideration of the work of (___Interviewer's Name___) in preserving and presenting family history and folklore, I agree that the tapes (photographs, documents, artifacts, etc.) described below may be deposited for future use by the above.

These tapes and their transcripts are the result of one or more recorded, voluntary interviews with me.

It is understood:

1. that (___Interviewer's name___) will allow qualified scholars and family members to listen to the tapes and use them in connection with research and educational purposes;

2. that no copies of the tapes or the transcripts will be made and that nothing may be used from them in any published form without the written permission of (___Interviewer's name___) except for educational and research purposes.

Tape #   Date   Place   Interview Subject

Signed: (Interview Subject's Signature)

Date: _____

Archiving

- **Anything worth collecting is worth preserving!**
- **Heat, humidity, and light are the enemies of archival materials everywhere.** Just like people, archival materials are happiest when the temperature is near 65 degrees and the humidity

is roughly 45%–55%. If you're comfortable, your archives are probably doing just fine.

• **Use Black and White Film Only!** As of today, no one is 100% certain that color photos or even slide transparencies will be permanent images. They just haven't been around long enough for us to bank on. Also investigate "archival processing" (a thorough washing of all films to remove developing and fixing chemicals).

• **Acid free file folders and photo albums** (and negative sleeves). You're not going to get the quantity discount of say, the Smithsonian, but despite the expense, these little goodies are the best things available to date. If the material is important to anyone, use them.

• **Archival Bibliographic Must**: Davies, Thomas L. 1977. *Shoots: A Guide to Your Family's Photographic Heritage.* Danbury, New Hampshire: Addison House.

Good Places to Start

Abernethy, Francis Edward, ed. *Texas Toys and Games.* Denton: University of North Texas Press, 1997.

Allen, Barbara, and Lynwood Montell, eds. *From Memory to History: Using Oral Sources in Local Historical Research.* Nashville: The American Association of State and Local History, 1981.

Briggs, Charles L. *Learning How to Ask: A Sociolinguistic Appraisal of the Role of the Interview in Social Science Research.* Cambridge: Cambridge University Press, 1986.

Brown, Linda Keller, and Kay Mussell, eds. *Ethnic and Regional Foodways in the United States: The Performance of Group Identity.* Knoxville: University of Tennessee Press, 1984.

Byington, Robert H. *Working Americans: Contemporary Approaches to Occupational Folklife.* Smithsonian Folklife Series, Number 3. Los Angeles: The California Folklore Society, 1978.

Camp, Charles. *American Foodways: What, When, Why and How We Eat in America.* Little Rock: August House, Inc., 1989

Carpenter, Inta Gale, ed. "Folklorists in the City: The Urban Field Experience." *Folklore Forum*, 1978.

Farrer, Claire R., ed. *Women and Folklore*. Austin: University of Texas Press, 1975.

Finnegan, Ruth. *Oral Traditions and the Verbal Arts: A Guide to Research Practices*. New York: Routledge, 1992.

Flynn, Robert, and Susan Russell. *When I Was Just Your Age: Remarkable Reflections on Growing up in Another Era*. Denton: University of North Texas Press, 1992.

Georges, Robert A., and Michael O. Jones. *People Studying People: The Human Element in Fieldwork*. Berkeley: University of California Press, 1980.

_____, eds. *Folkloristics: An Introduction*. Bloomington: Indiana University Press, 1995.

Goldstein, Kenneth S. *A Guide for Field Workers in Folklore*. Hatboro, Pennsylvania: Folklore Associates, Inc, 1964.

Graham, Joe S., ed. *Hecho en Tejas: Texas-Mexican Folk Arts and Crafts*. Denton: University of North Texas Press, 1991.

Humphrey, Theodore C., and Lin T. Humphrey, eds. *"We Gather Together": Food and Festival in American Life*. Logan, Utah: Utah State University Press, 1988.

Ives, Edward D. *The Tape-Recorded Interview: A Manual for Fieldworkers in Folklore and Oral History*. Knoxville: The University of Tennessee Press, 1974.

Jones, Evan. *American Food: The Gastronomic Story*. New York: The Overlook Press, 1974.

Jordan, Terry G. *Texas Log Buildings: A Folk Architecture*. Austin: University of Texas Press, 1978.

_____. *Texas Graveyards: A Cultural Legacy*. Austin: University of Texas Press, 1982.

Langness, L. L., and Gelya Frank. *Lives: An Anthropological Approach to Biography*. Novato, California: Chandler and Sharp Publishers, Inc., 1981.

Linck, Ernestine Sewell, and Joyce Gibson Roach. *Eats: A Folk History of Texas Foods*. Fort Worth: Texas Christian University Press, 1989.

Lindahl, Carl, J. Sanford Rinkoon, and Elaine J. Lawless. *A Basic Guide to Fieldwork for Beginning Folklore Students*. Bloomington: Folklore Publications Group, Folklore Monographs Series, Volume 7, 1979.

Morris, Brian. "Introduction," in *Anthropology of the Self: The Individual in Cultural Perspective*. London: Pluto Press, 1994.

Robinson, John A. "Personal Narratives Reconsidered," *Journal of American Folklore*, Vol 94, No. 371, January–March, 1981.

Sitton, Thad, George L. Mehaffy, and O. L. Davis, Jr. *Oral History: A Guide for Teachers (and Others)*. Austin: University of Texas Press, 1983.

Spradley, James P. *The Ethnographic Interview*. New York: Holt, Rinehart and Winston, 1979.

Stahl, Sandra K. D. "Personal Experience Stories." In *Handbook of American Folklore*, Richard Dorson, ed. Bloomington: Indiana University Press, 1983.

Stone, Elizabeth. *Black Sheep and Kissing Cousins: How Our Family Stories Shape Us*. New York: Penguin Books, 1988.

Toelken, Barre. *The Dynamics of Folklore*. Boston: Houghton-Mifflin Co., 1979.

Wachs, Eleanor. *Crime-Victim Stories: New York City's Urban Folklore*. Bloomington: Indiana University Press, 1988.

Watson, Lawrence C., and Maria Barbara Watson-Frank. "The Study of the Individual-Culture Relationship," in *Interpreting Life Histories: An Anthropological Inquiry*. New Brunswick: Rutgers University Press, 1985.

Zeitlin, Steven J., Amy J. Kotkin, and Holly Cutting-Baker. *A Celebration of Family Folklore: Tales and Traditions from the Smithsonian Collection*. New York: Pantheon Books, 1982.

Essays Illustrating Folklore

Phyllis Bridges

The Honored Dead:

The Ritual of Police Burial

The rituals for burial of the dead are among the oldest of folk patterns, and they are highly reflective of cultural beliefs and practices among a people. The rituals honor the dead, comfort the surviving, and demonstrate community values.

In the twenty-third book of the *Iliad*, the burial rites of Patroclus and the lamentations of Achilles and his followers are recorded. Homer tells us the rituals of burial from antiquity in his description of the actions of Achilles as he presides over the burial of his lifelong friend Patroclus:

> The horse led off, and after them came a mass of infantry one could not count. In the middle of the procession Patroclus was carried by his own men, who had covered his body with the

locks of hair they had cut off and cast upon it. Behind them Prince Achilles supported the head, as the chief mourner, who was despatching his highborn comrade to the Halls of Hades. . . . They made a pyre a hundred feet in length and breadth, and with sorrowful hearts laid the corpse on top. At the foot of the pyre they flayed and prepared many well-fed sheep and shambling cattle with crooked horns. The great-hearted Achilles, taking fat from all of them, covered the corpse with it from head to foot, and then piled the flayed carcasses round Patroclus. To these he added some two-handled jars of honey and oil, leaning them against the bier; and in his zeal he cast on the pyre four highnecked horses, groaning aloud as he did so. The dead lord had kept nine dogs as pets. Achilles slit the throats of two and threw them on the pyre. . . . This done, he gave a groan and spoke once more to his beloved friend: 'All hail from me, Patroclus, in the very Halls of Hades! I am keeping all the promises I made you . . .' (415–17).

So important to the ancients were burial rites for fallen heroes that truces were arranged and conflicts suspended until proper obeisance could be paid. Homer in the final book of the *Iliad* describes the courtesies arranged for the burial of Hector.

Works of literature from every age note the importance of burial customs. For example, the last speech in *Hamlet*, one given by Fortinbras, who has happened upon the carnage of the Danish court, shows the importance of death rites. Fortinbras says, "Let four captains/ Bear Hamlet like a soldier to the stage,/ For he was likely, had he been put on,/ To have proved most royal; and for his passage/ The soldier's music and the rite of war/ Speak loudly for him" (V.ii. 380–85).

Whether in antiquity, the Renaissance, or modern times, the folklore surrounding the death and burial of heroes is part of a ritualistic code which shows the innermost sensitivities and the most public displays of a community. For centuries the burial of fallen heroes, the honored dead of any group, has been formed out of an amalgamation of ancient lore and contemporary practice. Rituals arise out of the desire to show in a public and physical way the reverence and respect for the dead which are felt in a private and spiritual or psychological way by those who survive. Some times the rituals are brief and simple. For example, in March of 1993, when legendary stage actress Helen Hayes died, the theatre lights of New York were dimmed for a moment in homage to the contributions of Hayes. This action took but a moment, and the performances of the evening immediately commenced. In February of 1993, when professional wrestler and former world champion Kerry Von Erich died from suicide, the wrestling card of the evening was briefly delayed and the ringside bell sounded a ten count to signal the death of Von Erich. After the ten clangs of the bell, the scheduled matches began. Military services and fraternal orders hold elaborate rituals for the burial of their members.

Perhaps no professional group, outside the military, has a more highly developed ritualistic ceremony for the burial of the dead than the quasi-military law enforcement agencies. The funeral of a police officer who dies in the line of duty in one of the urban centers of Texas is likely to attract a crowd in the thousands. Law enforcement agencies all over the state send delegations. Between November 10 and December 18, 1993, two Dallas sworn officers were killed in the performance of their duties. Senior Corporal Richard Lawrence, age forty-six, was killed by car thieves at a far East Dallas apartment complex. Nineteen hundred persons attended the funeral. Representatives of fifty-three law enforcement agencies were present for the memorial service in Dallas, and the funeral service at his hometown in the Panhandle had to be set at the West Texas High School of Stinnett to accommodate the crowds. Just a month later, the Dallas Police Department lost another veteran officer in the line of duty when Senior Corporal David Galvan, age forty-eight, died in an auto accident as he was speeding to help another officer who was pursuing a stolen car. Twelve hundred police officers from forty-one cities attended the service.

Two deaths within five weeks of Dallas officers killed in the line of duty reflect the increasing danger and violence which threaten all in society but none more directly than police officers. Statistics kept by the Dallas Police Department in recent years reflect that the department loses to violent death an average of three officers per year. The average length of service for those who have died in the line of duty is 5.41 years, and the average age of the officers who die is 31.93. These statistics, along with the descriptions of the funeral customs practiced in the department, were shared with me by Senior Corporal Gene Hagen, a police chaplain, and Senior Corporal Verna Durden, a personnel officer. Hagen and Durden are involved in the funeral arrangements for every Dallas police officer who dies in the line of duty. Without their help, this study would not have been possible.

Since the founding of the Dallas Police Department in 1881, over sixty-five sworn police officers have died in the line of duty. Their deaths have come by shootings, stabbings, car crashes, plane crashes, heart attacks, accidents of various sorts. Most of the officers who have died are included in a book called *In the Line of Duty* by Officer Steve Elwonger. Elwonger relied upon the archives of the *Dallas Morning News*, the Dallas Police Department and the Dallas Public Library for his work.

The first Dallas officer to die in the line of duty was C. O. Brewer, who was ordered to arrest a man named Henry Miller for slander in 1892. In a scuffle during the arrest, Miller mortally wounded Brewer. The assailant Miller was arrested by other officers and taken to jail where a crowd of over one thousand angry citizens demanded to lynch him. To protect their prisoner, authorities were forced to fire at the crowd as they rammed the doors of the jail. Three people were wounded in the melee. Miller was later executed by hanging

In that same year, 1892, the second killing of a Dallas police officer occurred, and the intolerance of the people for such acts was once again clearly demonstrated. When Officer William H. Riddell was fatally shot as he was trying to serve a warrant on Franklin P. Miller at his shoe shop on Elm Street, a crowd gathered. The angry citizens wanted to burn the shoe shop down with Miller in it. The police chief arrived and dissuaded the crowd from setting the building ablaze, but as the chief took Miller into custody and loaded him in a wagon, a man from the crowd jumped in the wagon and threw a noose around Miller's neck. He was pulled out of the wagon. According to Elwonger: "Miller was half conscious when another citizen hit him over the head with a shotgun and broke the stock in two. Officers were able to place Miller back in the patrol wagon. While heading to the jail, another citizen jumped into the wagon and placed another noose around Miller's neck. Officers were able to lift the noose off as the citizen jumped out of the wagon" (Elwonger 11). Miller was later tried and found guilty and sentenced to hang. However Governor Culberson altered the sentence to life imprisonment, and fifteen years later Governor Campbell pardoned Miller on Christmas Day of 1908. Officer Riddell left a wife and seven children.

The first black officer to die in the line of duty was Officer William McDuff, who was shot to death on Christmas Eve of 1896, after less than two months on the force.

Dipping the flag. *Courtesy Dallas Police Department*

Officer Ernest Elmer Bates was killed in Dallas at the intersection of Elm and Akard on August 7, 1942, the first day that policemen were placed in the middle of the street to direct traffic.

Three Dallas police officers have been killed in plane crashes: Preston D. Hale in 1947, who was using a plane to search for a kidnapper when the craft crashed in a dairy pasture; and Lieutenant Robert L. Cormier and James "Chuck" Taylor, both of whom died when their police helicopter crashed into a communications tower as they were doing advance security work for the 1984 Republican Convention.

The first woman to die in the line of duty was Officer Lisa Sandel, who died in January of 1989 at Parkland Hospital, following injuries sustained in a car wreck while she and her partner were chasing a stolen car. Only twenty-six years old, Officer Sandel had been with the department for less than two years.

Probably the most famous of all officers to die in the line of duty in Dallas was Officer J. D. Tippitt, who was gunned down by Lee Harvey Oswald on November 22, 1963, the same day President Kennedy was assassinated. Tippitt was shot four times by a .38 revolver, and he died on the way to Parkland Hospital. Tippitt's funeral is said to be the largest ever held in Dallas. Cars were still in the church parking lot waiting to join the processional when Tippitt's hearse and the family car reached the cemetery several miles away.

The scores of deaths of officers in the line of duty over the past century in Dallas have aroused both public support for law enforcement and public outrage against the threats to officers' safety and thus community security. Central to the understanding of the high public profile given to police burials is an awareness of the sense of fraternity which law enforcement agencies feel for their own. The funeral ritual for police officers empha-

Twenty-one gun salute. *Courtesy Dallas Police Department*

sizes the self sacrifice of police work and the solidarity of sworn officers.

There are three levels of honors offered by the Dallas Police Department: Full Department Honors, which are reserved exclusively for those who are killed in the line of duty; Department Honors, which are accorded active members of the force who die on or off duty; and Ceremonial Honors, which are offered for persons such as city council members, civic leaders, or officers retired from other departments who live in the Dallas area. The twenty-one gun salute is a part of Full Department Honors, and is used only at services for those who are killed in the line of duty.

From the moment that an officer is wounded or disabled in the field until the moment of burial (called "service of committal" by the officers), there is a protocol that is followed. When an officer is wounded, injured, or killed on duty, there is an immediate, formulaic response: the officer's supervisor, a police chaplain, and the police chief are immediately informed. These individuals go at once to the scene of the officer (the scene of the crime, accident, or hospital). The first goal is to provide whatever support is needed and to inform the family and associates before the media can get the news on the air. The police move swiftly to get the family with the injured or deceased officer. In case of an injury and hospitalization, two officers are assigned to stay with the family around the clock for as long as needed. In the case of a death, two officers are assigned round the clock to stay with the family. Their job is to keep the media away, to assist with transportation for family, and to coordinate events with the family. Three shifts with two officers per shift handle the immediate needs of the family. There is also a battery of officers assigned to stand watch over the body of the dead officer around the clock from the moment of death until the funeral service. The posting of officers with the family and with the body is obviously a labor intensive effort. All expenses are covered by the department. The officers on duty are instructed to wear their Class A uniforms. These uniforms are also worn to the funeral service by all law enforcement officers.

Immediately upon notice of the death of an officer in the line of duty, fellow officers place black tape over their badges as a sign of mourning. The tape remains over the badge until the burial. The Police Department also sends out teletype messages to the home state of the dead officer as well as to all law enforcement agencies within Texas. The messages announce the time and place of the services and the directions. The Dallas Police Auxiliary ordinarily serves as hosts for visiting officers from other law enforcement agencies, and the auxiliary provides a meal for those who come from out of town.

As the family members of the fallen officer make plans for the service, the staff of the Police Department offers assistance and liaison with the funeral home and clergy, as well as making arrangements, subject to approval of the surviving family members, to demonstrate honors. Several funeral homes in Dallas offer deep discounts on services for police officers and firefighters who die in the line of duty. There is one funeral home that provides services free for those who are killed on duty. When there is a need for airfare to transport the body from Dallas to burial elsewhere, American Airlines has provided free transportation. Greyhound Buslines has also provided free transportation when large parties need to be transported for the burial of an officer. Private jets have sometimes been offered by Dallas entrepreneurs for use by the chief of police and his immediate staff when the burial of a fallen officer takes place out of state.

Services for officers killed in the line of duty are generally scheduled for times between 10:30 and 1:30 so that representatives from outlying law enforcement agencies can travel to and from the service on one day. Because over a thousand officers are often in attendance at a police service and burial, the filing past the coffin and the lineup of the processional require time. It frequently happens that the service will not be held in the usual place of worship of the deceased, for often the largest facility must be used to accommodate the crowds. For example, when Officer John Glenn Chase was killed in 1988 at the age of only twenty-five, the service had to be held at Marsh Lane Baptist Church. Almost three thousand people attended. The sanctuary was filled to capacity, and closed circuit television was beamed into every room of the church so that the mourners could see the service. It took more than an hour for the police officers in attendance to pass by the casket. Office Chase had been shot to death with his own gun in downtown Dallas. He begged for his life as his assailant fired on him. Some persons passing the scene yelled out their car windows for the gunman to shoot him again. There was such public outrage at both the killing of Officer Chase

"Taps." *Courtesy Dallas Police Department*

and the unconscionable conduct of the jeerers that the service for Chase attracted national attention. Motorists in Dallas turned on their car lights for several days as they drove through the streets as a sign of solidarity with the police. As officers from Dallas made their way across the country to Des Moines, Iowa, where Chase was buried, citizens and law enforcement personnel at every community, alerted by radio communication, came out to the highway and saluted as the cars moved through.

Whether the burial is in Dallas or another location, the Police Department works with the family to prepare the service. It is not unusual for the funeral or memorial service to be in Dallas and the burial elsewhere. Wherever the burial occurs, representatives from the Dallas Police Department attend and remain with the family until there is no longer a need for their services. The honor guard is made up of officers selected by the family and close friends of the deceased.

After the funeral or memorial service, the processional leaves for the cemetery in a designated order. Vans carrying flowers go first. The motorcycle officers go next. Sometimes there are as many as sixty officers on motorcycles forming the escort. Then the honor guard leads the way. Because the Dallas Police Department has mounted officers, horsemen are available to handle the riderless horse which is a part of the symbolism and pageantry of the processional. Already in place at the cemetery are the bagpiper and bugler. The family waits in the funeral car until all have parked at the cemetery. The uniformed officers assemble in a block formation and stand at parade rest until the body is taken from the hearse. As the body is carried by the pall bearers to the grave, the uniformed officers stand at attention and the family is escorted to the platform. The bagpiper plays "Going Home" as the family takes its place. All officers remain at attention and salute until the casket is placed over the grave on a platform. As the coffin is settled, the clergyman, following the wishes of the family, speaks. At the conclusion of the clergyman's remarks, a flag (either the Texas flag or the American flag—the choice made by the family) is held over the casket by the honor guard. The flag is then folded and handed to the police chief who presents it to the family. As the flag is handed to the family, the twenty-one gun salute begins. A team of eight persons handles the salute. There are seven persons who fire at the signal of their leader. Each person fires three rounds (all blanks) to make the twenty-one shots. Occasionally a family will decline the honor of the gun salute, particularly if gun fire has been a part of the scenario that has brought them to the grave. In Dallas, pistols are used. In some law enforcement agencies, rifles are used. As the last gun shots fade, the bugler plays taps. There is a flyover by the Dallas Police Department helicopters, and on occasion the missing man formation is used. After these rituals, the cler-gyman makes his final remarks or says a final prayer. The bag-piper then plays "Amazing Grace" as the family is escorted to funeral cars. The honor guard and liaison officers see the family home. A Dallas Police Department chaplain remains with the body until interment is complete.

The elaborate ritual of a police burial is often covered by the media. Probably no other service for working professionals at-tracts so much attention as the burial of an officer who is killed in the line of duty. The honors presented are worthy of a great warrior, a Patroclus or Achilles, and indeed most rank and file officers consider themselves to be working in a battle zone every day as more and more violence is unleashed on society.

The honors for those who are killed in action do not stop at the grave. Shortly after the funeral, the chief of police presents the Police Cross medal to the family of the deceased in a private ceremony at police headquarters. Portraits of all officers who are killed in the line of duty and painted by Fort Worth artist James

R. Spurlock are placed at the Dallas Police Academy, where they are a daily reminder to officers in training of the dangers of the work they have chosen. The names and dates of all officers killed in the line of duty are also engraved on plates and placed on a display plaque in the chief's office. A granite stone near the Bryan Log Cabin in downtown Dallas also records the names of all Dallas County officers and deputies who die in the line of duty. Police substations throughout the city also have memorials to the officers from their areas. At the national level, the date of May 15 is set aside as National Police Officer Memorial Day, and a service is held each year on that date cohosted by COPS (Concerns of Police Survivors) and the Fraternal Order of Police. All those officers who die in the line of duty are remembered on the Capitol grounds in Washington, and their names are inscribed on walls of honor. Between 120 and 160 police officers are killed each year in America in the line of duty. At the state level, there is a memorial ceremony every other year (odd years) in Austin. Locally, the Dallas Police Department schedules a day around May 15 each year to honor the fallen. The name of each officer who has died in the line of duty in Dallas from 1892 to the present is called out. As the name is called, an officer responds, "Killed in the line of duty, Sir." The decoration for the memorial service is a blue carnation floral arrangement in the shape of a police badge.

There are numerous memorial funds that attempt to help the survivors. The Dallas Police Association makes an immediate gift of $1000 to the family of any officer who is killed. The Fleetwood Memorial fund makes gifts at the state level. The Department of Justice has the Police Officers Survivors Benefit, which makes grants to survivors of officers disabled or killed in the line of duty. The Department of Labor can make grants if the officer was killed pursing an offender who was violating a federal crime. Surviving children are offered tuition and books at any state university in Texas. In addition, often private trust funds are established and donations sought from the community.

The efforts of the Dallas Police Department to honor their fallen comrades and assist the survivors are representative of human sympathy and ritual conduct in all places and times. The rituals followed in Dallas are well formed and predictable. They are, nonetheless, sincere and comforting. The rituals for remembrance of those who die in service to others through law enforcement can surely be found in many police organizations. The practices are likely similar throughout Texas, but perhaps they are less noticeable because the incidence of violent death of police officers is less common. For example, this past year the city of Irving had its first death of an officer in the line of duty. But in Dallas and other urban centers where life is very dangerous, the too frequent loss of officers brings the folk ritual of the burial of the honored dead to the fore.

Of all the incidents in which law enforcement officers have been killed in the line of duty in Texas, probably no other has reached the intensity of public furor that the Waco confrontation between the Branch Davidians of David Koresh and the officers of the Bureau of Alcohol, Tobacco, and Firearms (ATF). During the February 28, 1993, confrontation, four ATF officers were killed and sixteen were wounded. Police officers in Dallas, as well as others across the state, put black tape on their badges in mourning for the ATF agents who died. They wore the tape for four days. The political wrangling and finger pointing about the Mount Carmel fiasco took center stage for months. In May in Washington during the National Law Enforcement Officers Memorial service, over one thousand people gathered in memory of the four who died and the sixteen who were injured. Secretary of the Treasury Lloyd Bentsen and other dignitaries attended along with one hundred ATF agents from Texas and Louisiana. The

New York City Bagpipers band played, and the names of the four agents who died at Waco were added to the memorial wall where already 178 names of ATF agents had been placed in honor. The memorial service in Washington was open to the public. After the ceremony the Waco Police Department presented the Cross of Valor to the families of the slain and wounded. Families of the slain and wounded were taken to the White House for a private meeting with President and Mrs. Clinton and Vice President Al Gore. During that same week another memorial service for the ATF agents was held in Waco. The Waco service, however, was not open to the public or press. Only officers with badges and their immediate families were allowed to attend the Waco memorial service. Both the Washington and Waco services illustrate that whatever the format for the memorial the honor extended to those in law enforcement who are killed in the line of duty is considered an important obligation of the survivors.

Like Achilles centuries ago struggling to do right in the ritual of heroic burial for his fallen comrade, the officers of twentieth-century Texas can say to their departed, "I am keeping all the promises I made to you."

WORKS CITED

Elwonger, Steve. *In the Line of Duty*. Dallas: Taylor Publishing Company, 1991.

Kenneth W. Davis

Meaner Than Hell!

Three types of tales about "Meaner than Hell!" individuals locked away in private prisons reveal much about the way folklore continues to grow and spread in Texas. First are stories about famous killers who somehow avoid capture and therefore escape formal imprisonment but are nevertheless kept away from society by being locked up in jails maintained by their families or neighbors. Second, there are stories about lesser known killers who go to trial and win acquittal but who are so overcome by guilt they lock them-

selves away. A third group includes victims of rabid dogs. These hapless individuals insist on being locked away from their families to avoid attacking them and transmitting rabies. Recurring motifs make examples of these stories a significant body of lore.

One of these types is a tale I collected in mid-September of 1958 when I was driving to Nashville, Tennessee, to attend graduate school. Late on a hot afternoon, near the western edge of Texarkana, Texas, I stopped for gasoline at a small Conoco station whose operator was a shriveled, leather-faced, toothless gnome who was quite a talker. Because his eyesight was failing he couldn't read the official-looking parking sticker on my car's windshield. The sticker allowed me to park on the Tech Tech University campus; the station attendant thought it indicated something else. He asked me if I were one of "them laws" who was in town to look after "that killer." After I had signed the credit card slip, I assured him I was not a police officer and asked if he referred to the famous Texarkana killer who in the midst of World War II created terror throughout the Southwest.

The ancient worthy nodded agreement. Until then I had all but forgotten the grisly murders which made the pages of *Life* magazine. I asked what happened to the killer. The talkative man gave me a conspiratorial look and then answered in low tones as if to make sure no one else anywhere in the universe would hear the information he had to pass along. Between long pulls on an ice-cold bottle of Dr Pepper, he told me that the local police aided by Texas Rangers and the highway patrol quickly enough determined who the killer was but were unable to obtain enough evidence to indict him. Instead, they went to the man's wealthy parents and told them that if they did not lock their son away, some lawman—or someone else—would have to shoot the boy to protect people in the area and to save the state the cost of an expensive trial. So, the man continued, the killer's parents built a cement room, reinforced with steel rods, onto the back of their palatial home and locked the boy away. "That boy was meaner than Hell," my informant said, "but he's all locked up now." I asked where this house was located. The man said he had never seen it, but that his friends in the local chapter of the American

Legion knew for sure where it was. After another drink of Dr Pepper, he added that not too many months after imprisoning their son at their home, the couple died within two or three weeks of each other and left in their will provisions for their son to be fed and cared for. He then said that for some reason, the job of caring for the killer in this private prison fell to Department of Public Safety patrolmen who regularly stopped at the Conoco station to buy gasoline and a case or two of RC Colas. The attendant concluded his account with the comment that he had heard on good authority that the killer was "hooked on RC Colas."

I hurried on to get to Memphis before nightfall. Later in Nashville I let this intriguing information slip into the back files of my memory. Not until I began teaching folklore courses several years later did I recall this account of private imprisonment. What reminded me of the incident were numerous accounts my students gave me of people locked up in their homes for a variety of reasons.

The Texarkana killer tale is, of course, a kind of prototype. Several distinct features are prominent: The killer is from a well-to-do family. Because of his wealth, he avoided punishment in a state-operated facility. But justice was not thwarted. Although my informant did not mention the possibility that this killer's family had in effect bought off the police, such rumors circulated in Dallas in the mid 1940s. My uncle, the late James R. Duke, was parts manager for the Dallas Hudson Company. Famous Texas Ranger Lone Wolf Gonzaullas was a customer. He told my uncle the rumors that although the local police in Texarkana knew who the killer was, they would not attempt to arrest him because (a) they had too little evidence, (b) the family was too rich and influential, and (c) the family had agreed to maintain a private prison. In the minds of the folk who picked up and added to the rumors, there was a practicality to this alleged agreement among the local authorities and the killer's parents. The killer was no longer a threat to society, and the taxpayers were spared the expense of a long, ugly murder trial.

Ranger Gonzaullas also told my uncle some rather grim, darkly comic stories in the grand tradition of folk humor. Many people in Texarkana were quite properly scared almost sleepless because of the killer roaming about committing mayhem before he was supposedly locked away by his parents. In one such brief anecdote, a nervous young cotton gin worker was so scared that he started sleeping with a loaded six-shooter under his pillow. He soon discovered that having a gun under a thin pillow caused him to have a crick in his neck. So he put the gun in a chair by the head of his bed. One moonlit night at about 11 P.M., he awakened from a fitful sleep to see two giant hands reaching up from the foot of his bed. Terrified, the man grabbed the six-shooter and fired a shot. He blew off the big toe on his right foot. My uncle recalled that at this point, the fearless Texas Ranger dissolved in laughter.

Gonzaullas told another anecdote. On a dark, rainy night, a farmer living near the outskirts of Texarkana on the Arkansas side was awakened by menacing sounds of something bumping around in the front yard. The frightened man jerked open the front door, fired both barrels of his shotgun blindly through the screen door at the sounds, slammed the door, and lay all but frozen with terror until daylight. Then he discovered that he had killed his neighbor's elderly mule, a creature used only to plow gardens and amuse small children who rode on the back of the innocent and gentle animal. This farmer was so grief-stricken he packed his meager possessions in his Model A pickup and left Texarkana for good.

In these two anecdotes is the blending of the comic with the terrifying which is common in traditional folk humor in all parts of the world. The folk have the sense to laugh at what would otherwise be too terrible to cope with.

A second type of meaner-than-Hell-but-locked-up story is one that seems to have vast appeal to teenagers and young adults. At least a dozen students in my folklore classes submitted tales like the following conflation.

In a fit of rage prompted by jealousy, a Lubbock man brutally killed his wife. He was immediately filled with remorse and called the local police who with sirens screaming and red-lights flashing rushed to the scene. There, as they had been told, was the body of the deceased. Between sobs of apparently genuine grief, the killer made his confession and begged the officers to shoot him "like the mad dog I am"—so one informant reported. But the police merely took him into custody where his fate took a curious turn. His well-to-do brother, a prominent Dallas, Houston, or San Antonio lawyer, doctor, or accountant, flew to Lubbock, hired the city's most famous criminal defense lawyer, and got the killer released on bond. Soon the murder trial was held. Despite the morose murderer's insistence that he wanted to die for what he did, the clever attorney somehow persuaded the jury that the killing was justifiable homicide; and, wonder of wonders, the confessed murderer was acquitted. He was not really a free man, however. For even if he was not to be electrocuted— the fate he really longed for—or to be sent to the penitentiary, his second choice of punishment for his heinous crime, he was imprisoned by his sense of guilt. So what did he do? He built a house variously reported to be on Akron Avenue, on 37th street, or on Sixth Street, and locked himself in, vowing never to leave this self-made prison which would take the place of the real jail he deserved to be in.

Consider the similar elements in this account and in the story of the Texarkana killer. First, there is the wealthy family and suggestions that wealth can somehow subvert ordinary justice. Second, although the murderer escaped formal punishment, he was nevertheless punished and was no longer a threat to society. And there are, of course, numerous corollary stories. In one of these yarns, the killer yet lives in a circular house made of Austin cut stone in the 2300 block of Sixth Street in Lubbock. One youthful and perhaps overly imaginative informant told me that she had heard all through junior and senior high school that the round house had a sort of running area in it and that on moonlit nights, the guilt-ridden killer ran furiously about the indoor track howling like a wolf. Another informant assured me that he had seen the man peering from the round house's high, barred windows. The killer had red, beady eyes. As a folklorist, I am surprised by nothing and never challenge the veracity of informants. But I did drive by the supposed home-prison on Sixth Street. I was bemused to discover that it belonged to a colleague of mine on the university faculty, a professor of Agricultural Economics whose only moral failing so far as any of us knew was his support of President Dwight D. Eisenhower's farm program at a time when farmers were going broke with alarming frequency.

A third type of meaner-than-Hell-but-locked up story is also a mixture of the pathetic and a smidgen of the comic. As is the case with many folk tales, a variant of this one worked its way from the European oral tradition into the pages of fiction. Marjorie Kennan Rawlings in *The Yearling* gave an account of a man who was bitten by a rabid dog and chained himself to a tree after giving his wife and children orders not to release him regardless of how earnestly he might plead with them. A student from far west Texas who begged me never to reveal his name told me the following story of what happened to his great-grandfather shortly after 1900 in a small community near El Paso. The man was out hunting in late January to find game for his nearly starving family. He was about to abandon the hunt when he found a wild heifer he immediately shot and began to butcher. He was so obsessed with finishing the task he didn't hear a small pack of wolves which, attracted by the scent of fresh blood, hurried to the scene. Without warning, the leader of the pack jumped the man, bit him on his arms and face, then, frothing at the mouth, fell over dead. The other wolves grabbed the freshly butchered meat and hurried away. The man bandaged his wounds as best he could and began the trip home. As he walked along, he realized that he had been bitten by a rabid animal and knew what was in store. When he arrived home, he told his wife to lock him in the stoutly built granary and not let him out for any reason. The student added that in a bit more than a week, his great-grandfather developed rabies and began to howl like a wolf. In intermittent spells of lucidity, he begged his wife to shoot him. After watching her husband's agonies for several days, she sent for a wealthy rancher who had befriended her and her husband when their children were born. She begged the rancher to shoot her husband. Instead, the rancher and several cowhands roped the stricken man, tied him up, and took him to a doctor in El Paso who consulted several other doctors. They agreed that the humane course was to give the man a poison which would release him from his misery. Each doctor then put a lethal portion of a drug in a cup. After much difficulty, the doctors succeeded in getting enough medication into the man to "kill an elephant" as one of them said years later. But the man did not die. Instead, his symptoms subsided and he seemed to be recovering, yet he never regained his sanity. The wealthy rancher took pity on the man and his family, and built a secure, jail-like room in one of his horse barns where for many years, this victim of rabies lived a life of fits of violent rage alternating with interludes of child-like simplicity.

My informant told me that he heard the story from his ninety-five year old grandfather, son of the rabies victim. The elderly man ended his account with a rueful, comic comment that the doctor's decision to poison his father was the only time he knew of when doctors agreed on anything. The old man added that in this case, it would have been better for the victim if he had succumbed to rather than survived the physician's collective ministrations.

This third account of someone meaner-than-Hell-but-locked-up is about not a person who committed violence, but one who was a victim of circumstances which made him a danger to others as well as to himself. It resembles the other accounts also in that a person of wealth manages to keep the story's central figure from being formally institutionalized.

Like most people given to the study of and admiration for the folk, I heard from my childhood on through my early adult years stories similar to those I have recounted here. My maternal grandmother Laura Jane Perkins brought many mad-dog stories to Texas from her home in Gravelly Springs, Alabama. My Mississippi-born grandfather Henry Perkins was not a man to waste words on yarns he deemed nothing but a pack of lies. But even that stern old gentleman knew a story or two about killers who escaped formal punishment only to be kept locked away by family members. Accounts of people coping with rabies are common throughout the world. I heard a story of a victim of a rabid dog who chained himself to a tree from my paternal grandfather William Davis when I was barely six years old. I think he told it to warn me away from stray dogs.

Perhaps these varying accounts of people who for some reason are privately restrained—either willingly or unwillingly or through pressures from well-to-do or even poor family members—appeal to the folk because they show that not all problems have to be solved by the establishment. To the folk, these stories also suggest that although terrible things may happen, eventually there will be a righting of wrongs—or at least the innocent will be protected from people who are meaner than Hell.

Ken Untiedt

Gang Graffiti

A dozen or so years ago, when I was in high school, we had only two gangs. One was called "The Boys," the other, "The Chipmunks." They had little effect on our school's activities, and even less on those of the town. The Boys gathered each weekend in an empty bean field they called "The Farm," where they would drink beer and smoke marijuana. The Boys were primarily jocks and rich kids, and the only damage they did, besides scratching "The Boys" into a few desk tops, was to their own brain cells. The Chipmunks were formed as a parody of The Boys by a group of students we would now commonly refer to as nerds, and their sole purpose was to show the stupidity of The Boys' irresponsible, self-indulgent ways. As a result, the members of The Chipmunks, including

me, received regular beatings from the members of The Boys. However, this was the extent of our town's gang activity.

Today, gangs have found their way into nearly every town in America, regardless of size or location. Drive-by shootings are daily occurrences, and we repeatedly witness innocent victims fall at the hands of these increasingly violent groups of young people. The purpose of gangs is the same as it has been since the beginning of time: unity. Young people who do not have an adequate home life desperately need to belong to something, and gangs provide them with companionship, protection, and a sense of association. They create family environments for children who need them.

Studies of gangs are numerous, and the topics are fascinating. The psychology of these youngsters, the rules and internal organizations, criminal acts committed as initiations, and the gender-differentiated roles of gang members are only a few of the possibilities. One of the most interesting aspects of gangs, and one of the most revealing, is the language used by gang members, both spoken and written. Gangs have not only their own terminology, which they express in body language as well as vocally, but they also have their own literature. The graffiti they use can be complex and cryptic, and most people who see it have no idea what it means, but it is the most direct way for gangs to communicate to the general public, and to each other, that they exist. The following examples, which I have observed during my time as a Lubbock police officer, are typical of gang lore all across Texas.

Graffiti can be territorial, it can be used to send messages to the police or rival gangs, and it can be nothing more than an expression of an individual gang member's artistic ability. Style can be directly associated to the racial groups that dominate different gangs. Black gangs often use crude drawings and letters, with the artist's name appearing larger than the name of the gang. Hispanic artists are more creative, better at drawing elaborate picture-stories, and they pay more respect to their gang by signing their work with smaller letters than those used in the actual drawing.

When looking at graffiti, some general rules can be used to help decipher what is being communicated. Obviously, when a gang's name has been crossed-out with a large "X" in a different color of paint than what was originally used, it indicates that a rival gang is not pleased with the geographic placement of the work. Writing a gang's name backwards is also a sign that the drawing is by a rival gang. Two gangs' names painted next to each other tells of those gangs' alliance with each other. Blood dripping from a gang member's name, or even red paint sprayed crazily over it, can mean impending doom for that individual.

Gang terminology, which stemmed from hand signals, has found its way into gang graffiti. Originally, hand signals were developed to send secret messages, usually when gang members were being questioned by police on the street. Numbers were the easiest signals to give, and they are still used today. A picture of an eight ball means death, a two ball means a shooting, probably with a .22 caliber handgun, which is easily obtained on today's streets. A "45" is a .45 caliber, and a "38" is a .38, or a Saturday Night Special. Gang artists even paint pictures of hands making the signs for their gang.

However, there are many exceptions to the rules of gang graffiti, and even the most basic rules can change without warning or explanation. Keeping up with what gangs are saying through graffiti is difficult, but it is imperative that law enforcement agencies try to understand what is being communicated by these young people. A slip of paper found in a young person's pocket may seem to be nothing more than scribbles and funny pictures at first glance. But to someone who is literate in gang graffiti, it gives away important information regarding a "really bitchin'" party, with detailed instructions including the place, time, location, and what each person is required to bring. Reading on, we can learn that bowls of crack, booze and "ho's" are all provided. There are no mistakes as to who is welcome, and who is not. Oh, one last reminder in the post script—don't forget to "come packin'," just in case there is trouble, or the supply of chips runs out and someone needs to make a quick hit on the convenience store down the street for a refill on munchies.

Sometimes the pictures we see on walls are not simply postcards sent from one gang to another saying, "Glad you're not here." Often the pictures present segments of an on-going saga, much like chapters from a novel. Each scene tells a separate part of a modern urban epic. For instance, we can imagine a story about two gang-bangers, as we in the business call them. The story stars Gilbert and Raymond, with guest appearances from a police sergeant and Raymond's older brother. Gilbert and Raymond are rivals; Gilbert is a member of the VAB (Varrio Arnett-Benson), and Raymond is an East Sider (VES).

Our story begins with a painting on a supermarket wall, which explains in great detail how Gilbert is challenging Raymond to a fight. On another wall, this time a elementary school two weeks later, the scene depicts Gilbert's vow to kill Raymond because Raymond accepted Gilbert's offer and whipped him. The graffiti may only look like two billiard balls, an eight ball and a two ball. To the trained eye, however, it is Gilbert, complete with his trademark hat, flying his VAB colors, telling everyone concerned that he is going to shoot Raymond for humiliating him in front of fellow homeboys. This part of the story almost comes true a week later, except for the fact that Raymond and his brother Julio look an awful lot alike. Unfortunately for Julio, Gilbert shoots him by mistake. Unfortunately for us, the wound is not fatal and Julio, a "major scumbag," survives.

The story is temporarily on hold, because Gilbert is in prison. But alas, nothing is forever, especially in our country's corrections system, and Gilbert is released. Immediately the tale resumes. Within a month, on the wall of the local telephone company, the police sergeant who worked on the case that got Gilbert convicted is shown being "burned" by Gilbert, who is breaking free of his prison restraints. More threats to Raymond appear randomly for the next several months, until Gilbert is caught burglarizing a building in an attempt to frame Raymond, who has not yet been injured or bothered in any way. Gilbert is again sentenced and sent away. The story will be renewed before too long. Gilbert has only spent a total of two years in prison, and he will be paroled soon for good behavior while serving his time. The question that needs to be asked is, "What about the bad behavior while he is out?"

This is only one of the stories being told on the fences, walls, and garages of our town. Many other stories are also being told at the same time in towns everywhere. And not all of the graffiti is unpleasant to look at. Some of the artists are really good at what they do. Although they are violent juvenile delinquents, they can be quite talented. A few of the paintings may actually be called beautiful. It is incredible how some of these kids make use of multiple colors, blend new characters into an established motif, and create the illusions of depth and form. This form of folk art is comparable to works of the masters, and the most impressive fact is that it is all done hurriedly in the dead of night.

The only things that surpass the artwork are the names themselves. Once they were all traditional gang names, like The Bloods, The Crips, and names such as Varrio East Side, Varrio South Side, and Varrio Arnett-Benson, which are all based on their geographic area. Today, however, gangs have creative, fashionable names, which have very little to do with where their main

Varrio Arnette-Benson jacket with personal graffiti. *Courtesy Sgt. Dave Tillery, Lubbock Police Department*

Nortenos Catorce (Northside Fourteen)—The backwards S and the crossed-out *E* are directed towards Southsiders and Eastsiders, respectively. The crossed-out *C* is probably meant for The Wicked Crew, another local gang. *Courtesy Sgt. Dave Tillery, Lubbock Police Department*

force is located. Names like Wicked Crew, North Side Locos (a gang which is nowhere near the northern part of town, but the members thought the name had a nice ring), and Fiends of the Earth. These are great names.

The names of the individual gang members are even better. I know that many parents must have at least considered giving their children names like Monkey Boy, Baby T, Little Monster, and Slut Girl at birth, rather than waiting for them to go through all of the red tape of obtaining them in gang initiations. You see, this whole gang-thing is rich in tradition. Some kids will proudly tell you that they are fourth- or fifth-generation gang members. Their parents are not ashamed or embarrassed about them. They're proud of them! Imagine the respect you would get if you could tell your friends that your son was the youngest member of the Banditos. Yes, your boy had his "jumpin-in" at thirteen, and he killed his first cop at fifteen. No football scholarship or citizenship award could match that.

Nothing is as good as it used to be, though. Gangs are quickly losing many of their traditions. Turf-oriented gangs are no longer holding tight to their territory. Many have expanded so much that they have forgotten where they came from. They have lost touch with their roots, and what it was that made them a gang in the first place. I know East-Siders who live on the west side of town, and they don't even care. Many of them have no interest in the significance of their gang's name. When L. A. Bloods move to West Texas and bring along their original names, which come from the street numbers in Los Angeles, too much of the heritage is lost. There is no meaning left. Can't they have the names legally, or even illegally, changed to fit their new home?

Gang life is all based on commercialism now. Too many movies have been made about gangs for the real essence of gang life to have survived. There aren't any rumbles anymore. Kids these days drive past their enemies at high speeds and shoot at them

Numerous drawings, messages, and turf markings, with Varrio Southside appearing to dominate this central bulletin board. *Courtesy Sgt. Dave Tillery, Lubbock Police Department*

A two ball, indicative of a shooting, is wearing a hat that is a trademark of a particular gang member. *Courtesy Sgt. Dave Tillery, Lubbock Police Department*

with high-tech weaponry, rarely hitting the intended target. What kind of honor is there in that? And honor is what it used to be all about. It used to be that when someone showed you some disrespect, your gang fought that person's gang in hand-to-hand combat in order to maintain your reputation or the boundaries of your part of the city. The only victims were the gang members, who stole from themselves a chance at a normal, respectable role in society.

Today, everyone is a victim, from the school girl who gets killed by a stray bullet in a drive-by to the elderly lady who can't afford to move from a deteriorating neighborhood and watches it get slowly raped by uncaring youths too numerous to be affected by an ill-equipped police department. The rules have changed, so much that they seem to no longer exist at all. The new laws have little effect because of a poor corrections system, and the gangs know they can get away with their activities. They know that for the most part we are at their mercy.

The one thing that has not changed is the graffiti. It still tells the story, in its cryptic way, and if we are literate in the gangbanger's symbols and terminology, we can follow along, trying to keep up with the ever-changing system of gang life. The pictures we see on our buildings, fences, sidewalks, and park benches will continue to tell the story, with new chapters added every day. No details will be left out, if you know how to interpret the images. The graffiti will remain a constant part of the lore of gangs. Perhaps these poor, lost children will eventually find their way back to the mainstream of society. Maybe they can become productive members of our world. And perhaps one day, they will learn how to spell and use a "b" instead of a "v" for the word barrio. One can only hope.

Chris Goertzen

Gideon Lincecum, 'Killie Krankie,' and Fiddling in Early Texas

Gideon Lincecum (1793–1874), Texas pioneer and rough-hewn polymath, possessed among his many skills that of fiddling. His large and varied prose samples, much of which have been reproduced by Lois Burkhalter (1965) and by Jerry B. Lincecum and Edward H. Phillips (1994), allows us to witness much of his activity as a practitioner of botanic medicine, as an early scholar of Choctaw language and lore, and, above all, as a naturalist with a special interest in ants. Music remained in the lesser position of avocation, but it was one that he pursued avidly. He fiddled regularly, beginning in his teenage years or earlier, through the last year of his long life. His accounts of daily life during a post-Civil War sojourn in a confederate colony in Tuxpan, Mexico, make clear that it was his habit to fiddle for a good while nearly every

111

evening (Burkhalter 256, 266, 276 and 292). It is frustrating that he didn't choose to write about music more than he did. We are deeded just a handful of passing references and a pair of page-long narratives about fiddling, writings which together associate a handful of tune titles and several performance venues with him.

Investigation of Gideon's two narratives dealing with his fiddling fit into and perhaps even enhance our understanding of early Texas fiddling. By reproducing Gideon's main writings that discuss music and generally exploring Lincecum's tunes—and how and where he played them—we can see how he fit into musical life of his day. The tune most associated with him, "Killie Krankie," has lived and changed over time and leads to speculation concerning what Gideon's character and musical activities might have to do with contest fiddling in modern Texas.

The first excerpt originally appeared in "Personal Reminiscences of an Octogenarian," which Gideon published serially in *The American Sportsman* during 1874–75. This excerpt, from November 21, 1874, describes a serendipitous picnic in 1835 near Eagle Lake, which is about thirty miles west of Houston. Gideon, then living in Monroe County, Mississippi, had brought a few men from there to see if Texas would be a suitable place for a restless faction of his community to relocate. He stayed on after the party disbanded, and continued to explore on his own from March 8 through May 2 of 1835, basing a series of small trips at Burnham's Ferry on the Colorado River. He came to believe that this was in most ways "the most desirable part of Texas," with ample timber and good grass for stock, yet plenty of wildlife, though he harbored reservations concerning "unsettled" government and "predaceous" Indians (Burkhalter 316). Indeed, although the following excerpt presents an idyllic picture, the county where the picnic took place had been devastated by floods and cholera in 1833, and would be overrun during the Texas

Revolution just a few months after Gideon left (Shotto 45–46). He would wait until 1848 to move his family to Texas, and would locate not in this county, but rather a few dozen miles north, at Long Point (in Washington County, near present Brenham).

On the day of this particular picnic, Gideon was traveling alone. With the aid of a pair of Indians fortuitously (and warily!) encountered, he gathered a supply of venison and honey. A Mr. Heard, with whom Gideon had recently stayed, happened along with two neighbor families (his host must have been William Jones Eliot Heard, who had recently founded the nearby settlement of Egypt[2]). This group had a picnic planned. Gideon joined forces with them, and invited the families to camp overnight with him. I quote:

> The carriages were immediately unloaded, and the Negroes started back for a supply of blankets, more bread, coffee and so on. One of the younger men told the Negro to bring his violin—which was as much as to invite the neighborhood to come.
>
> [More folks, and Gideon's Indian acquaintances assembled gradually]
>
> Seeing the violin case thrown out amongst their pots and blankets, and not having had one in my hands for months, I was hungry for music. I opened the case and found a splendid violin, in excellent condition. I took it out, and going near to two or three ladies, said, "some of you were telling a newcomer what the wild man could do. With this good violin, I will furnish you with a little story that will bear telling as long as you live." I performed "Washington's Grand March" so loud that I could distinctly hear the tune repeated as it returned from the echo on the opposite lake shore. I could feel that my very soul mingled with the sound of the instrument. At the

time I was about to become so entranced as to be unfit for such jovial company, the handsome lady ran up and, slapping me on the shoulder, exclaimed, "Good heavens, Doctor! Where are you going?" I was startled, and turning up the violin, performed "Gen. Harrison's March," then "Hail Columbia" and then the "No. 1 Cotillion in the Beggar Set." They all went to dancing and continued until I quit.

Everything now being in readiness for eating, Mrs. Heard beat a tumbler with the handle of a knife, and the fiesta commenced. They ate, and bragged, and laughed, until the darkness came, and they had waked all the echoes of the old lake. Then they called up the Negro fiddler and tried to dance awhile, but the grass was too much for them. Then one of the ladies proposed that all should be seated and get the Doctor to treat them to a few pieces of his good music.

While they were fixing the seats, Oka-noo-ah was expressing to me the delight he had experienced, and how glad he was that he had accidentally found me in his journey. These people had treated him so politely, he should never forget it.

When the company were all seated, I inquired, "What style of music would you prefer; the lively, or the grave?" "Oh, give us your own musical taste; we don't want to hear anything we are accustomed to."

I was in high tune myself; and on that clear-sounding instrument, before that gleeful company, I poured forth the wild, ringing, unwritten harmony, that is only heard and learned by the student of nature from her sweetest songsters, in the deep unhacked forest of Florida, and the jungle-enveloped coast lands of Mexico. I continued before that silent audience for at least an hour. "Is it enough," I said? "Oh no; go on, go on," they all cried. I played on, till my musical appetite was satiated. When the music ceased, preparations for sleep were made, and all lay down for the night. . . . (10–12).

The second excerpt, centering on Gideon's regular performance of one tune, "Killie Krankie," comes down to us through the interpretation of Gideon's first biographer, Lois Burkhalter. She interwove description of this with an account of Gideon's last days; I will extract much of the material about music.

When Gideon was seventeen years old and clerking in an Indian trading post in Eatonton, Georgia, his employer, Ichabod Thompson, brought him from Savannah a black English violin as a Christmas present. It was the treasure of his life. Not being acquisitive of worldly goods, he made it the only possession he cherished throughout his life.

It was at dawn on Christmas of 1810 when young Gideon answered a knock at his door and found the kindly Ichabod Thompson standing outside with the violin in his hands. Gideon, barefooted and in his nightgown, stepped outside the door to accept the wonderful instrument, the dearest Christmas present of his life. He placed the violin against his shoulder and, disregarding the cold wind, played a Mississippi popular tune, "Killiecrankie" [Burkhalter adds in a footnote that Gideon spelled this tune title "Gillie Crackie"].

To commemorate this momentous occasion, every Christmas dawn thereafter, for sixty-three years, Gideon arose from bed wherever the day found him, and, as he was, in nightclothes and barefooted, played his Christmas tune three times. . . .

[He took as good care of the violin as circumstances allowed, taking pains to restring it whenever possible.]

In his younger days, when his house was full of visiting relatives and friends and all his musical children lived under his roof, the violin was a source of conviviality. In his old age it was a solace, a link with the happy days of his youth. . . . The violin—Gideon seldom belittled it by referring to it as a fiddle—soothed the aches and pains of his tired old body after a day's hard work in his Tuxpan fields: "I retire to my room, get out my old violin and the stimulus of half a dozen merry tunes sets up a healthy action in all the electric currents belonging to my old machine and all pains and aches are gone.". . . When he returned to Texas the old black violin was one of his few possessions which Gideon took with him. . . .

[Finally, as he lay on his deathbed in November 1874, suffering from paralysis,] he remembered all of the sixty-three Christmases he had played his happy Christmas tune on that old black violin. . . . Gideon chuckled as he recalled that he had camped near Willbourn's place on Chocolate Bayou. Mr. Willbourn, a very religious man, came to camp later that day to inquire about the weird daybreak music. Gideon explained he belonged to a new religious sect, and that playing the tune three times at daybreak was part of the devotional. "He thought it very strange and left. . . ."

Gideon remembered his sixty-third playing of the Christmas tune, in Long Point in 1873, which was to be his last. . . . In the doorway, the night-shirted old man, barefooted, stood on his weary old legs and played his violin:

O Killiecrankie is my song;
I sing and play it all day long,
From the heel unto the toe
Hurrah for Killiecrankie O!

And ye had been where I hae been
Ye wad na be so cantie O!
And ye hae seen what I hae seen
On braes of Killiekrankie O!
(Burkhalter 290–99; reproduced, partly in paraphrase,
in Lincecum and Phillips xxxi-xxxii).

Should we be surprised that Gideon Lincecum was a fiddler? Some of us may still harbor a picture of the fiddler as backwoods, maybe uneducated. That would be simplistic for today's fiddlers, and outright wrong for the eighteenth and nineteenth centuries. Most fiddlers from back then whom I've seen evidence of were store owners, lawyers, members of the various professions that Gideon explored (see also Sanders, "Honor the Fiddler!" 79 and "The Texas Cattle Country" 22). This should not really come as a surprise: becoming an accomplished instrumentalist in any culture is a specialization requiring some capital and considerable leisure. A young gentleman educated late in the eighteenth century would learn to fiddle along with picking up cards, small-sword, etc. By Gideon's generation, the flute had become more fashionable (Austin xvii), although ambitious lads who, like Gideon, were outside of urban centers or other channels for the latest trends might well stick to their fathers' instrument, the violin. Learning music in genteel—and would-be genteel—circles usually took place during the teenage years. When Gideon was given his English fiddle, in 1810, he was seventeen, and already knew enough to be able to immediately whip off a tune. At the time of marriage, most, but not quite all young

gentlemen retired their flutes, fifes, and fiddles, and young ladies their pianos, guitars, and harps (instruments were then
sex-specific, though some young men played the piano). Individuals for whom music had a special and enduring appeal might
continue playing, though not professionally. The whole point of
musical training was to foster appreciation of the finer things,
and that's precisely what adults were supposed to do: appreciate. The reason many slaves were trained to fiddle was to allow
upper class fiddlers to be gentlemen first and fiddlers a distant
second. A dance was an occasion for them to dance and to so-
cialize with their friends, not a time for sweating in the corner
for others' benefit.

The blacks who fiddled at the 1835 picnic at Eagle Lake may
stand for hundreds of slave fiddlers busy at white dances (see, e.
g., Stoutamire 27–32). Such occasions constituted the real beginning of the black-white musical interchange that would be so
important for American music. Blacks played white dance tunes —
but just what liberties did they take with these melodies, acci-
dently or not? When black-face minstrelsy boomed after
1835 — this would become the most popular stage entertainment
of mid-nineteenth-century America — the genre's white male quar-
tets claimed they were imitating blacks. Most of the blacks these
showmen had heard making music were most likely slave fiddlers. My guess — and this must remain a guess — would be that
blacks would have expressed their African heritage by favoring
the British (Scottish) tunes that were rhythmically more complex, and then taken additional rhythmic freedoms with these
melodies. Some of the early published music of minstrelsy is
extremely simple, portraying blacks as childlike, but more is
mildly exotic, and in fact Scottish. We can follow the black-white
musical interchange a few more steps. After the Civil War, black
black-face troupes began to appear. To earn a living, they had to
please white audiences, and thus to imitate the established white

troupes. Late in the century, minstrelsy expanded and dissolved into variety and vaudeville, but survived in its old-fashioned form in the medicine show. Performers such as Roy Acuff (a recently deceased country music star) learned from both black and white medicine show fiddlers and banjoists. By the time we get to Acuff's generation, we have white medicine show performers learning from black black-face minstrels who copied the whites who had in part imitated black slave fiddlers who had been trained to play white dance tunes. Could musical interaction have been avoided? That both Gideon and slaves fiddled at the 1835 picnic cited above was nothing unusual, just a tiny instance of this all-important black-white musical interchange.

Was this an isolated moment in Gideon's life, or part of a larger pattern? His parents owned a handful of slaves. He would own slaves, too, and would defend the institution of slavery, though now and again speaking of a slave as a friend. We don't know if any of his own slaves fiddled, but he must have regularly encountered black fiddlers. And he clearly was open to learning music from outside of Anglo culture. During his lengthy sojourns among the Choctaw, he absorbed songs and dances some of which he later taught to Alabama-Coushatta Indians (Burkhalter 47). His remarkable openness to influence and undoubted opportunity to hear black fiddling more than add up to likelihood of interchange. Other researchers have remarked on the ubiquity of black fiddlers in Texas later in that century, and into ours ("Honor" 83; Angle 62). Sanders described a white fiddler (born in 1846) who had "learned to fiddle . . . from a Negro slave belonging to [his] grandfather" ("Honor" 86). Gideon's documentation of black fiddlers at his 1835 picnic extends such evidence back in time, and cannot have described a unique occasion. The fiddlers he met must not have been the only black ones then living in Texas, and they must have interacted with white fiddlers other than Gideon.

Gideon's fiddle was from England. Most instruments sold in the U. S. during the eighteenth and early nineteenth centuries probably came from—or through—there, simply because England was then our main mercantile connection. Our main sources then shifted to Germany, then turned home late in the century, as manufacturing picked up in many spheres, and as musical instruments, along with all sorts of goods, became more readily available throughout the country courtesy of Sears and Roebuck, Montgomery Ward, etc. Of course, these days, most of our fiddles are either from the orient or once again from Germany. Mine is German—from a Dallas pawnshop.

Fiddling has long been coupled with dancing. Our first record of these activities in what would be the U. S. was through their being proscribed in a Virginia statute of 1618, which forbade Sabbath-day "dancing, fiddling, card-playing, hunting, and fishing" (Dulles 8). Fiddling and religion have frequently been at odds—hence Gideon's rascally pleasure on informing the religious Mr. Willbourn, who had overheard Gideon's playing one Christmas morning, that this was part of his particular sect's ritual observance of the day.

When Gideon performed "Washington's Grand March" so loudly that he could hear it echo from the opposite lake shore he was following fairly standard folk fiddle practice. Playing loudly allowed these generally solo players to be heard over "squeaking floors, shuffling feet, crying babies, and the sonorous voice of the caller" ("Honor" 82). This need has favored a piercing, insistent sound over the blended and much more uniform tone favored by art violinists; the variatous "folk" timbre is more easily achieved on less expensive instruments anyway. That Gideon felt his "soul mingled with the sound of the instrument" plugs into general romantic thought, as does his description: "I poured forth the wild, ringing, unwritten harmony that is only heard and learned by the student of nature from her sweetest songsters in the deep unhacked forest of Florida and the jungle-en-veloped coast lands of Mexico."[3]

I am not sure how much to make of Gideon's playing of "Killie Krankie" each Christmas. Music is a standard ingredient in all sorts of calendric rituals: Gideon was creating one of these, play-ing the tune thrice, barefoot, at dawn. And music is such a fine memory aid: that is why we have "our song," and why so much money is poured into the short tunes for commercials.

Now to Gideon's tunes. We get just a hint of his repertoire from his writings: "Killie Krankie" plus, from the picnic, "Hail Columbia," "Washington's Grand March," "General Harrison's March," and the "No. 1 Cotillion in the Beggar Set." "Killie Krankie" and the "Cotillion" are dance tunes. The other three, though of martial/patriotic origin, could be either for passive listening or could appear at a dance. A description of a dance held at a Vir-ginia plantation in 1773 went as follows: "About seven the La-dies and Gentlemen began to dance in the Ball-Room, first Minuets one round; Second Giggs; third Reels; and last of all Country-Dances; tho' they struck several marches occasionally" (Fithian 76).

Our five tune titles run a gamut from ubiquitous through uncommon to defunct. The commonest is "Hail Columbia," which began life as a popular tune entitled "President's March," writ-ten by Philip Phile in 1783 or 1784. It was so popular that an actor, Gilbert Fox, "who wished to have a full house" planned to assure this by having a friend, Francis Hopkinson, add "some stirring words" to this tune (Sonneck/Upton 171). This was in 1798. What was now a song was published several times that year as "The favorite New Federal Song," later that year taking text as title: "Hail Columbia." The tune was printed seventy-one times that I have seen before 1835, twenty-one of those texted and titled "Hail Columbia" (Goertzen 1982:10). It is the one of the five tunes that Gideon mentioned that most Americans alive today have heard. It is more distinctive than the other four. There is occasionally some sense to which tunes survive and which do not.

This example and the next two are from one of the more widespread instrumental anthologies of the nineteenth century, Elias Howe's *Musician's Omnibus* of 1864 (respectively pp. 16, 25, and 26). Howe gathered these tunes and many others from numerous other of his publications dating back to 1843. His earliest collections themselves conflate yet earlier and today rarer collections assembled by others. Thus, the versions of tunes reprinted here represent ones available in Gideon's day.

"Washington's Grand March" was first published in 1796 under the title "New President's March." It was soon reprinted as "President's New March," "General Washington's March," "Washington's New March," "Washington's March," and finally the title it settled into, "Washington's Grand March." It shared all of these titles with other pieces. Two tunes called "Washington's March" were especially popular; this was the second to arrive, and so it became "grand" when titles started to stabilize a few decades into the nineteenth century. The "grand" may mark the march as serving as a ballroom piece. This tune remained fairly popular well into the century, but was insufficiently distinctive to last longer.

Gideon mentioned "General Harrison's March." I've found nothing bearing precisely that title. If he remembered exactly which tunes he played on that occasion in 1835, his "General Harrison's March" may have been a tune published as "The Battle of the Wabash" (1814), which honored Harrison's victory over the Indians at Tippecanoe (Spaeth 41). If, on the other hand, Gideon was recalling representative tunes from that period of his life rather than exactly which tunes he played on a specific occasion, this reference may represent a casual retitling of an uncommon tune called "Harrison's Grand March," which I suspect was written between 1825 and 1835, and which can be traced in print back to 1843 (Howe, *Musician's Companion* I:106).[4] It's pretty generic, and has not survived in oral tradition.

The last tune named in the picnic description was "No. 1 Cotillion in the Beggar Set." This must have been just the first of many dances Gideon played that day, but we are deeded just the one title, one I haven't been able to locate. This simply means that if the tune was published (and the form of the title does suggest quoting from print), the source or sources in which it appeared are lost. This is not a big surprise; the vast majority of surviving American sheets and anthologies from this period are unique. Print runs were very short, too short to ensure an exemplar's survival in this case. The tune title must refer to Christopher Pepusch and John Gay's *Beggar's Opera* of 1728, the first ballad opera, which was performed many times over many decades in the colonies and young United States. Cotillions were dances in sets of five or six, each dance having a few simple figures. The tunes in a set of cotillions were in one key. (Sometimes one tune would be in the closest key to the main one.) Most were in compound duple time (usually 6/8), sometimes with a tune or so in simple duple time thrown in for minimal variety. These sets served a function at dances, but, as part of many tunes being mechanically recast in 6/8, have lost rhythmic variety and become rather unexciting. I couldn't find a "Beggar Set," and my experiments in arranging parts of one impoverished the original spritely tunes in the *Beggar's Opera*.

Now we'll consider the most interesting of Gideon's tunes, "Killie Krankie." This is most probably one or another tune named for a battle in Perthshire in 1689. At this battle, the King's forces lost, but, on the cavalier side, two important generals fell. These were John Claverhouse and Haliburton of Pitcur (both mentioned in many versions of the song text). Their deaths were a serious setback; the decline of the cause of James II is said to date from the battle of Killiekrankie.

The tunes called "Killiekrankie" were never particularly common in print in Scotland, and didn't make it into surviving American publications at all. Common tunes—published or not—tend to be stable, but rarer ones may escape a constant reassertion of the details of their identities and change in the mix of written and oral tradition that has long characterized British and American fiddling. For the times we are dealing with in this essay, this mixed tradition is useful—our study of the history of oral tradition must depend on crossover into written sources, which we assume—well, hope—present a fair amount of the picture. Gideon claimed that no member of his

family ever had "the advantage of a lesson in music in our lives" (Burkhalter 159), but this should not be taken to indicate that he didn't read music. It was his habit to be extravagantly self-taught in each area to which he turned his energy. He probably could at least puzzle out melodies from print, like many fiddlers throughout U. S. history.

The most likely candidate to be Gideon's "Killiekrankie" is the tune by that name that survives today in Scotland. This tune was originally instrumental. It may have been composed within a few years after the battle, which took place in 1692, and was published a half dozen times in the Scottish fiddle books of the late 1700s through the early 1800s. The example at the top of the illustration is from the most famous 18th-century Scottish fiddler, Niel Gow ([1784]:6). Robert Burns added a text to the tune in 1790 as one of many contributions he made to the *Scots Musical Museum*, a widely distributed national—and national-ist—song book compiled by James Johnson (I, 302). The melody of the song "Killie Krankie" follows the contour of the earlier fiddle tune: a change of key plus very slight adjustments of rhythm and contour allows easier singing. It still sounds like a fiddle tune. Scottish songs and dance tunes are closely related; texts appear and drop off regularly. Here, the two strains contrast somewhat in range, as is characteristic of fiddle tunes, and moments awkward for the voice remain, notably the leaps in the second strain (third brace).

Two other possible candidates should briefly be mentioned to be Gideon's "Killie Krankie," though each can be easily ruled out. A rarer fiddle tune invoking this battle, entitled "The Original Sett of Killecrankie," also flourished in eighteenth century Scotland (e.g., in Gow, *Part First* 7). This "Killecrankie" also appeared in the *Scots Musical Museum*, but supporting a text unrelated to that of the more common "Killiekrankie" (Johnson #256). Overall, I have encountered it much, much less often than the first form, and it has passed out of use. It was probably not Gideon's tune.

We have one more real possibility, a better one. Another originally Scottish tune called "Money Musk" was extremely popular in Britain and in the Northern U. S., but seems to have been much rarer in the South. The rarer a tune, the less firm its grip on its title. In our only surviving distinctively southern collection of fiddle tunes from the nineteenth century, a rural Virginia music merchant named George P. Knauff drew on local oral tradition. His very first tune, which he called "Killie Krankie," is really "Money Musk" (I,1). This association of tune and title wouldn't have extended to the north, where "Money Musk" was a hit. But Gideon's "Killiekrankie" was said to be a Mississippi tune. If the tradition that Virginian Knauff drew on was pansouthern, perhaps Gideon's tune sounded like "Money Musk." However, Gideon's "Killie Krankie" had words attached: It is difficult to imagine singing anything to the sawtooth contours of "Money Musk" (for examples of this tune, see, e. g., Bayard 329–301).

The more common of two Scottish tunes called "Killie Krankie" remains the most likely candidate for Gideon's Christmas performances. It has never quite gone out of use, though it has changed in small ways. In today's sung versions, contours are often smoothed slightly (the biggest and most interesting change is in the second strain, where octave leaps are excised in favor of repeating earlier material). And minor changes in rhythm allow graceful diction. The modest changes in the tune reflect performers—and editors—choosing to make this less of a fiddle tune, and more of an integrated and linear song. These are all kinds of changes that are routine in oral tradition, and which are unsurprising in print when print is allowed to follow practice rather than forcing the reverse.

"Killie Krankie," when considered as a fiddle tune rather than as a song, would have been classified as a reel, a genre most surviving members of which are now called hoedowns, breakdowns, etc. in the United States. Our tiny selection from what must have an extensive personal repertoire includes a cotillion, this one reel, and three marches. Decades after the picnic at Eagle Lake, Gideon in 1868 visited his youngest daughter's home in Richmond (just west of Houston). She owned a cabinet organ, and borrowed a violin for her father to play. They performed for an audience which Gideon thought "not as fascinated by their music as it was amazed at a seventy-five-year-old man with a long white beard nimbly playing waltzes, cotillions, reels and marches on a violin" (Burkhalter 251). Our five tune titles include no waltzes, but mention the other three genres that evidently formed the enduring core of Gideon's repertoire. Waltzes and reels (i. e., breakdowns) remain at the center of Texas fiddling today, while cotillions are gone, and marches persist both in a few specialty numbers such as "Bonaparte's Retreat" and as an important influence on the rags that are fairly common in contemporary Texas fiddling. In short, the sample of tune titles deeded us in Gideon's writings comes remarkably close to being representative of this nineteenth-century Texas fiddler's repertoire as he himself defined it, and also overlaps with the general Texas fiddle repertoire as it is shaped today.

• • •

Evaluation of a few ways that Gideon Lincecum's remarks on fiddling fit plausibly into the early history of Texas-style contest fiddling—the most widespread style of fiddling in the modern United States—might modestly enhance our understanding of the factors encouraging the formation of this style. Its origins are sufficiently murky, and the style sufficiently important, that enlisting even the tiny amount of information deeded us by Gideon becomes a worthwhile exercise. The three interdependent factors explored include the frontier social and musical milieu, the consequent interest in contests of all kinds, and the influence of Scottish culture and fiddling.

J. Olcutt Sanders, while describing square dances that took place in West Texas cattle country about a century ago, also told us much about factors shaping Texas fiddling of that and earlier times. Since population centers were few and far between, social gatherings were infrequent but lengthy, and fiddlers—thin on the ground—came from long distances to play. Between such occasions, much of the playing that these fiddlers did was for their own enjoyment ("Honor" 78–79). Many on the frontier, and certainly fiddlers, were self-reliant and creative, and might well have described themselves as Gideon did himself, as "not formed by nature for any kind of government" (Burkhalter 7). When fiddling for themselves, these iconoclasts must have varied tunes to keep their solitary activity interesting, and they must have sought out tunes that rewarded variation. Early Texas fiddlers might not have been by nature any more inclined to do these things than were fiddlers elsewhere in the United States, but the demographic situation that left them playing alone as much or more than other American fiddlers, when added to cussedness manifesting itself as innovation, created the sort of environment in which little two-strain tunes could start growing into more involved compositions.

Long trips to have fun might have seemed wasted if the resultant gatherings hadn't been stretched a day or two also. That many attending such gatherings were competitive extroverts—nineteenth century cowboys loved pitting their skills against one another—inspired structuring the festivities around contests of various kinds, particularly but not exclusively rodeos. Many or most men attending had the sorts of skills tested in a rodeo, but fiddlers remained too few to constitute the critical mass for a fiddle contest. One would play at the evening square dance, and be in but not yet of the competitive atmosphere. This remained true decades later, when these gatherings were remembered in Old Settlers' Association festivities. Cheri Wolfe Geisler, quoting J. Marvin Hunter, mentioned an Old Settlers' Association fest in Bandera County in the 1920s that featured a spelling match, a hog calling contest for men, a cow calling contest for women, a barbecue, and a square dance (24). Soon thereafter, as transportation became much easier and populations denser, fiddlers finally could have their own contests, contests they had long been ready for in many ways.

A last nineteenth-century factor that was critical in influencing future Texas fiddlers' musical inclinations is ethnic—the Scottish influence. Many early Texans were partly or wholly of Scottish extraction. Gideon was one-fourth Scottish; one grandmother was also Jim Bowie's aunt. Enough Scots were important in early settlement that many Texas county names are Scottish family names. Scots were known for individualism, and often for interest in preserving Scottish folkways such as versions of the Highland Games, first held in their modern form in the mid-eighteenth century in order to "preserve the colorful culture and traditions of the Scottish people" (Gordon 169, 172). Scottish tunes, which tend to have been relatively complex in the context of America's legacy of British fiddle tunes, may have come by their ear-rewarding intricacy because of the remarkably early Scottish practice of *listening* to dance tunes in order to wax nostalgic. It would have been natural for early Texas fiddlers to latch onto such tunes during the long hours they played solely for their own enjoyment, and for later Texas fiddlers to revive such tunes as fodder for contests. A long tradition of fiddle and bagpipe contests in Scotland[5] may have followed Scots and

Scottish tunes around America, and the variation common in Scottish performance joined naturally with that intrinsic to jazz and blues, and to Texas' special contribution to the black-white musical mix, Western Swing.

Gideon played mainstream American tunes on mainstream British models for dancing at the 1835 picnic at Eagle Lake, but it is no accident that he chose an uncommon and uncommonly graceful Scottish tune, "Killie Krankie," for his solitary annual Christmas ritual. In the list of "Texas Fiddle Favorites" given by Sanders in 1941 (88–89), after a short dozen tunes he classified as "from the British Isles, but more or less naturalized by now," he listed over a hundred as "American favorites, most of which originated in the South." Among the best-known of the many "American favorites" that actually came from Scotland are "Turkey in the Straw" (a rhythmically thinner predecessor was called "The Rose Tree" in eighteenth century Scotland; Goertzen and Jabbour 126), "Leather Britches" (previously "Lord Macdonald's Reel") and "Billy in the Low Ground" (the Texas—and now national—version of which hearkens back to Scotland's "The Braes of Auchtertyre").

Music occupied only a tiny corner of Gideon Lincecum's prose, but clearly was important in his life, and enhanced the lives he and his fiddle touched. The little he tells us about fiddling in early Texas is immediately much of what we know on the subject. His ancestry, temperament, and even his repertoire all fit well into the hazy picture of the roots of Texas contest fiddling, the most widespead and influential of modern American fiddle styles.

NOTES

[1]This essay expands a paper delivered on May 1, 1993 during "Telling Our Stories IV: Voices from Old-Time Texas: The Gideon Lincecum Bicentennial Celebration and Humanities Conference at Austin College." I thank Jerry Lincecum (Professor of English and descendent of Gideon) for inviting me to participate in this event, my alma mater, Austin College, for flying me out, and Cecil Isaac (retired Music Professor at Austin College, who influenced my entry into the academic study of music) for suggesting my name to Jerry. I also thank Steve Green for commenting on a draft of this article.

[2]Heard, a Captain in the revolutionary forces at San Jacinto, continued to have a strong role in the community after Texas achieved independence. He helped raise funds for a project to make the Colorado River more navigable in 1837, then became Chief Justice for Colorado County in 1838 (Shatto 54, 63–65). He was probably classified as both farmer and stock raiser, as were most early settlers in order to get the largest possible land grants under Mexican colonization laws (Harrison 20–21).

[3]Gideon probably intended "harmony" to be an attractive substitute for "musical sound." But if he in fact meant harmony, he could have been referring to the fact that, in British-American fiddle tunes, melodic lines often were configured in such a way that harmonic implications were transparent, making chordal accompaniment redundant. Our first musicologist, Benjamin Franklin, remarked on this in a letter of June 2, 1765, addressed to Lord Kames of Edinburgh: "I have sometimes, at a concert, attended by a common audience, placed myself so as to see all their faces, and observed no signs of pleasure during the performance of a great part that was admired by the performers themselves; while a plain old Scotch tune, which they disdained, and could scarcely be prevailed on to play, gave manifest and general delight. Give me leave, on this occasion, to extend a little the sense of your position, that 'melody and harmony are separately agreeable and union delightful,' and to give it as my opinion that the reason why the Scotch tunes have lived so long, and will probably live forever (if they escape being stifled in modern ornament), is merely this, that they are really composition of melody and harmony united, or rather that their melody is harmony" (Sonneck 79).

[4]That Howe was reprinting this tune from somewhere, and doing so in a hurry, is evidenced by his having omitted the tune's last few measures.

[5]Niel Gow, Scotland's most famous 18th-century fiddler, "won a prize for fiddle playing open to all Scotland" at a contest held in 1745 (Collinson 214).

WORKS CITED

Angle, Joe. "Fiddlers: A Texas Tradition." In Francis Edward Abernethy, ed., *Some Still Do: Essays on Texas Customs*. Publications of the Texas Folklore Society Number XXXIX. Austin: Encino Press, 1975, 58–73.

Austin, William. *"Susanna," "Jeanie," and "The Old Folks at Home:" The Songs of Stephen Foster from his Time to Ours*. New York: MacMillan, 1975.

Bayard, Samuel P. *Dance to the Fiddle, March to the Fife: Instrumental Folk Tunes in Pennsylvania*. University Park: Pennsylvania State University Press, 1982.

Burkhalter, Lois Wood. *Gideon Lincecum 1793–1874: A Biography*. Austin: University of Texas Press, 1965.

Collinson, Francis. *The Traditional of National Music of Scotland*. Nashville: Vanderbilt University Press, 1966.

Dulles, Foster Rhea. *A History of Recreation*. Second Edition. New York: Appleton-Century-Crofts, [1965].

Geisler, Cheri Wolfe. "Two Generations in the Texas Fiddling Tradition: An Analysis of Interlocking Symbolic Systems, 1900–1940." M. A. thesis (folklore), University of Texas, Austin, 1984.

Goertzen, Chris. "Philander Seward's 'Musical Deposit' and the History of American Instrumental Folk Music." In *Ethnomusicology* 26/1(1982):1–10.

Gordon, Harry. "Scottish Texans and the Highland Games." In Francis Edward Abernethy, ed., *The Folklore of Texan Cultures*. Publications of the Texas Folklore Society Number XXXVIII. Austin: Encino Press, 1974, 166–73.

Gow, Niel. *A Collection of Strathspey Reels*. Edinburgh: author, [1784].

____. *Part First of the Complete Repository of Original Scots Slow Strathspeys and Dances*. Edinburgh: Niel Gow and Sons, 1799.

Harrison, Rosanne. "Mexican Land Grants." In Colorado County Historical Commission, Compiler, *Colorado County Chronicles: From the Beginning to 1923*. 2 Vols. Austin: Nortex Press, 1986, 19–29.

Howe, Elias. *The Musician's Companion*. 3 Vols. Boston: author, 1843.

____. *Musician's Omnibus*. Boston: author, 1864.

Johnson, James. *The Scots Musical Museum* (1853; first printing 1790). 3 Vols. Rpt. Hatboro, Pennsylvania: Folklore Associates, 1962.

Knauff, George P. *Virginia Reels*. 4 Vols. Baltimore: Willig, 1839.

Lincecum, Jerry Bryan and Edward Hake Phillips, eds. *Adventures of a Frontier Naturalist: The Life and Times of Dr. Gideon Lincecum*. College Station: Texas A & M University Press, 1994.

Sanders, J. Olcutt. "Honor the Fiddler!" In J. Frank Dobie and Harry H. Ransom, *Texian Stomping Grounds*. Publications of the Texas Folklore Society Number XVII. Austin: Texas Folklore Society, 1941, 78–90.

____. "The Texas Cattle Country and Cowboy Square Dance." In *Journal of the International Folk Music Council* 3(1951): 22–26.

Shatto, Janice. "Early Settlement." In Colorado County Historical Commission, Compiler, *Colorado County Chronicles: From the Beginning to 1923*. 2 Vols. Austin: Nortex Press, 1986, 30–57.

Sonneck, Oscar G. "Benjamin Franklin's Musical Side," In *Suum Cuique: Essays in Music*. New York: Schirmer, 1916, 59–84.

Sonneck, Oscar, and William Treat Upton. *A Bibliography of Early American Music*. Washington, D. C.: Library of Congress, 1945. Rpt. New York: Da Capo, 1964.

Spaeth, Sigmund. *A History of Popular Music in America*. New York: Random House, 1948.

Stoutamire, Albert. *Music of the Old South: Colony to Confederacy*. Madison, Wisconsin: Fairleigh Dickinson University Press, 1972.

Texas Gazeteer. Wilmington, Delaware: American Historical Publications, Inc., 1985.

The Bluebird Mare from Sterling City

Patrick Dearen

She kicked to the sky with a tornado-like fury that made her the rival of any bucking horse in history.

To hundreds of would-be riders, she was known as the Blue Filly, Bluebird Mare, or Sterling City Mare, and in the 1910s and 1920s she bucked her way ramrod across Texas and into the legends of early rodeo. Throughout, she dominated so completely that the extent to which a rider was "fork-ed" (hard to dislodge) was measured not by his number of finishing rides of the Blue Filly, but merely by how many *jumps* he had lasted. For in her entire decade-plus of competitive bucking—in Texas fairs and traveling "wild west" shows—only a handful of cowboys survived long enough to make significant, documented rides, and some of those only with extenuating circumstances. Riders simply were awed and overmatched the moment snubbers withdrew to let them face alone this dust devil of a horse.

In rodeo history, only a few other horses have demanded such respect, even fear, and theirs are the names of the most famous broncs of all: Midnight, Five Minutes to Midnight, Hell's Angel. Midnight (1910–1936), thirteen hundred pounds of coal-black fury, so terrorized riders from Oregon to New York that his tombstone bears the epitaph "There never lived a cowboy he couldn't toss." Five Minutes to Midnight (1924–1947) earned his own epitaph as "the cowboy's pal" from his tendency of spilling a rider viciously and then gently nuzzling him. Hell's Angel, a demon of an animal, would kick the rear of the chute to propel himself forward, thus taking the offensive so violently that few riders could survive.

For many observers, that storied threesome epitomized everything that a bucking bronc should be. Yet, the Sterling City Mare—despite a reputation limited only to her Texas bucking territory—may loom as the barometer against which even those legendary horses must be judged.

"I've seen Five Minutes to Midnight pitch, and I've seen Midnight pitch, and I've seen Hell's Angel pitch, but I've never seen anything like that Sterling City Mare," said Paul Patterson (born 1909), a one-time Pecos River cowboy and later folklorist who saw the Blue Filly in a wild west show in Rankin, Texas. "They were famous, but they didn't have the moves that that Sterling City Mare [had]. I've never seen anything to beat her."

The story of this nonpareil bucking mare is also the story of horsemen—breeders, ranchers, trainers, snubbers, riders—and of spectators, who carried the memories to generations thenunborn. It all began with horse rancher Alonza Austin Eddins, who, upon his wife's death in 1904, settled along Sterling Creek southwest of the isolated West Texas town of Sterling City. During his three-year stay he acquired a strain of horses part Steel

Dust (a Quarter Horse family established in 1849) and part Percheron (a draft breed imported to the United States in the early 1850s).

"They were not a mean strain of horses—most of them broke right gentle—but they sure could buck," recalled Eddins' son, L. B. "Bill" Eddins (born 1901). "I had an older brother [Addison Eddins] that made quite a bronc rider, and he said they pitched about as hard as any strain of horses he ever rode. When I was about twelve years old I tried to ride one, a big ol' colt. He threw me higher than that ceiling."

On September 2, 1907, Alonza Eddins' eighteen-year-old daughter, Ina Claire, married Harry Tweedle, a nearby rancher who had moved to the encompassing county of Sterling at age three in 1886. As a wedding gift, the elder Eddins presented them with three horses of that strain, including a blue-colored mare. In about 1912, Tweedle bred her to a vicious stallion, part Thoroughbred and part Spanish.

The foal, a filly, had an attractive blue coat (darker on the quarters), eventually earning her the name "Bluebird." As she matured she had the finely chiseled head and firm, powerful musculature of her Percheron forbearers, and the Steel Dust's wide shoulders and haunches. This blend of draft horse strength and stamina and Quarter Horse agility and courage—coupled with a mature weight of twelve hundred pounds or more—soon would intimidate and confound a multitude of bruised and shaken riders.

She made no early impression on the Tweedles, however, and they sold her as a yearling to fellow Sterling County citizen Oscar Findt, a cowboy and one-time government trapper. Findt ran her in the pasture for a year, then tried to break her as a two-year-old, only to find the seemingly gentle filly a real outlaw under the saddle. Not only did she have a bloodthirsty hatred for being ridden astride, but she possessed the sheer power and savage kicks to throw him repeatedly.

Rare was the horse that proved unbreakable, but Findt could do nothing but turn the Blue Filly out to pasture again while the story about her pitching prowess spread throughout the county. A young cowboy named Boots Franklin heard the talk and hired on with Findt, who, within a few weeks, charged him with breaking the animal. As a crowd looked on, the Blue Filly repelled Franklin's every effort by unceremoniously dumping him to the ground. At the urging of astounded observers, who never had seen such brutal kicks and elemental power in a horse, Findt decided to take the Blue Filly into Sterling City and train her to buck.

Adjacent to his brother's wagon yard south of the courthouse square, Findt set up a rope corral sixty feet square and five feet high, with steel corner posts supporting four strands of one-inch rope. He placed her in a training regimen that included regular exercise, a careful diet supplemented by three dozen raw eggs a day, and actual bucking experience under a saddle tied down to a "kitchen"—a flank strap which makes a horse kick high. To accomplish saddling and mounting in those days before chutes, he relied on snubbing: securing her alongside a second horse whose rider "eared" the filly into submission by biting her ear. In the next several months, Findt bucked the Blue Filly regularly with dummies and any horseman with the daring to test her. By the age of three—at which time she weighed almost eleven hundred pounds and stood about fourteen and a half hands tall—she had developed into a truly fearsome bucking horse. Before, she had dislodged riders with native ability and raw strength; now, she felled all comers with an ease that bespoke finesse and a maturing power in her catapult-like kicks.

"She was a very powerful horse and she pitched like hell," noted renowned Southwest historian J. Evetts Haley (born 1901), who later would see her perform in Midland, Texas.

Still, in an era in which only barnstorming broncs gained widespread recognition, the Blue Filly remained relatively unheralded until the spring of 1916, when monthly "Trades Days" in Sterling City sponsored bronc busting events. For a $5 fee, according to a contemporary advertisement in the *Sterling City News-Record*, a rider could enter the competition that rewarded the winner $20, with the second- and third-place finishers receiving $15 and $10, respectively, and the owner of the best bronc $5.

Findt may not have entered the Blue Filly in the April event— at which Frank House of Sterling City rode highly regarded "Skyrocket" to a finish—but a more noteworthy bronc busting loomed only a few weeks away. In conjunction with the May 1, 1916, Trades Day, the Rankin and Cullender Horse Show brought its eighteen-person troupe to Sterling City. This traveling wild west production, part side show and part rodeo, boasted not only of a "famous Mexican bandit," but also of a vicious bucking horse called Montana Bill, or Montana Bald, owned by Fred Roe.

A crowd gathered hours before the performance, just to watch the broncs parade about the makeshift arena erected on the town's outskirts. A lot of the talk reportedly centered on a comparison of the outlaw horses with the Blue Filly, and Findt agreed to let Delbert Walling of Rankin and Cullender take a ride at her. Walling, a Robert Lee, Texas, native who stood about six-three and weighed more than two hundred pounds, demanded—and received—one important stipulation: that the filly be saddled with only two cinches, not a "kitchen."

Without a flank strap to predispose Bluebird to unleash her violent kicks skyward, Walling succeeded in riding her around the arena twice before calling for the pickup horse. Despite the somewhat tainted ride, Bluebird's budding reputation did not suffer; conversely, her favorable comparison with the show's wild broncs and the crowd interest at a quarter a head only served to give Findt the idea to take his bucking mare on the road.

It would have been a great promotional gimmick to tout the horse as unridable, but just as it was true that "there never was a cowboy that couldn't be throwed," it was also true that "there never was a horse that couldn't be rode." In fact, only six weeks after Walling's two-cinch ride, H. A. "Cotton Picker" Huckleby took a memorable seat on the Blue Filly in Findt's rope corral. A *Sterling City News-Record* article of June 16, 1916, recorded the event: "'Cotton Picker' rode the 'Blue Filly' last Monday [June 12, 1916] to a finish. Out of 17 men to 'ride at' the 'Blue Filly' 'Cotton Picker' is the second man to keep his seat without 'pulling leather.' We give 'Cotton Picker' credit for being a fine rider."

Nevertheless, Findt proceeded with his plans. Enlisting the aid of his brother Ben, he formed a traveling wild west show around the nucleus of the Bluebird Mare from Sterling City, or, more simply, the Sterling City Mare. Initially they played only in nearby cities such as San Angelo, Big Spring, or Brownwood, but as rider after rider slammed to the dirt and the Blue Filly's fame grew, Findt took his mare to rodeos, fairs, or goat ropings throughout the state. But whether the site was the birthplace of rodeo—Pecos—or a sprawling metropolitan cow town—Fort Worth—it was a mismatch when even the best of riders dug their spurs into the rock-hard sides of this phenomenal bucking mare. This was especially true in those early rodeo days when a rider sometimes faced not a mere ten seconds in the saddle, but a seeming eternity that ended only when the horse stopped pitching.

And as the months became years, the Bluebird Mare transcended historical fact and entered the realm of legend, for neither man nor devil seemed to be able to stay atop her.

"It was impossible—that was a booger, that Blue Filly," re-called Robbin "Bob" Burns (born 1903), who would travel by horse into Sterling City to watch her buck.

"There never did but just one or two people ride her in her prime," noted Billy Rankin (born 1906), who saw the Blue Filly in the town of Rankin.

"At her best, there didn't *none* of them ride her," argued Hubert Williams (born 1906), who frequently watched her buck in Ster-ling City.

"Boy, could she buck! Kick? *That high*," remembered long-time cowboy Ralph Davis (born 1909) with a gesture skyward and awe in his voice. "And her tail would come over and hit you right in the back every time."

Under the saddle, this outlaw mare exhibited two other memo-rable characteristics that endured the passage of three quarters of a century.

"You can't imagine how she squealed when they got on her and when they turned her loose," said Oliver "Son" Cole (born 1913), who saw her pitch in Sterling City.

"She just absolutely couldn't stand that flank strap—all time she was pitching, she'd be urinating," recalled Paul Patterson. "And if you sat pretty close, why, you might get a shower."

Although D. L. Hunt remembered that in those "hard times" he and other youngsters would sneak in to watch the Blue Filly's frequent Saturday performances at Sterling City barbecues, spec-tators generally paid admission or donated in a hat to get past the encircling cars. However, no matter the setting, the greatest flow of greenbacks always came from gambling, with bets placed on whether the rider lasted a specified number of jumps or rode her to a finish to collect an advertised prize. Billy Rankin, famil-iar with the mare's habit of urinating as she pitched, once seized upon that knowledge in placing bets with first-time onlookers in the town of Rankin.

"Kid-like—that was back when I was a kid—I'd bet somebody a dollar that he rode her till she wet," he recalled. "You know, that'd mean 'ride the pee out of her.' But the first jump she made, she hit the ground a-slinging water."

In order for the legend of this bucking mare to have abided beyond the lifetimes of the very cowboys who dared her, she must have possessed qualities that immediately set her apart as extraordinary. "She just come out of there kicking so gol-durned hard, wasn't no place to sit," said eyewitness Vance Davis (born 1906). "They eared her down and saddled her, tied that rope in her flank, and turned her out and, man-a-mighty, that was the fastest bucking son-of-a-gun *I* ever saw."

But beyond the rapidity of her "jumps" were the power and technique behind her phenomenal kicking ability.

"She just stood on her forefeet and kicked with her hind feet, and you'd think she was going over [head first], but she didn't," detailed Alphonzo Dunnahoo (born 1901), who saw her buck with a dummy in the saddle in Loraine, Texas.

"When she hit the ground," added Paul Patterson, "she would be sometimes just absolutely vertical. When she'd kick, her feet reached as far as they'd go, [then] they'd give a jerk—nearly jerk your neck in two."

"She'd get way up like that," embellished Robbin Burns, "and then she'd give that second kick and you couldn't stay there."

"She was so stout," said Hubert Williams, "that she jarred you loose."

Even if a rider still somehow hung on, he faced almost certain disaster with the ensuing brutal blow to his back by the upward-curving cantle at the rear of the saddle.

"She would kick right straight up in the air and come right straight down, and that meant the cantle of the saddle was sticking right straight horizontal to hit you right in the small of the back," explained Patterson, echoing the recollections of Williams and Burns. "It took really some rider to ride her."

Despite her tendencies under the saddle, the Blue Filly was far from an outlaw bareback. "She was gentle as a dog till they put that rope in her flanks," remembered Vance Davis.

To stir up interest at the admission gate, Findt often startled crowds by contrasting the fearsome bucking mare with her pet-like alter ego.

George H. McEntire, Jr. (born 1908), who saw Bluebird frequently in Sterling City, described her as "one of the most gentle, easy-going ol' ponies there ever was. When it came time for the featured attraction of the riding event, in would come the Blue Filly with about five little girls riding her bareback. And they'd slide down her hind legs holding on to her tail, go between her legs, crawl under her, do just everything in the world that you shouldn't do. Then [the snubber] would ear her down and they'd put the saddle on and the kitchen cinch. They'd put the ol' boy on her, turn her loose, [and] she'd throw him off. They'd pick her up, take the saddle off, and then here'd come the little girls. They'd jump back on her, ride her around the arena as gentle as a dog, a little pet, and then go on back outside."

If youngsters weren't available, then one of the Findt brothers or even Oscar Findt's wife might do the bareback honors along the street leading to the arena.

"My mother said she'd ride that horse in parades and everything else," noted Nan Findt [born 1925], the daughter of Oscar Findt. "A woman could ride her as long as she rode with both legs on one side."

To some individuals who carried the memory of the Blue Filly on into the sunset of the century, she loomed remarkable in her personality.

"Harry Tweedle kept this pony during the wintertime, the off-season, and he used her from time to time as a rustling horse to

The Bluebird Mare, "gentle as a dog," held by snubber Ollie Carper. *Courtesy Patrick Dearen*

gather the other horses, just for a little exercise," recalled McEntire. "He'd be lopin' along out through the pasture on Bluebird [presumably bareback and sideways], and he could feel her begin to tighten up, get a little stiff. He knew durn well what she was fixin' to do. And about the time ol' Harry would loosen up and get ready to bail out, thinking she'd jump, she'd smooth out and go lopin' on. She was just *playing* with him. She had a personality that was absolutely unbelievable, and also a sense of humor."

While the Blue Filly never gave a bronc buster occasion to smile, the caliber of the riders who tested her remains unclear. In the days of unorganized rodeo (the Cowboy's Turtle Association was not formed until 1936), saddle bronc riders generally were fulltime working cowboys, who may not have been in positions to hone their skills as finely as today's professionals. On the other hand, the much larger pool of working cowboys in the 1910s and 1920s meant a greater likelihood of extraordinary riders surfacing. Too, in a pre-mechanization era that saw their livelihoods revolve around horses, working cowboys faced the best and the worst of broncs either in breaking the animals, saddling their "mounts" of seven every roundup or trail drive, or riding the "rough strings" that no one else dared.

A good example of that day's brand of rider was Arthur Schnaubert, whose father served as first sheriff of Upton County, Texas.

"Arthur Schnaubert didn't care for rodeoing; he just liked to work cattle," remembered fellow cowboy Paul Patterson. "He could stand in the stirrups and just let a horse pitch a little, and then just throw his leg on over and ride him. He'd ride a horse without even looking at him—and that's twice as hard because you can't tell which way the horse [is pitching]; if you can't see him jumping you can't stay with him good."

Reportedly, Schnaubert once lasted nineteen jumps on the Blue Filly, while another top rider of the area, Dave Armstrong, supposedly bested even that lofty figure.

"Dave Armstrong was eighteen, and he was a good bronc rider and weighed 118 or 128 pounds," recalled Billy Rankin. "In Midland, he took a seat at her and rode her twenty-three jumps."

Nevertheless, neither Armstrong nor Schnaubert ever came close to establishing mastery over the Blue Filly, as was evident when the Findt brothers brought their show to the town of Rankin one year. "A lot of people came out to see the best riders we had in that country, Dave Armstrong and Arthur Schnaubert," remembered Patterson. "Well, Dave lasted four or five jumps on her and Arthur about six or seven."

Another superior West Texas rider of the day was Virgil "the Concho Kid" Bright, who gained notoriety for being one of the few men ever to ride the Bluebird Mare to a finish.

"He was, I guess, about the best rider in that whole country in those days," recalled longtime cowboy and one-time calf roper Douglas Poage (born 1906). "He'd ride steers and turn around on them backwards and all the way around on them while they was bucking."

It was in Big Lake, Texas, that Poage witnessed the Concho Kid's ride of the legendary mare. "Man! He spurred the dickens out of her," Poage remembered. "He'd knock the fire out of his cinch rings while he was riding her."

Darrell Garrett (born 1900), who often saw the Blue Filly buck in Sterling City, recalled a second time the Concho Kid "rode" the horse. "Few people called it a ride," noted Garrett, "for this was the only time in her career that Bluebird was ever saddled and didn't buck."

In a more typical performance on another occasion, remembered Robbin Burns, the Blue Filly unleashed her phenomenal kicks and sent the Concho Kid flying in only "a few bucks."

Another cowboy credited with a "finishing ride" of the Blue Filly was Jim Gilstrap, who reportedly spurred her between the ears in knocking her down.

While Schnaubert, Armstrong, the Concho Kid, and Gilstrap were remembered for their notable efforts astride the Blue Filly, other riders had to endure the "hoorawing" (mock jeering) of crowds filled with cowboys. A man named Curly, for example, once took a seat on the Blue Filly in Sterling City. "In about the second or third jump," recalled Robbin Burns, who witnessed the ride, "you could see money and knives and everything leaving [his pockets], and off he went."

John Crisp, on the other hand, at least avoided the standard bruises when he challenged the Blue Filly in Findt's rope corral. Thrown high, he came tumbling down to hook both legs over the top rope and just dangle there, head-down, to the guffaws of the crowd.

Equally unique in the career of the Bluebird Mare was the time she bucked completely through those ropes to wreak the same havoc she usually levied on her riders.

No one ever got a closer look at the Blue Filly's awesome power and incredible kicks than official snubbers Harry Tweedle,

Albert Ballou, and Ollie Carper. Carper grew so enamoured with the horse that he decided to dare her himself—but only after taking measures to minimize her chances of throwing him.

"He had his stirrups hobbled—they tied them there at the girt," remembered Hubert Williams, who watched the ride in Sterling City. "He thought he could stay on. He stayed on, all right, but he couldn't get loose. Liked to popped his head off before they could catch her and stop her from pitching [after ten or twelve jumps]. They had to snub her to get him loose."

Other riders who tasted the dirt at the hooves of this bucking legend included Frank House, Jack Fritz, Red Graham, Marvin Churchill, Leslie Bugg, Sam Munn, Bill Armstrong, and Emery Latham. But of the hundreds of times snubbers eared her down to let someone ease into the saddle, none burned itself into the memories of onlookers the way it did on a warm June day in 1922.

The scene was a corral just west of Sterling City, and the rider a scraggly-bearded man with the nickname "Wild Bill" or "Wildcat Bill" and a reputation as champion bareback rider of the world. In an era before organized rodeo, that reputation may or may not have been deserved, but his performance that day certainly testified to it. Though his last name (possibly Wyche) has not survived the decades, no one who was there ever forgot the ride he made with a block of wood clenched between his teeth and whiskey on his breath.

Working his way through the area on a previous occasion, Wildcat Bill—like every passing cowboy who fancied himself a "fork-ed" rider—had made a point of testing his mettle astride the Blue Filly. In that attempt, remembered Oliver "Son" Cole, the brutal impact of the cantle against his back had thrown him hard to the ground. But Wildcat Bill obviously was a rider who benefited both from experience and a study of a bucking horse's technique.

"She threw him off and he said, 'I'll come back and ride her,'" recounted Cole. "He told us, 'If I can't ride her, I'll send my sister. She can.'"

Now, as Wildcat Bill readjusted the stirrups and climbed into the saddle for his 1922 attempt, he carried with him a carefully devised strategy to neutralize the devastating impact of cantle against back.

"Wild Bill's method of riding the Blue Filly," detailed Robbin Burns, "was with short stirrups and moving from one side to the other of the cantle of his saddle as she made a buck." Therefore, explained onlooker Cole, the cantle "didn't hit him in the back" as it did other riders.

"Boy! He rode her just as pretty as you ever saw anybody!" recalled Hubert Williams.

Nevertheless, the Blue Filly still had plenty of fight left when Wildcat Bill decided to end the ride. After staying with her an unheard-of thirty-one jumps that carried them twice around the corral—and as Findt rushed out to save the horse's reputation—Wildcat Bill hollered "Catch her!" to the pickup man.

"I was standing right beside him when he got off and you could just see his temples beating—the Blue Filly had gotten Wild Bill's wind," noted Burns. "Wild Bill made the remark when he got off that she was hard to ride and if anyone wanted to ride her, there she was."

Despite Wildcat Bill's extraordinary strategy and exceptional agility that carried him into legend that day, there were some observers who did not believe he had ridden the Blue Filly at her best.

"She didn't pitch like she had been pitching, because she was getting old," said Williams. "They'd just got her up off the grass [pasturing her in the off-season]. I don't think they'd been practicing her any."

Another factor contributing to Wildcat Bill's successful ride may have been the condition of the turf. John I. Blair (born 1908), who was at the arena that day, claimed that the dirt was so deep that the mare could not get the firm footing necessary to effect her devastating kicks.

In 1924, Oscar Findt took the Blue Filly to Big Spring, Texas, where 365 ropers converged for a three-day goat roping. Each afternoon and night, his horse turned outlaw under the saddle to dominate every rider. The performance so impressed a Big Spring man named Mallie McDougal (some say Tom McDougal) that he approached Findt about purchasing the horse. Although Findt had turned down bids for years, his desire to spend more time with his family and the generosity of McDougal's offer led him to sell.

Findt's role in the story of the Bluebird from Sterling City was over, but her career was not. For the next several years, McDougal bucked the famed mare throughout the region against all challengers, but despite her advancing age, her legend as an unparalleled bucking horse grew ever-stronger.

Only in death, at approximately age 17 in 1929, did this gentle mare that kicked furiously to the sky yield at last to the riders who would carry their respect and awe of her into the twilight of their lives.

[The story of the Bluebird Mare was presented by Patrick Dearen at the 1993 San Angelo Texas Folklore Society meeting. It was published in 1994 in Western Horse Tales (Don Worcester, editor) and is reprinted with permission of Republic of Texas Press, a division of Wordware Publishing, Inc., Plano, Texas.]

Robert J. Duncan

The Night the Stars Fell

Daddy used to tell a distant, barely-remembered family story about the night the "stars fell." He said that our ancestors in Kentucky thought the end of the world was at hand. William A. Owens, in *This Stubborn Soil*, mentions that his great grandmother Missouri Ann Cleaver was born "about the time the stars fell" (Owens 14). The song "Stars Fell on Alabama," by Mitchell Parish and Frank Perkins was published in 1934 ("Stars" 212–14).

Carl Carmer's novel entitled *Stars Fell on Alabama*, also published in 1934, says in its preface:

Many an Alabamian to this day reckons dates from "the year the stars fell"—though he and his neighbor frequently disagree as to what year of our Lord may be so designated. All are sure, however, that once upon a time stars fell on Alabama, changing the land's destiny (Carmer xiv).

All of these allusions refer, almost certainly, to the Leonid meteor storm of November 13, 1833. ("Shower" is almost too tame a word.)

In 1990, I noticed a reproduction of a wood engraving in the Texas State Historical Association's newsletter, *Riding Line*. It accompanied a letter asking for help in documenting that this meteor storm had been observed in Texas. Don Olson, an astronomy professor at Southwest Texas State University, in San Marcos, said in his letter to the editor of *Riding Line* :

This meteor shower, widely observed throughout almost all of the eastern United States, was a spectacular event with "shooting stars" and exploding fireballs appearing at rates estimated as high as 150,000 meteors per hour—"as thick as snow coming down in a snow storm" (Olson 9).

Olson said that he and David Evans had written an article entitled "Early Astronomy in Texas" for the April 1990 issue of the *Southwestern Historical Quarterly*. They were not able to cite a Texas observation of the phenomenon. I immediately wrote to Olson, because I had read of a sighting of the meteor shower in the 1959 TFS publication, *Madstones and Twisters*. The article, by F. S. Wade, tells of "Uncle" Ad (Adam) Lawrence, who lived on a ranch west of the Brazos River in 1833. An old Spaniard visited Lawrence and claimed he was one of Jean Lafitte's pirate band. He said that the U. S. Marines had captured Lafitte on Galveston Island. The Spaniard and two companions had hidden Lafitte's treasure in two small cannons and buried them deep in the sand of Galveston Island near a hackberry tree. The three men vowed to return for the treasure together after several years, when things had blown over. Word had reached the Spaniard that his two friends were dead. He told Uncle Ad that if he would go with him to Galveston to locate the treasure, he would split it with him.

Wade, who wrote down the story many years later, said:

The second night's camp was on the prairie. A full moon was shining brightly. Uncle Add [sic] said he could not sleep. After a while he looked at the old Spaniard, who was sleeping on his back, his shirt open in front. He saw a great scar across the man's breast, and his face had many scars on it.

Suddenly it came to him that his companion was not a mortal but the devil, leading him to destruction. While looking in horror upon the scarred sleeper he heard an owl hoot in a near-by bottom: a timber wolf uttered a doleful howl, then the heavens seemed to be on fire and the stars fell in showers (Wade 144, Speck 139–40).

Dolph Fillingim wrote Francis Abernethy a letter (November 29, 1972) in which he says that his grandfather William Fillingim saw the meteor storm. William was a teen-ager traveling through Alabama with a wagon train the night the stars fell:

He said when the stars began to fall that night the people that he was traveling with got under their wagons to protect them from the falling stars. When they stopped falling, they got out from under the wagons and looked to see if there were any stars left up above, but it seemed like all the stars were still up there.

Richard Devens, in a book entitled *Our First Century*, published in 1876, quotes a Southern plantation owner:

> I was suddenly awakened by the most distressing cries that ever fell on my ears. Shrieks of horror and cries for mercy, could be heard from most of the negroes [sic] of three plantations, amounting in all to some six or eight hundred. While earnestly and breathlessly listening for the cause, I heard a faint voice near the door calling my name. I arose, and taking my sword, stood at the door. At this moment I heard the same voice still beseeching me to rise, and saying, "O, my God, the world is on fire!" I then opened the door, and it is difficult to say which excited me most—the awfulness of the scene, or the distressed cries of the negroes. Upwards of one hundred lay prostrate on the ground, some speechless, and others uttering the bitterest moans, but with their hands raised, imploring God to save the world and them. The scene was truly awful, for never did rain fall much thicker than the meteors fell towards the earth; east, west, north, and south, it was the same.
>
> In a word, the whole heavens seemed in motion (Devens 330).

Olson and Evans reported:

> During the 1910 apparition of Halley's Comet, journalists sought out old people who might have witnessed the previous apparition in 1835. In Austin, one elderly black woman, Aunt Lavinia Forehand, recalled seeing the comet, and dated it as "two years after the stars fell" (Evans 436).

Aunt Lavinia was a slave in Murray County, Tennessee, in the 1830s.

Ray Williamson, in his book *Living the Sky, The Cosmos of the American Indian*, says that the Sioux Indians made a buffalo skin painting to document the meteor shower:

> The scanty evidence available suggests that native Americans did record particular events. This is relatively rare, but we know of at least two historic examples: the unmistakable paintings of the Leonid meteor shower of 1833 made on a buffalo skin by the Dakota Sioux and a depiction of the solar eclipse of August 7, 1869. The Dakota Sioux and other Plains Indian groups were interested in both of these ephemeral events and used records of them as part of their so-called winter count to remind them of other events that took place during the same year. (Williamson 194)

Garrick Mallery, in *Picture-Writing of the American Indians*, catalogs five pictures depicting various views of the 1833 meteor shower:

> The five [Dakota] winter counts next cited all undoubtedly refer to the magnificent meteoric display of the morning of November 13, 1833, which was witnessed throughout North America. . . .
>
> Fig. 1219.—It rained stars. Cloud-Shield's Winter Count, 1833–'34. White-Cow Killer calls it "Plenty-Stars winter."
>
> Fig. 1220.—The stars moved around. American-Horse's Winter Count, 1833–'34. This shows one large four-pointed star as the characterizing object and many small stars, also four-pointed.

Fig. 1221.—Many stars fell. The-Flame's Winter Count, 1833–'34. The character shows six stars above the concavity of the moon.

Fig. 1222.—Dakotas witnessed magnificent meteoric showers; much terrified. The Swan's Winter Count, 1833–'34.

Battiste Good calls it "Storm-of-stars winter," and gives as the device a tipi with stars falling around it. This is presented in Fig. 1223. The tipi is colored yellow in the original and so represented in the figure according to the heraldic scheme (Mallery 723).

Devens discusses the "One Hundred Great and Memorable Events" that occurred in this country between 1776 and 1876. He devotes a chapter to the meteor shower of 1833.

Extensive and magnificent showers of shooting stars have been known to occur at various places in modern times; but the most universal and wonderful which has ever been recorded is that of the thirteenth of November, *1833, the whole firmament, over all the United States, being then, for hours, in fiery commotion!* . . . During the three hours of its continuance, the day of judgement was believed to be only waiting for the sunrise, and, long after the shower had ceased, the morbid and superstitious still were impressed with the idea that the final day was at least only a week ahead. Impromptu meetings for prayer were held in many places, and many other scenes of religious devotion, or terror, or abandonment of worldly affairs, transpired, under the influence of fear occasioned by so sudden and awful a display (Devens 329–30).

Nineteenth-century sketch of the night the stars fell, November 13, 1833.

Many people remembered the prophesy in *Revelation 6:12* and *13*:

And I beheld when he had opened the sixth seal, and, lo, there was a great earthquake, and the sun became black as sackcloth of hair, and the moon became as blood,

And the stars of heaven fell unto the earth, even as a fig tree casteth her untimely figs, when she is shaken of a mighty wind.

It didn't help matters that there had been an unexplained very dark day just a few decades before, on May 19, 1780. We now attribute that dark day to a huge forest fire (Devens 88–96).

Professor Denison Olmsted at Yale was an eyewitness to the meteor shower of 1833. He described the display as comprising three varieties of meteors:

First, those consisting of phosphoric lines, apparently described by a point. This variety was the most numerous, every-where filling the atmosphere, and resembling a shower of fiery snow driven with inconceivable velocity to the north of west, and transfixing the beholder with wondering awe.

Second, those consisting of large fireballs, which at intervals darted along the sky, leaving luminous trains which occasionally remained in view for a number of minutes, and, in some cases, for half an hour or more. . . .

Third, those undefined luminous bodies which remained nearly stationary in the heavens for a considerable period of time; these were of various size and form (Devens 331).

Devens says:

> At Poland, Ohio, a luminous body was distinctly visible in the north-east for more than an hour; it was very brilliant. . . . At Niagara Falls, a large, luminous body, shaped like a square table, was seen nearly in the zenith, remaining for some time almost stationary, and emitting large streams of light.
>
> At Niagara, no spectacle so terribly grand and sublime was ever before beheld by man as that of *the firmament descending in fiery torrents over the dark and roaring cataract!*
>
> At Charleston, S. C., a meteor of extraordinary size was seen to course the heavens for a great length of time, and then was heard to explode with the noise of a cannon (Devens 332).

Dr. Ashbel Smith, a physician in Salisbury, North Carolina, wrote to Professor Olmsted that he saw the display while traveling in the country in his sulkey on a professional visit:

> By far the most magnificent meteor seen on the morning of the 13th, in this vicinity, crossed the vertical meridian about 3 o'clock A. M. Its course was nearly due west, in length by conjecture, about 45 degrees, and at a distance of about 25 degrees south from the zenith. In size, it appeared somewhat larger than the full moon rising. I was startled by the splendid light in which the surrounding scene was exhibited, rendering even small objects quite visible; but I heard no noise. . . . The track of the meteor adverted to, was visible at least twenty minutes. . . . By its continuing to have a southern declination from me when first and last seen, (my course in traveling hap-

pened to be towards it, and in the same plane) I concluded it was probably several miles high (Olmsted 379).

Most observers reported no sound accompanying the meteor shower, but several reported a noise like the explosion of a sky-rocket (Olmsted c. 392–93 and Devens c. 332 for following information, unless documented otherwise). In Richmond, Virginia, a crackling sound was reported. Some other events coincided with the meteor shower. At Harvard, there was supposedly rainfall without clouds. Several people in various locations reported a precipitation of a jelly-like material. What appeared to be Aurora Borealis was observed in Connecticut and New Hampshire. There was an earthquake in England (Milne 120). Ironically, the Leonid meteor shower of 1799 in Cumana, Venezuela, had been accompanied by a severe earthquake (Packer 155).

The trails of the 1833 meteors were predominately white, but a number were other colors. Olmsted said, "The trains left by the exploding balls, were usually of a yellowish hue, but sometimes [they were] reddish." An observer at Dover, New Hampshire, reported:

. . . an appearance of the Aurora Borealis, early in the preceding evening, which continued until 4 o'clock in the morning, when it suddenly broke into streams of strong light, spreading into columns, changing into a thousand different shapes, varying their colors through all the tints of the rainbow, and shooting from the horizon almost to the zenith. This scene was followed by a splendid exhibition of fireworks. Luminous balls might be seen darting about with great velocity, leaving behind them a train resembling that of a comet. The whole was closed by the formation of a triumphal arch which vanished before the coming of morning light (Olmsted 397–98).

Leonid meteor showers are so named because they appear to originate at a point in the constellation Leo. They are associated with the Tempel-Tuttle Comet and recur at intervals of thirty-three years, always in mid-November, and were recorded as far back as 903 A.D. The unusual clarity of the atmosphere over most of the country on the morning of November 13, 1833, apparently was one reason this particular Leonid display was so stunning. Olmsted says:

> The morning itself was, in most places where the spectacle was witnessed, remarkably beautiful. The firmament was unclouded; the air was still and mild, the stars seemed to shine with more than their wonted brilliancy . . . (Olmsted 363).

Devens says that a calculation was made that "not less than *two hundred and forty thousand meteors were at the same time visible above the horizon of Boston!*"

The *Christian Advocate and Journal,* published exactly a month after the meteor shower, says:

> It seemed as if the whole starry heavens had congregated at one point near the zenith, and were simultaneously shooting forth, with the velocity of lightening, to every part of the horizon; and yet they were not exhausted; thousands swiftly followed in the track of thousands, *as if created for the occasion* (*Christian Advocate* 41).

What was it like that evening, before the fireworks started? I called Don Olson and asked. He plugged the date into his computer: the evening of November 12, 1833, a Tuesday and the Wednesday morning of November 13. The detail that I heard

over the phone was eerie. Don said that, using Dallas as a hypothetical observation point, on that long ago evening the sun set
at 5:30. The moon set very early: at 6:40 P.M. The moon was only
a very thin crescent of three percent that evening anyway, but
after 6:40 there was no moonlight at all. The constellation Leo
rose in the east a few minutes after midnight. When the meteor
shower commenced a few hours later, Leo was well up in the
sky.

This scenario contradicts the F. S. Wade/Uncle Ad Lawrence
story of the full moon, but since that story was off the mark by
ten days anyway, perhaps it comprises a composite of two events
that happened on the trip.

Actor Edwin Booth was born on November 13, 1833. One of
his biographers, Richard Lockridge, says:

> Edwin was born . . . in the deep country outside Balti-
> more . . . and that night there was a shower of meteors
> which amazed the servants in their shanty behind the
> tragedian's house. He was born with a caul, and that set
> the servants to nodding. They said young Edwin was born
> lucky, and mumbled to the young mother that the caul
> must be kept. For many years Mary Ann Booth . . . saved
> that object which promised high fortune to her son, and
> it was passed on to him, an indistinguishable thing but
> perhaps a symbol of destiny. The meteors, which were
> even more spectacular, could not be saved. But they could
> be remembered (10).

When Booth toured the West with a road company that played
mining camps, there was a rash of fires. Lockridge says:

> The camps began to catch fire just as the players quitted
> them. It was vexing and inexplicable. Perhaps there was

among them some one who liked to see sparks fly upward. Five camps flew upward in quick succession and
the miners began to speak of Booth grimly as the "fiery
star" (60).

If only it had not been Edwin Booth, but his brother John Wilkes,
what a story we would have! Supermarket scandal sheets could
have had a field day with stories of an alien invader from outer
space as a presidential assassin.

W. P. Zuber, who later would gain fame with his story of Moses
Rose's escape from the Alamo, was a thirteen-year-old boy living
in Grimes County in 1833. He didn't witness the meteor shower,
but his mother did. She was suffering from an eye infection. She
got up during the night and put some medicine in her eyes. Her
attention was attracted to the falling stars out the window, but
she assumed that she was having an optical illusion caused by
her illness, so she went back to sleep. The next day she learned
about the meteor shower from neighbors and realized what she
had actually seen (*Austin-American Statesman*, May 18, 1910).

Mrs. Harriet Powers (1837–1911), a black woman in Athens,
Georgia, made a quilt (ca. 1895–1898) that depicted the 1833
meteor storm, along with other unusual and Biblical events. Of
the meteors, Mrs. Powers said, "The people were frighten [sic]
and thought that the end of time had come. God's hand staid
[sic] the stars. The varmints rushed out of their beds"(Vlach 47).

Gary Kronk says:

The night of November 12–13, 1833, not only marks the
discovery of the Leonid meteor shower, but sparked the
actual birth of meteor astronomy. . . .

New information continued to surface following the
1833 display which helped shed new light on the origin
of the Leonids. First, a report was found concerning F. H.

A. Humboldt's observation of thousands of bright meteors while in Cumana, South America during November 12, 1799. Further digging around this date in other publications revealed the spectacle was visible from the Equator to Greenland. . . . In 1837, Heinrich Wilhelm Matthias Olbers combined all of the available data and concluded that the Leonids possessed a period of 33 or 34 years. . . .

The interest of the astronomical world began focusing on the predicted return of the Leonids as the decade of the 1860's began. Most important was Hubert A. Newton's examination of meteor showers reported during the past 2000 years. During 1863, he identified previous Leonid returns from the years 585, 902, 1582 and 1698. During 1864, Newton further identified ancient Leonid displays as occurring during 931, 934, 1002, 1202, 1366 and 1602. He capped his study with the determination that the Leonid period was 33.25 years . . . (Kronk 1–2).

The Leonid meteor showers do recur about once every thirty-three years, always in November. The fraction of a year in excess of thirty-three does not indicate a shift in the time of year; it simply reflects the fact that the meteor showers are occasionally thirty-four years apart.

Eschatology, the study of doomsday prophecies, occupies a space somewhere between religion and folklore. It's as ancient as the Old Testament and as recent as the Branch Davidian stand-off at Waco. Just as Mark Twain said about the reports of his death—that they were greatly exaggerated (or at least premature), so far the predictions have not been borne out. As we approach the second millennium, we will, no doubt, see many more predictions of this kind.

And world without end.

Amen.

BIBLIOGRAPHY

Carmer, Carl. *Stars Fell on Alabama*. New York: Blue Ribbon Books, Inc. and/or Farrar & Rinehart, Inc., 1934.

Christian Advocate Journal, December 13, 1833, quoted in *Bible Readings for the Home Circle*. Battle Creek, MI: Review and Herald Publishing Co., 1888.

Devens, Richard M. *Our First Century*. Springfield, MA: C. A. Nichols & Company, 1876.

Evans, David S. and Donald W. Olson, "Early Astronomy in Texas," *Southwestern Historical Quarterly*, vol. XCIII, no. 4 (April, 1990).

Fillingim, Dolph, letter to F. E. Abernethy, November 29, 1972. Fillingim twice states the year of the meteor shower as 1835, but this may have been a reference to the 1833 event that somehow got off by two years as it was handed down within the family.

Kronk, Gary W. Internet article, "Meteor Observing Calendar," under "November," "Leonids." This is a slightly condensed version of his out-of-print book, *Meteor Showers: A Descriptive Catalog* (1988).

Lockridge, Richard. *Darling of Misfortune, Edwin Booth: 1833–1893*. New York and London: The Century Company, 1932.

Mallery, Garrick. *Picture-Writing of the American Indians*. Vol. II. New York: Dover Publications, 1972.

Milne, David. "Notices of Earthquake Shocks Felt in Great Britain," *Edinburgh New Philosophical Journal*, vol. XXXI (1841).

Olmsted, Denison. "Observations on the Meteors of November 13, 1833," *The American Journal of Science and Arts*, vol. XXV (January, 1834).

Olson, Donald W. Interviews and letters during the spring of 1990.

Owens, William A. *This Stubborn Soil*. New York: Charles Scribner's Sons, 1966.

Packer, David E. *English Mechanic*, Vol. LXXIV (September 27, 1901).

Speck, Ernest, ed. *Mody Boatright, Folklorist*. Austin: University of Texas Press, 1973.

"Stars Fell on Alabama," words by Mitchell Parish, music by Frank Perkins, reprinted in *The New York Times Nostalgic Years in Song*, edited by Irving Brown. New York: Quadrangle/The New York Times Book Co., 1974.

Vlach, John M. *The Afro-American Tradition in Decorative Arts*. Cleveland: Cleveland Museum of Art, 1978.

Wade, F. S. "The Adventures of Ad Lawrence," *Madstones and Twisters* (PTFS volume XXVIII), edited by Boatright, Hudson and Maxwell. Dallas: SMU Press, 1958.

Williamson, Ray A. *Living the Sky, The Cosmos of the American Indian*. New York: Houghton Mifflin Company, 1984.

Rail
Tales:
Some are True

Two Strong Men Stood Face to Face

"There is neither East nor West, border nor breed nor birth," wrote Rudyard Kipling, "When two strong men stand face to face, though they come from the ends of the earth."

This is the story of a fast freight engine and two strong men, Ted Finklea and Dewey Williams, when they stood face to face back in the 1940s. Both were crack locomotive engineers on Southern Pacific's Dallas Division. The company's officers as well as the employees liked and respected them. They were personal friends of long standing.

But let us here set the stage for our story.

Dewey Williams had been promoted to traveling engineer and

was now on the "other side of the fence," that is, an officer of the company. The Dallas Division extended from Houston through Dallas to Denison, Texas, and part of his and the trainmaster's duties was traveling over the division, monitoring the performance of employees and enforcing the company's rules. Dewey often drove his black 1938 Buick in his work.

Ted Finklea was a freight engineer assigned between Houston and Hearne. But, while Ted was well liked and respected, his conductor on this particular trip was not. This man liked to stir up mischief without involving himself. "Let's you and him fight" best describes him. Crew members tolerated him; the company brass watched for an opportunity to fire him.

Two streamlined, steam powered passenger trains, the Sunbeams, ran daily between Houston and Dallas, 252 miles in 252 minutes. Maximum authorized speed was seventy-nine miles per hour. The orange, yellow, black, and red cars and engines raced over Texas prairies like gorgeously plumed Phoenix birds. Gray-haired and steely-eyed Tom Spence was Superintendent; he was very fond of No. 13 and No. 14, the two Sunbeams, and he would definitely fire any person caught jeopardizing the on-time performance of his darlings.

No. 342 was a freight train that arrived in Hearne about 4:00 P.M. daily. Shippers used this schedule to get their products from the Midwest, Colorado, and Oklahoma to the ports on the Gulf Coast. The practice was to call No. 342 to leave Hearne at 6:30 P.M., the arrival of the northbound No. 13. This gave No. 342's crew two hours to run the seventy miles to Hempstead, get into the siding and take water before southbound No. 14 was due.

But at *no* time did anyone even think of a train's leaving Hempstead ahead of No. 14, for to do so would surely delay him, and Nos. 13 and 14 were just not delayed on the Dallas Division, not even yellow blocked, without bringing the wrath of God, or worse yet, the wrath of T. M. Spence, down on the offender's head.

Now on with the story.

Our hero Ted Finklea was called at 6:30 P.M. for No. 342 one day, and No. 13 was smack on the money, coming up through the south end of Hearne yard with a streamer of smoke and steam vapor laying back along the train, the numerals 13 staring starkly from the indicators, her engine a colorful red-orange onrushing tower wearing long skirts. Dirt swirled, trash danced along the rails beneath her and in her wake as she scurried through the yard toward Bremond and her meet with No. 14. When man created the steam engine—and got it hot—God breathed the flame of life into its firebox, and it became a living thing. This is a feeling that could come to anyone watching the Sunbeam go by.

No. 342 was ready and the air tested. The conductor, way-bills in his hand, was highballing. Finklea released the air and began easing the engine forward. The engine was a Mike (Mikado MK-5) which was out of the back shop just long enough to be well broken in and at its peak performance. MK-5 engines were ideal for our prairie country. They were oil burning steam engines with four pairs of drivers and carried 190 pounds of steam. They sometimes doubled as passenger engines. Manifest freight trains were allowed sixty m.p.h. when Mikes were pulling them.

And this Mike was a stepper. Consider this: though No. 342 had to pull Sutton hill just out of Hearne yard, slow through Bryan, College Station, and Navasota, and reduce speed through the Navasota River bridge, still the train was in the approach to Hempstead by 7:50 P.M.

We had no radios then; communication was by whistle and hand signal. As No. 342 approached the mile board, Ted put the air under them and blew the two long blasts and one short to tell everyone concerned that he intended to let No. 14 by there. The head brakeman shouted over the roar of air exhausting from the brake valve, "They're highballing from the caboose!"

Reliving that event for just the moment, Ted grinned a little and said, "I knew better than to do what I did, but, like Flip Wilson says, 'The devil made me do it.'"

"And I thought, 'If that so-and-so of a conductor wants a ride, I'll give him a ride!'—and I blew one long blast." That long blast told the world that he was going down the main track and would leave ahead of the Sunbeam.

Little did anyone know that standing under the eaves of the depot were two men in business suits, Dewey Williams, the traveling engineer, and the trainmaster.

"Get up on the tender," Ted pointed to the fireman and shouted over the engine noise, "Have the manhole cover off when I stop, and get all the water you can in three minutes." Down the main track the big train went, stopping precisely under the water spout the first try. Three minutes—HOOO! HOOO!—they were moving. It was now 8:02 or 8:03. No. 14 was due in Navasota at 8:17. The cars were creaking and moaning and clanking and shuddering like they always do, the shining surfaces of turning wheel flanges reflecting the dim station lights as they rolled past.

Ted was a busy man, his left hand notching the lever along the quadrant that "shifted" the engine to higher speed, his right hand moving between the control for sanding rail, the throttle, and the whistle cord and his eyes reading the steam pressure gauge, the back pressure gauge, and the water glass. He was giving the Mike his best, and she was giving him her best, her beginning chuff-chuffs quickly becoming short staccato barks and then the overpowering roar that comes when speed passes sixty m.p.h. Now Ted "had 'em in the wind." He listened to the jingle, the rumble, and the roar as they steamed along the prairie, flames licking the firebox door.

Then the head brakeman, a new man, yelled through the engine's roar, "Say, Ted, I saw a couple of guys in business suits standing under the eaves of the depot watching us take water, and now they are following us in a car." "What kind of car?" "A black Buick, and the conductor is waving a washout" (signaling stop now!).

Everybody on the division knew Dewey's black Buick. Ted was trapped! Now Ted didn't feel so good. He told me, "I knew right then that I was fired, but there was no turning back." He held a hand that had to be played out. Ted kept the throttle back.

He went on, "And that dumb washout signal from the conductor. Everybody knew that it was just a feeble effort to dodge responsibility for instigating my snafu at Hempstead."

No. 342 was flying—and so was the black Buick. Dewey and the trainmaster were traveling over the speed limit on a pre-World War II highway of two lanes, both of which needed maintenance. The two officers were in far greater danger in their rocking and rolling Buick than anyone on No. 342 or No. 14.

Then they were approaching Cypress, the Buick and the train. Ted called to the brakeman, "I'm going to let No. 14 by at Cypress. Listen carefully. By going down the main track and backing in, I can keep from showing him a yellow block. You drop off at the far switch. When the caboose is past the switch, line it for the siding right then, because I'll be backing in."

And they did just that. No. 342 pulled by and backed in. No. 14, right on time, never saw a yellow block.

While Ted was thus backing No. 342 into the clear, the fireman said, "Ted, that car that's been a-follerin' us has stopped beside the highway, and the driver is walkin' this way." Ted told me that when he had the train in the clear, he stopped the engine, walked across the gangway, and looked down. There stood Dewey, looking up, hands on hips, gold watch chain across his vest, cigar jutting just so, and hat pushed back from his fore-head.

"That's a mighty good engine you've got there, Ted," said Dewey.

"And that's a mighty good car you're drivin', Dewey," was all that Ted could think to say.

For the record: a retired engineer told me at a railroad retir-ees reunion that he was the fireman on No. 14 that night, and that at no time did he see a yellow signal set by No. 342. The company offered Finklea a thirty-day suspension if he would involve the trouble making conductor, but he declined. Though he had some job insurance, it was not enough to cover the six months pay he lost before he was reinstated.

A Tragedy

D. R. Day was a young S. P. fireman in the early 1940s. He had an uncle and a cousin in engine service. He married the pretty daughter of a section foreman and fathered two pretty little daughters before going away to war.

While Day was in military service, the S. P. upgraded the Austin Sub Division track for "Mike" (Mikado MK-5 class) en-gines which were faster, higher, wider, and longer than Consoli-dations and could pull longer and heavier trains.

But those wider cabs left little space between the cab win-dow and the steel stanchions of the overhead steel bridges the engines had to cross. In fact, the space was so narrow that a person in the cab of a moving MK-5 could hold a large cabbage head just out the window and watch it smash into cole slaw when it struck the steel bridge.

Of the many who went to war, Day was one of the lucky ones. He came back to his family and to his job. He marked up on No.

239 and No. 240, overnight freights between Houston and Austin.

Allen Johnson, a retired engineer living in Austin, recalls that it was on D. R. Day's second trip that No. 240 was double headed (two engines pulling) from Austin to handle a heavy train, the lead engine being a smaller engine operated by an engineer named Collins. Allen himself was Collins' fireman. The second engine was one of those Mikes with the wider cab. "Smokey" Dennison was engineer and young Day the fireman.

Crews watch their trains for sticking brakes, hot boxes, shifting loads, etc. The best inspections are made when the train is rounding a curve. The rear brakeman and the head brakeman position themselves on the side that is on the inside of the curve and thus get a good view of each car for a moment or two before having to focus on the next. At night the men watch for flames which indicate an overheated bearing (hot box) and for flying sparks which signal a brake beam dragging or a wheel derailed. The fireman in the cab also watches when he is not busy with his firing duties.

Shortly after leaving Austin yard, eastbound trains enter a curve to the left, and, just past the curve, cross one of those narrow steel bridges over Walnut Creek, and begin a steep five-mile climb to Daffan.

And so it was that No. 240 that night left Austin about 8:40 P.M., Engineers Collins and Dennison pushing their engines to get a run at Daffan hill, and Firemen Johnson and Day busy fueling the fires to build steam for the climb. The two brakemen were in position to "look 'em over" around the curve.

The stars that night were big and bright deep in the heart of Texas. As he moved about in the cab, Day's white cap, catching the starlight, looked like a ghostly blob jouncing in the dark cab window.

By about 8:55 P.M. the two coupled engines were entering the bridge, headlight gleaming, reflections of flame flashing from their fireboxes. Their combined exhausts were making a rapid drum beat of sound which overpowered all other sounds except the occasional lonesome wail of the whistle blowing for a road crossing. The cab was very dark and very noisy. Most of the train was still rolling around the curve.

Engineer Dennison was watching ahead; Fireman Day must have turned around on his seat box and leaned from the window to better inspect the train. It was then that Old Man Death, the Grim Reaper, placed two icy fingers on the back of the head of Fireman D. R. Day.

Certainly young Day had no inkling that while he was looking back at the train his head was like the head of cabbage, and the area back of his right ear was aimed right into that steel beam of the bridge. After all, this was only his second trip since his returning from military service and finding the MK-5 engines working into Austin.

In the dark and the noise, no one saw or heard what happened.

Some minutes later, when the train was a considerable distance up the five mile grade, Smokey Dennison began "blowing the lead engine down" (signaling "stop"). The lead engineer, Collins, ignored Smokey's whistled signals until the heavy train was pulled over the crest of the hill at Daffan. No. 240 stopped fairly near the road crossing.

Allen Johnson said that Collins had "beaten" a lot of water out of his engine, so he, Allen, as fireman, never dreaming of ongoing tragedy, tended his engine before going to the second engine to find why Smokey had signaled stop.

He found Smokey was still on his seat box, in fact, he never moved from it during the entire episode. Day lay with his left leg

No. 13 Sunbeam leaving Houston in November, 1945. *Courtesy Emery Gulasch*

Crossing the Brazos on the Dalsa Bridge, near Varisco, Texas. *Courtesy Stuart L. Schroeder*

Derailment of freight train
north of Ennis. *Courtesy Allen
M. Johnson, Austin*

partly in front of the left seat box, and his body lay on the deck angled toward the right side of the engine. Allen said that in the back of Day's right ear was a crease made by the bridge that was wide enough and deep enough for him to have laid his two fingers in it.

Young Day was a large man, and his body took up most of the moving-about room in the cab. Allen saw he was alive, pulled him to a different position and propped him up.

Meanwhile, someone made his way to the dispatcher's telephone located in a small booth at the Daffan siding. I was the dispatcher to whom he reported the accident. I called an ambulance from Austin. Young Day died at Brackenridge Hospital about 4:00 A.M.

No. 240 stopped at Elgin for water. While J. W. Denges, the fireman sent to finish the trip, was taking water on the Mike, he noticed something white caught under a walkway on the tender. He picked it up; it was D. R. Day's white cap.

Bottle of Wine, Fruit of the Vine

Ralph Essary is a retired mechanical foreman living in Ennis. He and I exchange inspiring bits of history like this yarn he sent me.

Years ago (and perhaps still) wine was shipped bulk in railroad tank cars. Railroad detectives examined the seals on the cars at terminals to protect against theft. Employees, knowing they could draw jail time for liberating the contents, yielded not to temptation. But the empty tanks returning home were not so monitored. Yard and road crews—not to mention hoboes—knew that a consignee never got the last drop of juice out of a car.

Our story took place during World War II, a time when many men were at war, and manpower was scarce.

When an empty wine car arrived, men in the Espee (Southern Pacific) yard in Ennis had a routine. A car inspector would tag the car to the "RIP" (repair) track. When the switchmen delivered the car to the RIP, someone would watch the foreman's office while others jacked the car so that the remaining fruit of the vine would run to the discharge valve. Car mechanics, machinists, clerks, storekeepers, switching crews all came with their bottles and jugs for a share in the windfall of liquified manna.

One day after filling their bottles and jugs, the men caught up with their work early. They began to sample the stuff they had meant to take home. Even the foreman was drawn into the frolic. Everyone was tipsy.

The Master Mechanic, J. E. Frels, hard as nails, could not contact anyone on the "horn," so he came down "off the hill" to see what was wrong. Now this "Boss Man" had come up on the old San Antonio and Aransas Pass Railroad at Yoakum, and he was tough. At first he couldn't believe his eyes. He wanted to fire the whole bunch when he remembered there was no way he could replace them.

Before any of the partying animals spotted him, he sneaked back to his office to fume. The Ennis yard's biggest bash went unreported.

Beating the Bookie

It was a different America then. Back in the 1930s a person driving a Hudson or a Studebaker or a Packard could listen to Bob Wills' band playing "San Antonio Rose" on the car radio as he drove to the post office to mail a letter and two post cards for a nickle.

A man could get five o'clock shadow if he didn't shave with Gillette Blue blades. Those failing to bathe with Life Buoy soap would certainly have B.O., and all of us wondered where the yellow went when we brushed our teeth with Pepsodent. Smokers would walk a mile for a Camel if they didn't reach for a Lucky instead of a sweet. Silver dollars were in circulation, and a man mooching a smoke and a light was often asked sarcastically, "Need a dollar to strike it on?"

Our public figures had words of wisdom for us. Franklin Roosevelt advised us we had nothing to fear but fear itself; Will Rogers quipped that when Congress makes a joke, it becomes a law; Gracie Allen confused us with "There's so much good in the worst of us, and so many of the worst of us get the best of us, that the rest of us aren't even worth talking about." And Mae

West told us that it wasn't the amount of men in a girl's life that mattered, it was the amount of life in her men.

And while the use of telephones was increasing, the nation depended primarily on Postal Telegraph and Western Union for its long distance communication. Western Union wires were strung along railroad rights of way. And such was life in the Ellis County town of Ennis where a couple of young Southern Pacific telegraphers, "Slats" and "Catfish," solved a financial problem in an All-American way.

Because of the Depression, Slats was down to earning a meager living working part-time. Catfish still had a full-time job and would advance Slats the necessary when his cash ran short. But one time Catfish was down to ten dollars when Slats needed to pay some bills. But Catfish had a plan.

On one of the main corners downtown stood Hashop's Drug Store where townsfolk socialized over coffee and cherry-cokes, and two blocks down and around the corner was the Western Union office.

Next to Hashop's was the bookie joint. "Bookie Joint?" you ask. Yes, horse racing was legal in Texas, and in those Depression days, some folks kept finding funds to have fun playing the ponies. There were race tracks at Alamo Downs (San Antonio), Arlington Downs between Cow Town and Big D, and Epsom Downs in dear old Houston, out around Aldine.

Race results were telegraphed to the Ennis bookie from Western Union's Dallas office. Western Union's telegrapher in Ennis copied the results, repeated them to Dallas to verify his copy, then enclosed the results in an envelope, licking and sealing the flap. A messenger ran the telegram around the corner and up the street to the bookie shop where bettors were waiting, and where the bookie signed for the telegram. The bookie opened the envelope, read the contents and settled the bets.

And so it came to pass that on a certain day, about the time the racing results were to be telegraphed from Dallas to the bookie at Ennis, Catfish connected the Western Union telegraph wire through his local telegraph instruments, phoned Hashop's drug and asked to speak with Slats. Slats answered and listened to the racing results coming over the wire, walked around to the bookie joint and placed his bets before the racing results arrived in the envelope and the betting closed.

Slats won! Nearby bettors and losers congratulated him. With his share of the winnings Slats made a sizeable payment on his room and board bill. A week or ten days later, Slats won again. On the third try the bookie told Slats that, though he didn't know what was going on, he would accept no more bets.

But our heroes were happy with what they had, for they had paid off a board bill, recovered Catfish's few dollars, and each had a comfortable amount of money in his pocket.

A Bull Durham Cough

One year in the early nineteen nineties, at the annual S. P. Railroad Reunion at Columbus, Texas, I was one of a group of about five or six standing and talking "railroad" when we were joined by a friendly man whom I know, but whose name I cannot recall. At one point, the subject of conversation must have touched on work trains or on gambling, because our friend told us this tale.

"One time I was on a work train on the Rockport Branch handling track material for an extra gang. When we got off duty each afternoon, we would tie up the engine and caboose on a track next to a gin. Someway we had access to the gin, and we played cards in there until bed time. Some of the men on the extra gang joined us, and word got around, and some of the locals who enjoyed cards joined us for a game. We had a lively den of iniquity going there.

"I was looking out the door one afternoon, and saw one of the locals who had played the night before walking across the pasture toward the gin.

"When he got inside, he closed the door and pulled out a big ole pistol, and said, 'I got cheated here last night. One of you fellows has that ten o' clubs, and I'm gonna find out who it is that's got it, and I'm gonna shoot him.'"

Here our friend hesitated like he suddenly wished he had kept his fool mouth shut. Then he confessed:

"And I had that card—in my pocket."

The rest of us laughed in surprise. Someone asked, "I can see that you didn't get killed. What did you do?"

Our tale teller replied, "You've heard you gotta know when to hold 'em; know when to fold 'em? Well, when I saw him coming, I put my hand in my pocket and began folding that card as small as I could. Back then I smoked Bull Durham, and I had 'at ole Bull Durham cough, and when he told us what he was gonna do, I slipped the card in my mouth and got to coughing, and when I stopped, I had swallowed that card."

Big Dan

Like ninety-nine percent of us who went to work for Espee, Big Dan was as poor as Job's turkey when he hired out as a track laborer somewhere on the Victoria Division, I think it was around El Campo. A big fellow wanting a better life, he soon figured out how to get there. One day the Roadmaster came by in his track car. Dan noticed the car was driven by a laborer. Not long afterward, our hero was driving the track car. In a few short years he was on some official's staff, and a fairly short time later he was on the General Manager's staff in Houston. Big Dan had mastered corporate politics. But, alas, he never mastered train operations.

Not long after G. W. Kelly became General Manager, Big Dan received one of those side ways promotions to Superintendent of Safety—and away from train operations. Maintaining and improving safety standards is an important job, but it pretty well excludes a person from train operations, and train operations is the "smoke" in the proverb "the smoke gets in your blood."

In the spring of one year about 1950, Mother Nature dumped countless tons of water over Texas, especially over the Brazos watershed. At the time there were not enough dams along the Brazos to control such floods, and, like the "Old Mizz-oo" in the song "Shenandoah," the "Ole Brazz-oo" became a mighty river.

Southern Pacific Lines bridge the Brazos at a number of places between Waco and the Gulf. Mr. Kelly and several of his staff drove from Houston to Waco to begin monitoring the Brazos flood waters. Track and bridgemen were alerted. A train of track material was made up at Austin. For some reason, Big Dan, Superintendent of Safety, was among those in the G. M.'s party.

After the river crested at Waco, the General Manager's party headquartered at Hearne to watch the Dalsa bridge which carried a huge volume of transcontinental freight. Though both the Little River and the Little Brazos had added their waters to the flood, the Dalsa bridge withstood the torrent.

But the Brazos would add the waters of the Yegua and the Navasota before it reached the next bridge, the Chappell Hill bridge near Highway 290 between Hempstead and Brenham. And this bridge was a problem bridge.

The soil in which the piling was driven shifted from time to time. S. P.'s best engineers had tried without success to stabilize the bridge. Speed over it was restricted to 15 m.p.h. The line was later abandoned because of the bridge.

Mr. Kelly and company now headquartered at Brenham. New instructions were issued. No. 240 (read Number two-forty) would leave Austin in time to be at the bridge before the crest and would have about twenty car loads of rip-rap to strengthen the shoulders of the roadbed.

No. 240 was at the bridge as planned, about 2:00 A.M.

The weather was not cold; the rain was slow and steady. The blackness of the night was pierced here and there by the lights of flashlights, lanterns and flares. Red and green marker lamps glowed on the caboose. The steam locomotive with the twenty cars of rock stood at the approach to the bridge, sounding like a huge tea kettle coming to a boil, its air pumps cutting on and off with their "thung-thung-thung-thung." The locomotive headlight lit up the blackness ahead, highlighting the silvery steel span and casting huge black shadows from it like some ghostly spider web.

Remember Big Dan, Superintendent of Safety between El Paso and New Orleans, between Denison and Brownsville? The role model for safety? He was there, at the West end of the bridge, near the engine, bulls eye lantern in hand, in boots, yellow slicker covering his burly body.

Mr. Kelly and his advisors watched the rising waters, decided the bridge was in peril; it needed the extra weight of the rock to hold it against the flood. He gave the order. The engineer acknowledged by blowing the whistle two shorts—whoo-whoo, and pulled the train slowly forward onto the bridge.

The Superintendent of Safety then performed a most unsafe deed. He boarded the caboose as it rolled by. His duties did not require his presence on the bridge; he was not experienced in boarding moving freight cars; he was encumbered by boots, slicker and lantern; it was nighttime, and the grab irons were wet.

A few feet out on the bridge, Dan lost his hold on the grab iron, and his burly body fell over the upstream side of the bridge. He held on to his lantern. Everyone who saw it was transfixed as the lantern submerged then surfaced, submerged then surfaced under the bridge and then downstream.

But a kindly thorn tree held up its limbs in Big Dan's way, and he managed to hang on to it and seat himself in its thorny boughs. Just as Jesus Christ had his crown of thorns, Big Dan had his throne of thorns—and his lantern was his scepter.

Mr. Kelly sent men to Hempstead for the volunteer fire department. They also awakened store owners and bought all the rope they could find.

Volunteer firemen tied the rope to a boat and payed it out while others in the boat guided it to the lantern's light. When our hero was in the boat, it was pulled to bank. Big Dan was saved.

The bridge was saved, too. The heavy rock saved it.

When the excitement was over, No. 240 and the General Manager's party proceeded to Houston. As I recall, it was not long afterward that a new Superintendent of Safety was appointed. I don't know what ever happened to Big Dan.

Dennis Read and Bobby Nieman

Dance Halls
of East Texas:
From Oral History

The dance halls of East Texas arose as a result of the oil boom. Many of the first dance halls were at the sites of the boom and thus did not have a very long life span. Some of them lasted only a year or so. In areas such as Kilgore and Longview, where the boom lasted for a much longer period of time, permanent halls were built. These dance halls were primarily the ones that existed at the beginning of World War II. The dance halls of East Texas tended to reflect the type of boom unique to oil. In the gold and silver booms in California and Nevada, while bringing all classes of men and women to the area, the lure was for instant riches on the individual level. Miners became wealthy overnight. The wealth was spread around. As a result, cities like Virginia City and San Francisco developed elaborate, gaudy dance halls that reflected the general advancement of wealth. In the oil boom, only the oil companies and the landowners got rich. While the boom provided lots of jobs in the middle of the Great Depression, the oilfield worker knew that he was not going to walk away wealthy. He made good money and had money to spend, but he never made a fortune.

As a result, the dance halls tended to remain small and not ostentatious. In fact, many of the dance halls were hardly more than bars with a dancing area. A number of these were clustered into areas that had their own place names: Two such areas were "Death Valley," between Longview and and Gladewater on what is now U.S. 80, and "Honky-Tonk City," between Longview and Kilgore on present Texas 31 near where Interstate 20 crosses. These honky-tonks were rough places to go to. Fights and killings were quite common during the 1930s and 1940s. Gambling and prostitution were also prevalent at many of the places right through the Second World War. Only a few of the dance halls ever achieved any sort of respectability.

Private clubs were less common. These clubs were attended by a generally higher socio-economic class of people. Private clubs required memberships. At least one of these, the Petroleum Club of Longview, is still in operation.

The largest club of those boomtown times, the Palm Isle, established in 1935, exists today in a different building as the Reo Palm Isle in Longview, the original building having burned.

Depending on the particular club, the music was either by jukebox, a band, or a combination. Many East Texas entertainers established their own groups and made the rounds of the honky-tonks. The individual popularity of some of these groups was heightened by their playing on KOCA radio out of Kilgore. Many entertainers from outside the area played in East Texas honky-tonks during the period before they became famous. Elvis Presley is a good example of this. One of the main reasons they played this area was the Louisiana Hay Ride in Shreveport. Another was that, especially for Kilgore and Longview, these halls were a good stopover for the big-name bands on their way from Dallas to Memphis or Atlanta, on a route which many groups traveled.

Death Valley had half a dozen clubs in its strip. Among them were Cunningham's Club, Maude Jefferson's, Paine's Club, and Dreamland. Maude Jefferson was a very large woman and ran her club by herself. The club was built around a large tree that grew in the middle of the building. During at least part of World War II this club, as were many such clubs, was off limits to military men. One night about eleven o'clock a group of soldiers arrived at the club in jeeps. They proceeded to tear the club to shreds. Military Police had to be called to quell this mini riot. The MPs arrested the soldiers and drove them off in the jeeps that they had brought. Violence was a common feature. Paine's Club had a road completely around it. One night a group of cars started driving around the club and shooting out all the windows. When the shooting was over there was broken glass everywhere (Faith).

Honky-Tonk City had about the same number of clubs as did Death Valley. Among the clubs were the Beer Bottle Inn, Blanche's Place, Top Hat, and Orange Front. These were often starting points on the way to the more notable Mattie's Ballroom, which was on the old Kilgore Highway. A road connected the two highways. A local resident of the area who lived at the intersection of the old Kilgore Highway and this connecting road recalled that there were wrecks every week-end night at that intersection. The wrecks were the result of people who had gotten to some state of inebriation at one of the Honk-Tonk City clubs and then headed for Mattie's Ballroom (Harder).

Gregg County became the focal point of dance halls in East Texas due to liquor, even more than the fact that the boom was there. Gregg County, through the end of World War II, was one of the few counties between Dallas and Shreveport going east and west, and between the Oklahoma border and Houston that was wet. Not only could beer be bought and sold, but liquor stores were allowed. As a result, most of the clubs sold beer. They also allowed people to bring in bottles and pay for setups (Brown). And some of the clubs had liquor stores attached to the club. To satisfy the legalities of the situation, one could enter the liquor store, buy something, then exit the store and enter the club by another door. Mattie's Ballroom and Paradise Club both had attached liquor stores (Green 1995).

The "big band" movement had its effect on the rise of the dance halls. By 1938, big band music and dancing was the rage. Everyone wanted to dance. This remained true even through the war. However, the war had a major impact on the availability of musicians. So many horn players were drafted that many groups went out of existence. There were not enough musicians for a large band. Country and western bands did not have the same problem, because their bands were smaller (Brown).

Gambling was a major problem. Many clubs had back rooms, or upstairs, for gambling. Some even had slot machines in the main area. Aubrey Freeman ran several clubs that had gambling. He ran the Lake Lamond Club and the Lake Harris Club in Longview, and the Shadowland Club in Kilgore (Green 1995). Freeman was a very personable man and was well liked by all people (Brown). Garth Green related that Freeman would furnish him money to gamble with. He acted as a kind of "shill." Green related that it was fun to gamble with someone else's money. Both Garth and Bob Green relate playing at both Lake Lamond and Lake Harris Clubs when they were raided by Texas Rangers. The Rangers would put one man up by the band while they were taking away the gambling equipment and shutting down the club. Garth tells that once, while the Rangers were

using axes to tear down the gambling equipment, Aubrey Freeman had the band continue to play "Quiet Heat" very loudly.

Dinner clubs were quite rare. The Paradise Club in Kilgore
was one of these. It was owned by a Canadian citizen named
Walter Carr. He ran this club for about fifteen years. The club
was one of the larger clubs. About one hundred couples could
dance at a time. In 1940, the war had already started in Europe,
and this included Canada. Carr had not yet received his U.S.
citizenship. As such, he could not return to Canada or he would
have been drafted. His father came to visit. Carr wanted to take
his father back to Canada, and to visit other members of his
family. Since he could not cross the border, he asked Bob Green
to go with him. The three of them drove to Idaho. Green transported Carr's father across the border, and then brought other
members of the family to visit him (Green 1995).

The other dinner club was Curly's which was on Highway 80
in Longview, across from the Petroleum Club. Frank Melton and
his wife ran the club. He had previously owned a cafe in
Henderson. When Henderson voted to be dry, he closed his cafe
and went to Longview to open Curly's (Green 1995).

Since most of the clubs were relatively small, live entertainment came mostly from local people. The Garth Green Band was
organized in Longview in the early Thirties. They were made up
primarily from the family of Green boys. There had been seven
children in the family. There were three sets of twins. This band
operated until 1941. The band was disbanded at that time due
to the draft, which had begun in October, 1940. The brothers
went into the service and played for USOs during the war. The
band was reconstituted after the war.

Al Dexter was another local entertainer and song writer.
During the war he wrote the song "Pistol Packing Mama." However, after the song became a number one hit in 1946, he had to
sue to get his rights. Ham Faith recalls that Dexter was telling

everybody that he was going to get $100,000. They all said, "Sure, Al, sure." No one believed him. He did get $85,000. After that, Dexter quit playing local clubs and began playing bigger clubs in the larger cities.

Ham Faith had his own group called the Highway Ramblers. This group also started in the early Thirties. The band continued into the war. When the band could no longer be sustained, Faith joined with Rex Hughes, another country singer, to form the country duet of "Ham and Spam." Spam did the singing (Brown). Frank "Buster" Mondella had his own band. In fact, he still plays in a big band group in Longview. Other area bands included the Knute Blevins band, Raymond Roan Band, Ernie Prichard Band, and Chan Chandler's Band. After the war Ernie Prichard became an executive with Cadillac. As the war progressed most of these bands stopped because of a lack of players.

One band that did not have to disband was the Collegians, later called the B. K. Thomas Band. Thomas was employed by Kilgore College. This band was made of Kilgore College and Kilgore High School students. They played at school events and at clubs. Kilgore High School did not have a band, so the high school students who were in the Collegians did not have a conflict. This band played all through the war (Brown).

Another interesting band came as the result of the war. Harmon General Hospital was founded in Longview to treat the war wounded. The base had a very good band. They played at school and civic events, and many of the band members played in area dance halls to make extra money (Brown). Another local entertainer made the big time. His name was Fred Lowery and he was a whistler. He got his start in the Thirties at the Continental Club. In the late Thirties, he joined the Horace Height Band. He played with them when the group played at the Palm Isle during the Forties (Brown).

There were several clubs that deserve special note. The Patio Club in Longview was unique. Couples danced under the stars on a patio. It was a very nice and quite popular place. The Continental Club was another upscale club. This club could accomodate several hundred couples. It was located at what was known as Pitner's Junction between Henderson and Kilgore. The club was run by a man named Nash, and his wife. The Airport Club in Kilgore was located next to the Kilgore Airport. This airport was used as a training field for Naval aviators going through flight school at Kilgore College. A rather unusual club was the Loma Linda. It was located on the old Gladewater Highway between Kilgore and Gladewater. This was a very small, and quite intimate club, intimate in more ways than one. Only about twenty to thirty couples could dance. The interesting feature was the small booths that people used. These booths had curtains that could be drawn to give complete privacy and were frequently used as trysting places (Green 1995).

When dance halls of East Texas are mentioned, there are two individuals who stand out over all the rest. The first is Hugh Cooper. Cooper lived his entire life in Henderson and Rusk County. During the oil boom he had a "wild hare idea" that a ballroom would be a good type of entertainment. He did not have any money so he borrowed and built the first Cooper Club in 1935. This club was located on west Main Street in Henderson, which was the old Tyler highway. This club was a big, barn-like building which could hold about three thousand people. Shortly after building the Cooper Club, Hugh Cooper arranged a contract with a national booking agency, the Music Corporation of America, MCA, for the exclusive first rights to any name group coming into East Texas. As a result, Cooper was the first to bring the major name bands and combos to East Texas. This was a significant element in this area's social life and musical development.

Cooper was a religious person and ran his club very strictly. He himself did not drink or smoke. He did not sell any liquor at any of the three clubs he was to own, although he did allow people to bring in setups when he had the Palm Isle. When he was forty-six in 1946 he married Hazel Harding, a resident of Henderson and twenty years his junior, and became a devout Baptist.

In 1937, the Cooper Club burned down. He immediately built a new Cooper Club farther out on west Main. The second Cooper Club was approximately the same size as the first one. He ran this club for about two years. In 1939 he bought the Palm Isle, which had been built in 1935, and sold the Cooper Club. The individuals who bought the Cooper Club tore down the building and moved it to Texarkana.

Hugh Cooper's Palm Isle was located on Highway 31 in Longview. It was the largest club in East Texas. Hugh told his wife that he had almost five thousand people in the building when Wayne King played there (Cooper).

With Hugh Cooper as its owner, the Palm Isle soon improved its reputation. Since Cooper had exclusive rights to name groups, a long line of major big bands played at the Palm Isle. In 1942, Cooper was inducted into the military. He first leased the Palm Isle to Mattie Castlebury, of Mattie's Ballroom, and then in November of 1943 Hugh Cooper sold the Palm Isle outright to Mattie Castlebury.

Mattie Castlebury, the belle of the oil-field dance halls, came like a whirlwind to East Texas. She had already had dance halls in Borger, Breckinridge, Burkburnett, Conroe, Ranger, Rule, and at least one in the Cromwell, Oklahoma, area, to mention a few. Mattie was born Mattie Sular Miley in Corsicana, Texas, in 1890. She was the oldest child of George Washington Miley, a farmer, and Martha Ward Miley. She had two brothers and two sisters

(Texas Census of 1900). Sometime after 1900 the Mileys moved to Oklahoma and Mattie married Robert J. Arthur of Virginia. Robert fathered the only two children she would have, Robert Henry and J. C. Arthur (Texas Census of 1910). Sometime between 1910 and 1920 this marriage failed.

How Mattie started in the dance hall business is currently unknown. She did introduce a unique twist to her clubs that brought her a great deal of business, some legal problems, and a large amount of gossip. Mattie brought in "taxi dancers." These were young women who would dance with men who came to her clubs. The men would buy tickets, select one of the taxi dancers, and give her a ticket for a dance. The taxi dancers got paid by the number of tickets they collected (Green 1993). Because of these taxi dancers, the rumors of prostitution follow her even today. However, long-time Gregg County Sheriff Noble Crawford knew Mattie Rogers as well as anybody in East Texas, and he completely refuted all allegations in this area (Crawford). And everyone who knew Mattie agreed with Sheriff Crawford.

Mattie was a consummate businesswoman with a great sense of public relations. When she first tried to talk the popular Garth Green Band into playing at Mattie's Ballroom, the Greens were reluctant. Finally, they agreed to play on the condition that she did not advertise in the newspapers that they were going to play her club. So Mattie proceeded to drive through Longview with a bull-horn announcing that the Garth Green Band was to play. In the end, the band got a laugh out of it since many of their followers showed up at Mattie's on opening night.

Mattie's Ballroom had the best dance floor around the area (Brown). Like Hugh Cooper, Mattie had very strict rules about behavior in her club. Many young teens went to Mattie's because it was safe. She did not drink or smoke. She did not swear or allow people to swear around her. Profanity would get one an invitation to leave (Green 1993).

While Mattie was an attractive woman, she was tough enough to take care of trouble. One night a group of baseball players and a group of men from a rodeo began a fight in the parking lot. She took out her .45 and shot it in the air. This brought the fracas to a quick halt (Green 1993).

Her favorite song was "Sophisticated Swing" and her favorite band during the Depression was the Garth Green Band. In fact, she asked the band to play for her funeral. However, when she died the band was not aware of her death, and so was not able to fulfill her request (Green 1993).

When Mattie leased, then bought the Palm Isle from Hugh Cooper, she got access to all of the bands, big and small, that had been playing there. One of the reasons that she was able to keep these bands was that, like Cooper, Mattie was scrupulously honest. The bands trusted her (Brown). Mattie promoted the bands in her new dance hall widely, advertising as far away as the Chicago newspapers. Mattie's Palm Isle went on to gain a national reputation as a music and dance center.

In 1949, Mattie contracted cancer. As her illness worsened, she sold the Palm Isle in 1951. Mattie died in 1954. But her memory is very much alive. Mattie has grown to be a part of the legendry and history of East Texas in a unique way. To East Texans she was Mattie, the Queen of the East Texas dance halls.

BIBLIOGRAPHY AND INTERVIEWS

Arthur, Mrs. J. C. (Lilian). Video tape interview by Dennis Read and Bobby Nieman. Americana Research Center, Longview, Texas. 13 November 1993.

Brown, Mr. Beverly E. Audio tape interview by Dennis Read. Americana Research Center, Longview, Texas. 21 March 1995.

Census of Texas 1900 Soundex, Navarro County, Precinct 3, Vol. 85, ED102, SHHET 22, Line 37.

Census of Texas 1910 Soundex, Wheeler County, Vol. 111, ED221.

"Cooper Club filled an entertainment void in area." *Rusk County History.* Rusk County Historical Commission: Henderson, 1982. 48–50.

Cooper, Hazel. Audio tape interview by Dennis Read. Americana Research Center, Longview, Texas. 20 March 1995.

Crawford, Noble. Video tape interview by Dennis Read and Bobby Nieman. Americana Research Center, Longview, Texas. 25 October 1993.

Faith, Harlan "Ham." Audio tape interview by Dennis Read. Americana Research Center, Longview, Texas. 13 March 1995.

Green, Garth. Audio tape interview by Dennis Read. Americana Research Center, Longview, Texas. 14 March 1995.

Green, Robert "Bob." Audio tape interview by Dennis Read and Bobby Nieman. Americana Research Center, Longview, Texas. 23 August 1993.

Green, Robert "Bob." Audio tape interview by Dennis Read. Americana Research Center, Longview, Texas. 20 March 1995.

Harder, Joe. Interview by Bobby Nieman. Americana Research Center, Longview, Texas.

Larson, Sallie. "Reo Palm Isle celebrates 55 years of fame." *Longview News-Journal.* 9 February 1990. Section D: 1–4.

The Oil Field Camp

James Winfrey

Writers of history, folklore, and fiction have described scenes of many Texas oil booms and boom towns of the past one hundred years. Walter Rundell, Jr., in *Early Texas Oil*, documented the story from Oil Springs near Nacogdoches in 1869, through Corsicana in the late 1890s, Spindletop in 1901, Ranger, Burkburnette, the Permian Basin and several others down to the East Texas field in 1930.

James A. Clark and Michel T. Halbouty under the title *Spindletop*, wrote the definitive work on the father of all Texas booms and then documented the East Texas field in *The Last Boom*. Boyce House in *Roaring Ranger* related facts and folklore of that celebrated boom. Mody Boatright and William Owens devoted two chapters in their *Tales From the Derrick Floor*, to boom towns. Boatright's *Folklore of the Oil Industry*, is all about characters and life shaped by oil booms. Elmer Kelton in *Honor At Daybreak* vividly describes life in a West Texas boom town of the 1920s, with its tent city. In *Letters of a Texas Oil Driller's Wife*, Ella Lane Carl tells about how it was in Borger and Pampa in the late 1920s. The most factual account of the life of an itinerant oil field hand from the early 1930s to the mid 1960s is *Roughnecks, Drillers and Tool Pushers*, by Gerald Lynch.

With all that has been written about oil booms and life in the oil fields, so far as I know, the oil field camp which was common throughout Texas for more than thirty years has not been described outside of company internal publications.

From Spindletop until the 1920s, most of the oil development in Texas was along the Gulf Coast and in west central Texas, where leases for drilling were typically farms. During that time there were many independent oil operators, the fields were not large, and no one company operated a large part of a field.

Beginning in the late 1920s, and continuing through the next twenty years, more effective exploration devices and deeper drilling brought discovery of our great Texas oil fields, which are now far along to depletion. The major oil companies were able to put together large enough blocks of leases in these big fields to make possible orderly development.

To efficiently operate producing company-owned drilling rigs, build tank batteries, and build and operate the rest of the infrastructure, the company had to have a field organization of experienced, reliable, and loyal employees. People who have never worked in The Oil Patch cannot appreciate the skills of the roughnecks, drillers, rig builders (who erected the derricks), roustabouts and other craftsmen whom it takes to get the job done. The original meaning of the term "The Oil Patch," as noted by this writer in 1944 in "Oil Patch Talk," was for the oil field only, the site of drilling and producing operations, *not* for the entire industry, as the term is now journalistically used.

Since almost all of the major oil fields were in rural locations and some were far from any town, the oil field camp was born of necessity. While it was good business for the company, it produced a paternalistic society with management genuinely interested in the well-being of employees. The District Superintendent was directly responsible for safe and successful operation of his camp.

After confirmation wells had been drilled following a discovery and after geophysical surveys indicated the probable size of the field, a campsite would be selected and a surface lease obtained from the land owner. With an eye toward future expansion, civil engineers planned the camp layout for location of first essential buildings: bunkhouses and bathhouses for single men, company houses for key personnel, a campsite for employee-owned houses and the necessary office buildings.

The office, warehouse, and pipe racks would be built first, a water well drilled, roads built and surfaced with shell, gravel, or caliche, and water and gas lines laid. All of this would be done in a remarkably short time. All wooden buildings, and that included everything except shops and pump houses, were prefabricated in contract shops and assembled by contractors. The buildings, including company houses, were delivered in finished pieces of floors, siding, ceilings, etc., and assembled on creosote blocks. The finished buildings were painted company colors. Shops were usually corrugated sheet iron on a steel frame.

Bunkhouses were in twenty-bed units, with ten beds on each side of the room. There were windows for ventilation, since this was before air conditioning. There was room for a foot locker at the end of each bed, but there was no room for chests or closets to hang clothes. Workers paid ten cents a day for these accomodations and were furnished sheets, pillows with cases, and blankets weekly. While I was a roustabout making sixty-eight cents an hour, ($27.20 for a forty-hour week), this was a great bargain.

The bathhouse was a separate building, a short distance from the bunkhouse. There was always plenty of hot water.

The crum boss, the official name for the custodian, was the absolute authority for what went on in his bunkhouse. At our Conroe bunkhouse, his nickname was "Deacon." He saw to it that the place was kept clean and straight and that there was no disorderly conduct. No alcohol was allowed in the bunkhouse. He had few problems with his guests. This was in the early 1930s, and nobody wanted to jeopardize his job.

Children's view (John Stradinger and Jo Ann Winfrey) from the Tomball Field Camp, 1945. *Courtesy Standard Oil (New Jersey) Co. Collection, Photographic Archives, University of Louisville (Kentucky)*

Gambling was allowed in the bunkhouse, but it was closely controlled by the crum boss. He checked on the players to keep outsiders from playing. There was an occasional crap game on a blanket on the floor. Savvy players made the expert even rollers bounce the dice off a wall.

Bunkhouse crap shooters, of course, talked to the dice. Their language was probably no different from any other crap game in rural Texas: Two ones is snake eyes. A two and a one is thirty days in the county jail. Four is Little Joe from Chicago. Five is a fever. Six is Sister Hicks or sixty days in jail. Seven is a natural on the first roll or crap out. Eight is eighter from Decatur, the county seat of Wise. Nine is ninety days in jail. Ten is Big Dick

Oil field company houses in the Tomball Field Camp, 1945. *Courtesy Standard Oil (New Jersey) Co. Collection, Photographic Archives, University of Louisville (Kentucky)*

from Baltimore. Eleven is a natural. Twelve (two sixes) is box cars.

Poker was the favorite game, usually played on a bed. House rules were twenty-five cents ante, table stakes, pot limit, and dealer's choice. Most dealers called for five-card draw or five-card stud, with the Joker working in aces, straights, and flushes. A few dealt draw poker with deuces or one-eyed Jacks wild, and some liked seven-card stud. One thing was sure, the crum boss shut the game down at 11 P.M. and turned out the lights.

The general run of poker players were strictly amateur, but I knew of one exception. He was a company fleet-truck driver we knew as Poker Red. He was one of the drivers who hauled pipe from the suppliers to the various fields where there was drilling activity. He was said to have been a sergeant aide to one of the company's high officials in World War One, so he could do about what he pleased. He was good natured and was well liked. Poker Red played in the bunkhouse twenty-five-cent-ante games occasionally, but he was usually a sweater. It was rumored that he played in big money games away from camp.

Poker Red always had a big roll of bills in his pocket and served as the roughneck's loan shark. We were paid on the tenth and twenty-fifth of the month, and some of the boys would run out of money by the first Saturday after payday. Poker Red helped them with a loan of nine dollars with the agreement that ten dollars would be paid back the next pay day. They did not seem to mind paying exorbitant interest for this financial service.

A few weeks after I was promoted from roustabout to Junior Petroleum Engineer (twelve to sixteen hours a day, seven days a week, for $135 per month), I got to move to a two-man room. Later, when I was made a District Petroleum Engineer, I was assigned a bunkhouse private room, one large enough to hold a chest of drawers and a rod to hang my clothes on. I still used the common bathhouse, which was detached from the bunkhouse.

While this was rather spartan, I considered it high living. Of course, it was not as nice as the Federal Courts now require for felons in Texas prisons.

The typical oil field camp included a mess hall, which was located within walking distance of the office and bunkhouses. My company designed and built our mess hall and furnished it with all the necessary equipment: tables and chairs, kitchen utensils, dishes, flatware, and linens. Operation was by a contractor who supplied the food and labor and who was responsible for the menu. Meals for daylight employees were served at early morning, noon, and evening, with sack lunches provided for roustabout gangs and drilling crews who could not come in at noon. Evening and morning tour drilling crews were served at odd hours to fit their schedules.

During the early 1930s, we were served three big meals for one dollar per day. Meals were nothing fancy, but this was good country cooking and plenty of it. There was one company camp mess hall in a remote section of southwest Texas in the 1940s that was so famous that employees of other companies and oil field salesmen came there to eat rather than going to town to a cafe. Outsiders were allowed to eat in company mess halls but were usually charged more than company men.

The oil field company camp was located in or near the field being developed, which in Texas was typically in a pasture. The campsite was always fenced, ordinarily with barbed wire. Access was through cattle guards. Some camps in west Texas rattlesnake country had snake-proof fences.

The layout of company houses varied with the terrain, but they were always spaced far enough apart to afford privacy.

The camp in the Thompson's field where we lived in the late 1930s was located on Rabb's Ridge, in the Brazos bottoms, seventeen miles down a rough gravel road below Richmond. While it was fairly remote, it was a beautiful site, among ancient liveoak trees. We were three miles from Thompson's Switch, where there was a small railroad station on the sulfur line of the Santa Fe and a post office in Hample's general store. There was a two-room, two-teacher county school in the camp for first through sixth grades. Older children were bused to Richmond, as were the Boy Scouts for their weekly meetings.

As in all other camps, there was an office with the warehouse attached, along with the usual pipe racks, machine shop, and domestic water, gas, and sewer systems. There was a tennis court and a recreation hall which was used primarily for monthly safety meetings and company training courses for employees. There were also parties, covered dish suppers, and children's programs.

The typical company recreation hall was provided with several heavy square tables made by the company carpenter for use by the domino players, which was the most popular game for the working men.

The company encouraged employees to raise vegetables by providing garden space and a completely equipped canning kitchen attached to the recreation hall. It included pots and pans, pressure cookers, and a machine for sealing tin cans.

The company houses for key personnel were prefabricated and all looked alike. They were erected on creosoted wooden blocks, three feet above ground, had weather boarded siding, sheetrock interior, and asbestos shingle roofs. The design made for quick and efficient erection and dismantling.

Our house at Thompson's, which was typical of the time, had four rooms and one small bathroom. There was a living room, kitchen and two bedrooms. Our breakfast table was in the kitchen. This house also had a six-by-twelve-foot front porch and a small screened back porch. We lived reasonably comfortably, although without insulation, air conditioning, or central heat, we were hot in summer and cold in winter.

One of the best things about living in a company house was the rent, which was three dollars per month per room. Rent included gas (which was odorized for safety), water, and electricity.

Our backyard clothes washing equipment included two number-two wash tubs on a wooden bench, a wash board, and an old fashioned cast iron wash pot, heated with a gas jet. We had an excellent solar powered dryer, that is, clothes lines strung between welded-pipe tee posts. Fortunately, after our first child came, my wife had a black woman to help her for three dollars per week.

We disposed of garbage in a burning pit which had a continuously burning gas jet.

The hourly paid people, who generally did not rate a company house, were provided with a large lot in an area separate from but near the company houses. They were allowed to build a house any way they chose, and were connected with water, electricity, and sewer service, the same as company houses. Some of their homes were better than the company house where we lived. Most had large gardens and some had a fenced lot for a cow or horse.

A big event at Thompson's was the squirrel barbecue during the fall squirrel hunting season. Hunters were asked to save their kills for a week and bring them to the picnic grounds by a small lake in the field. I was not much of a hunter, but I carried a .410 gauge shotgun around in my company car. We would have seventy-five to a hundred squirrels ready to be cooked. There was also a fish fry with buffalo and catfish from the Brazos, cooked in our cast-iron wash pot which was also used to boil our babies' diapers.

During the World War II years, we lived in the company camp in the Tomball field. It was located three miles from the town of Tomball, and was in an environment much different from

Thompson's. While all of the many company camps were basically the same, each had its unique character, somewhat reflecting the ideas of the District Superintendent. Being close to a town which had all of the goods and services available in a country town of that era, as did Tomball, added much to convenient living.

Most of the company houses in the Tomball camp were located facing a street circling a grassy park. Outside one row of houses there was a small shallow lake. Tall pine trees were scattered throughout the camp.

The employee-owned homes were located at a site about a half mile from the main camp and were referred to by some of the residents as "the po-boy camp." Near it in a motte of pines, was a very nice Boy Scout hut. The District Petroleum Engineer was expected to be the scout master.

Our house in the Tomball camp was of the same four-room design as at Thompson's, except for a big improvement in a large glazed porch across the back, with connections for our first Bendix washing machine. We had a bermuda grass lawn and a one-car garage for the first time.

For obvious reasons, the Assistant Superintendent had a five-room house and the Superintendent, a six-room house.

While the men rarely got together outside of the job except for safety meetings, a little dominoes, and a Christmas party, the women with their small children visited every morning over coffee, both at Thompson's and Tomball.

At Thompson's they met in one of the homes at 10 A.M. after having set the table, so they could rush home and have the meal ready at twelve noon when their husbands came for lunch.

During the canning season at the Tomball camp, the mothers took quilts to the recreation hall-canning kitchen to bed down the little ones while they worked and visited.

The ladies of the Tomball camp had a garden club and put on an annual flower show in the Recreation Hall.

On special occasions during good weather, the entire camp residents at Tomball and guests from town were invited to a picnic on Spring Creek, at a site which is now a Harris County park.

When we were living in company oil field camps, we were fairly isolated from the world except by radio, but we felt safe and secure, and we made friendships in the camps fifty years ago that we still cherish.

A group of men and women, now in their sixties, who grew up in the Tomball oil field camp have an organization called "Oil Patch Kids." They meet annually for a big party.

By the late 1950s, the need for oil field camps had diminished. With the advent of good roads, many employees preferred to live in town and commute. District offices were being consolidated and moved into town for economic reasons. By the mid 1960s, the oil field company camp which had been common throughout the Texas, Louisiana, Mississippi, and New Mexico oil country for thirty years was practically gone. Most of the company houses were sold to employees who moved them into small towns or to their farms.

In 1982, fifty years after I hired out as a roustabout, I returned to the Conroe and Tomball fields. Only small offices at the gas plants remained. There was not a trace of the camp sites, which had been taken over by pine forests. I know of no surviving traditional oil field camp. The only bunkhouse type living quarters in the States are on offshore mobile drilling rigs and production platforms and on the North Slope of Alaska.

Thus has ended an era in the ever changing history of the oil industry in Texas.

BIBLIOGRAPHY

Boatright, Mody C. and William A. Owens. *Tales From the Derrick Floor.* Garden City, NY: Doubleday and Company, 1970.

Boatright, Mody C. *Folklore of the Oil Industry.* Dallas: Southern Methodist University Press, 1963.

Carl, Ella Lane. *The Letters of a Texas Oil Drillers Wife.* New York: Comet Press Books, 1959.

Clark, James A. and Michel T. Halbouty. *Spindletop.* New York: Random House, Inc., 1952.

_____. *The Last Boom.* New York: Random House, Inc., 1972.

House, Boyce. *Roaring Ranger.* San Antonio: The Naylor Company, 1951.

Kelton, Elmer. *Honor at Daybreak.* New York: Doubleday, 1991.

Allen Turner and Richard Stewart

Noises in the Attic:
Adventures of Some Texas Ghosts

The Last Laugh

Summers along the Gulf Coast are slow and sultry and Saturdays are for sleeping late. But any plans Nana Flennesson, a young resident of the tiny Brazoria County town of Bailey's Prairie, might have had for sleeping-in were abruptly ended that morning in 1968 when she heard the distinct sound of children's laughter coming from an adjoining room.

That room was occupied by her three-year-old cousin, Tommy, and all Nana could conclude was that Christian and Travis, the young children of her neighbor, Ima Jean, had come over to play. "We didn't lock our doors back then," she said, "and the boys always played back and

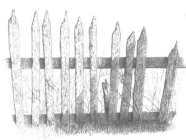

forth." What troubled Nana, though, was the early hour—it was about seven A.M.—and the fact that she and Ima Jean had agreed the children shouldn't visit one another without permission.

Although the women were neighbors, a field separated their houses, and a sluggish creek, notorious for the aggression of its water moccasins, ran nearby.

As Nana slipped on her bathrobe and shoes, she continued to hear the muttering, laughing children. But when she entered the nursery, she found Tommy fast asleep, and the voices seemed to be coming from the kitchen. "I was fussing by this point,'" she recalled. "I was calling for Christian and Travis to come out right then."

The kitchen was empty. So were the dining and living rooms as she pursued the voices through the house. They sounded as if they belonged to children delighting in playing hide and seek. Then she heard the voices in a loft.

"That compounded the problem," she said, "because they all were forbidden from going into the loft, which was reached by a spiral stairway. It was dangerous." But when she reached the loft—by now she was thoroughly awake—no one was there either. "I was thinking, 'What in the world?' when I heard the voices coming from the patio."

This time the door was locked. Nana unlocked the door, then heard the voices coming from the banks of the creek. "The creek banks were fairly cleared off," she said. "The problem was the snakes. I was thinking that if they didn't get snakebit, I would kill them. I could hear the laughing; the leaves were rustling like they were running through them. The children were laughing, twittering like they were talking behind their hands."

Nana was perplexed. Her neighbor's boys, ages five and seven, were well-behaved, and given the withering tone in which she was addressing them, they normally would have surrendered and pleaded for mercy. But no one was there. "Suddenly it dawned on me that that door had been locked," Nana said. "I went inside leaving them laughing on the creek bank. It was genuinely unsettling."

All told, she had followed the voices around her house and property for more than five minutes.

She found Tommy—"a little tow-headed sweetie"—sitting up in bed, pointing with his thumb toward the creek. "Auntie Nana, can I go play with those kids?'" he inquired. "He was looking at me with his big bright eyes, and I said, 'No.' Something wasn't right."

She telephoned Ima Jean.

"Where are Travis and Christian?" she asked.

"Why?" responded Ima Jean.

"Just tell me where they are."

"They're in there watching cartoons," Ima Jean said.

"They weren't over here—?" Nana began.

"Did you," Ima Jean nervously interjected, "hear something?"

Pale and feeling foolish the women rushed to compare notes.

"You heard the laughing children—thank God!" Ima Jean exclaimed.

She confessed to Nana that she had heard the frightening laughter on several occasions. Even her mother had heard and commented on the mysterious voices.

Eager to find an explanation for the phenomenon, the women quizzed Eugene Addison, a longtime Bailey's Prairie resident employed by Ima Jean and her husband. "Those are the laughing children," Addison matter-of-factly informed them.

The laughter, he told them, often had been heard in the area. Many locals studiously avoided walking through the pasture across Oyster Creek from the women's houses. That property, Eugene said, had been the site of a house destroyed by fire in the nineteenth century. As many as nine children perished in the blaze.

"He just shrugged his shoulders like we were crazy," Nana said. "It was like everybody knew about what had happened across the creek."

"I had heard that story since I was a boy, and that was a long time ago," Eugene, now an Angleton resident, said. "That was fifty years ago, and that's a story the old people used to tell. I never heard the children, and I don't believe in ghosts, but those others thought the story was true."

Screwing up their courage, Nana and Ima Jean probed the pasture, discovering what they believed was the foundation of the burned out house. "It looked like railroad ties that had been the base of the cabin," Nana said. "They were charred and were just about at ground level. We found the stubs of two crepe myrtles that people liked to put in front of their homes. And we found shell—it might have been some kind of walkway. The ruins of the house were on the fence line right between our houses. We said, 'Well, laughing children we didn't mind, but if they were screamers, we'd be out of here.'"

Nana heard the laughing children several other times while working in her yard. And, on one occasion a guest tending the patio barbecue pit heard the voices and expressed concern for children playing near the treacherous creek. "He had called to them and they wouldn't come up," Nana said. "He wanted me to get Ima Jean to take charge or for me to do something about it. I just went out and told them, 'Go home!' and we never heard the laughing children anymore."

"I value my reputation for sanity," Nana said, "but this really did a lot for me. I used to laugh when people would tell stories about the supernatural, but now I'm more open-minded.

"I think I'm sane, I'm well-educated and I don't drink. I can't tell you what happened; I don't know that it was ghosts or that it wasn't ghosts. But I can tell you that it existed. Whatever it was really was there."

A Graveyard Visitor

England Twine is a tall, quiet, black octogenarian who lives surrounded by his family in a modest frame home beside a farm road in the old farming community of Jamestown, near the Newton-Jasper County line. In a perfect world he might have become a diplomat, a professor or—as he dreamed in his younger days—a professional basketball player. But Twine did not grow up in a perfect world.

He grew up, rather, during hard times in the East Texas piney woods, hearing his grandmother's stories about slavery days. When he grew up, he worked at whatever jobs he could to make enough money to feed his family. Mainly, he farmed cotton, scratching out a crop on a few acres that had once been dense forest. He did other jobs too—when he could get them. He helped build some of the dirt roads that still snake through the forest near his home. Sometimes, he dug graves.

This was long before there were funeral homes with machines that could excavate a grave in a few minutes. The tiny cemeteries hidden in the woods around his home are filled with his handiwork. Many are marked with cement headstones he crafted by hand.

Sometimes while digging a grave, England would unearth a skull from an earlier burial. A lot of those graves never were marked, their occupants doomed to an eternity of anonymity. When that happened, the unflappable grave digger would just scoop out a little shelf in whatever grave he was working on at the time and place the remains securely in the niche. He isn't—and never has been—a man to frighten easily.

There was one occasion, though, when his courage was sorely tested.

He talked about the episode not long ago while standing in the soft shadows of late afternoon in one of the oldest Afro-American cemeteries of the area. In the stillness, his quiet voice floated across the peaceful scene like a soft breeze rustling the moldering leaves that carpeted the ground.

It seems that one of his boyhood friends was a rounder who always promised that if he died first, he would come back to haunt England. "He told me he'd try to run me," England said. When they were both still young men, the friend was killed by a jealous husband—a classic rounder's end— and was buried in the very graveyard in which Twine stood to tell his tale.

Several years later, England was alone in the cemetery near the close of day digging a grave. It was then, he said, that his friend's spirit came back to keep his promise. He came, England said, in the form of a lizard. Not just an ordinary lizard, mind you, but a giant reptile more than a foot long. "It was," England said sixty years later, the biggest lizard I ever saw."

"He was just looking at me and scratching on the ground," England said. "I knew that was him, so I went to talking to him. I said, 'I know that's you come back to run me. Tell me, you ought to know, where is there money buried around here?'

"He run back up that tree until I couldn't see him any more and pretty soon he came down as a rush of wind. He swirled around and then blew right out into the woods over there. That'll sure make the hair stand up on your head."

Office Ghost

Nick Ramon, now the head of a Harlingen housing agency, prides himself on being a rational man—a man who checks things out, knows the score, seeks rational causes to events and devises effective strategies. Thus, the events that occurred in Brownsville in the early 1980s still leave him uneasy. They were the type of occurrences that leave practical men beginning their day with a recitation of the 23rd Psalm—"The Lord is my shepherd, I shall not want"—just to achieve peace of mind.

The events that centered around Nick, then the head of the Community Development Corporation in Brownsville, began innocuously enough about 1981, two years after he opened his office in a nondescript, modern one-story building.

"I'd be down there on Saturdays and I'd hear noises," he said. "It would sound like footsteps, someone walking down the hallway. Or it would be doors closing. Not slamming, just shutting. But I didn't pay it much attention. I just thought it was my imagination. I am a very rational person, and I just thought I was overworked. I'd just go on with what I was doing."

Nick no longer could ignore the events though when he and a colleague, a city appraiser, saw an apparition in October of that year. "We had had a fund raiser one night and about five of us were down at the office late—about 10:30—counting the money. We were in a room with the door shut and locked when I began to feel that there was a presence moving toward us.

"I felt that it had walked up to the doorway, and then I saw a figure of a person—a man—lacking shape and form standing in the doorway. He had the outline of a head, but no real features. He was over six feet tall, and I would say it looked like fog. I had a very strong feeling of a presence being there. I turned to the other fellow and he looked at me and our jaws just dropped. The others in the room were facing the other way, but they immediately asked us what was wrong."

The apparition vanished after a few seconds, Nick said. "I had a feeling that it was under some kind of restraint," he said. "It was kind of like the feeling you have when you see a dog on a leash that's too short for it. You kind of feel sorry for it."

Nick said he likely would have attributed the manifestation to an overactive imagination had it not also been witnessed by the second man. Disconcerted by the episode, he said he called a staff meeting. "I told them what had happened, that we had had some very strange events occur in the building and asked them if they had noticed anything odd." He was somewhat taken aback by the office workers' response.

Secretary Yolanda Garza reported that a roll of toilet paper had rolled across the restroom floor of its own volition. Counselor Ruben Reyna had heard the sounds of an ancient organ playing in the night and had felt he was being pushed from the building. Once, he told Nick, a radio had changed stations without human assistance.

Another female staffer reported that a vacuum cleaner stored in the restroom mysteriously had turned itself on while she was alone in the room. Still another worker reported that a manuscript had launched itself from a desktop and floated through the air.

Nick himself noticed lights flickering on and off even though no human hand touched the switch.

Ever the logical man, he consulted an architect to determine whether there was a normal explanation for the strange noises heard in the building. "Buildings do creak," he said. "They do breathe. But the architect checked the plans and looked things over and said there was no reason for these things to be happening. A building shouldn't breathe that much. We had the wiring checked. There was nothing wrong that we could discover."

Finally, Nick consulted a priest. "He came in and blessed the building," he said. "And, yes, I was reciting the 23rd Psalm every morning when I came in. I asked him about things that I could do myself. The Psalm at least made me feel calmer." Nick lit candles, anointed himself with oil and even tried to converse with the presence, asking it to leave him alone.

But strange things kept happening.

One evening, Nick and his wife arrived at the office to retrieve some record albums. "There was an exterior window in the office," he said, "and as we drove up, the interior was illuminated by the car's lights. I left the car lights on when I got out to go inside. My wife stayed in the car. When I got to the door, I could look inside."

What he saw terrified him.

"The water fountain—the kind with a five-gallon jug of water on top—was bubbling like someone was drawing a drink," he said. Then the cooler began rocking. "We didn't go inside. We decided to leave well enough alone," Nick said.

About the same time, Nick told the *Houston Chronicle's* Evan Moore in 1985, the presence followed him home. "Like, one time it got in the car and rode home with me," he told Moore. "You could feel it, a sort of presence. The next day, my little girl saw it. She said a man stuck his head in her door and said, 'You want to come out and play?' and that's when it was really frightening."

As word of the haunting spread—the story made headlines in supermarket tabloids—mediums began to offer explanations for the unsettling occurrences. Landlord Andy Cortez told Moore that a Matamoros curandera, or folk healer, reported that a man and woman had been killed in the spot years earlier. She even named names. The curandera wanted to hold a seance in the building, but as Andy—in a conference call with Nick and the healer—listened to the proposal, his face grew hot and itched fiercely. When he looked in the mirror minutes later, it was covered with angry red splotches. Paranormal or merely an emotion-fueled eruption, the dermatological problem was sufficient for Cortez to deny permission for the spirit session.

Nonetheless, Nick said, "A Pentecostal preacher approached me and said he wanted to spend some time there to see if he could figure out what was going on. He did, and when I saw him the next morning, he said he had the strong feeling that a woman was buried there. Not in the building, but on that site. And that she was coming back so people would be aware that she was there. She wasn't evil or destructive, but she just wanted her presence made known."

That's about the time Nick decided he and his fifteen-member staff should move. "We couldn't get any work done," he said, "morale was really wrecked." Before they vacated the offices, the staff joined hands in a circle and asked the presence not to follow them.

"I can laugh about all this now," Nick said, "but, believe me, we weren't laughing then."

As publicity grew—the *Reader's Digest* even carried a story about the strange events in Brownsville—some townsfolk accused Nick of being a headline grabber.

"That wasn't the case at all," he said. "I had absolutely nothing to gain from talking about this, and quite a lot to lose. I never called it a ghost. I don't know what it was. I can't explain it, but I can assure you that these things happened."

[The above tales were taken from the copyrighted but unpublished manuscript, "Transparent Tales: An Attic Full of Texas Ghosts," by Allan Turner and Richard Stewart.]

John Lightfoot

Repo
Man

A repo man is a repossessor of automobiles whose
owners have become delinquent in their payments
to banks, credit unions, finance companies, and
both new and used auto dealers. The life of a repo
man has always been thought to be dangerous
and exciting. Each one you talk to has tales of
violence (both real and threatened), close escapes
from danger, and hilarious repo stories. But since
then-Assistant D.A. Johnny Holmes convicted a
policeman of attempting to murder a repo man
in 1971, no fatal or near fatal violence against
repo men had occurred in Houston—until February 25, 1994.

At 3:30 A.M. that morning (most repos
take place late at night when the
delinquent owners are hopefully
sleeping) fifty-four-year-old
Tommy Morris was attempting to

repo Jerry Casey's 1988 Ford pickup truck for Charlie Thomas Used Cars. Thomas also owns Charlie Thomas Ford and owned the Houston Rockets basketball team until he sold it in 1993. As Morris was hooking up the truck to his wrecker, Casey, firing from his house, shot Morris through both lungs with a .30-30 rifle. Morris made it two blocks from Casey's house before collapsing and bleeding to death. All my information about the Morris shooting and the subsequent no-billing of Casey comes from stories reported in the *Houston Chronicle* and Houston repo man Jim Douglass.

One month later a Houston grand jury no-billed Casey in the shooting of Morris. The grand jury believed Casey's assertion that he thought Morris was a car thief, not a repo man. An 1880s Texas law allows Texans to use deadly force against thieves after dark. But Houston-area repo men, Morris' widow Donna Morris, and the Texas Association of Professional Repossessors (TAPR) believe that justice was not done. They believe Casey knew his truck was being repossessed and that he should have been indicted for murder. TAPR was organized seven years ago to lobby the legislature for more reasonable laws pertaining to repoing vehicles.

Grand jury testimony revealed that Casey had not been warned in advance that his truck was going to be repossessed, but on February 25, 1992, a different repossessor had towed off another vehicle Casey had purchased. On that occasion, however, Casey had been several months behind in his payments. This time Casey was only three days behind. Charlie Thomas lot workers' position was that sufficient notice of possible repossession was given at the time of sale. The sales document states that an auto may be repossessed if the owner is only one day behind in payments.

Casey testified he was awake with stomach problems when he spotted the wrecker outside his house, ran to get his rifle (which had a telescopic sight), and fired two shots. But Houston repo man Douglass testified Casey couldn't have possibly gotten the shots off that fast since it only takes a repo man seven seconds to attach the vehicle to his wrecker and drive off. Donna Morris and Douglass said Casey must have known who was taking his truck and why. Assistant District Attorney Larry Standley was quoted in the *Houston Chronicle* (February 26, 1994) after the no-billing as saying, "People in Harris County are particularly paranoid about crime. You have to be extremely careful around other peoples' property."

Morris' widow said Texas' old law about defending your property with gunfire at night might have been fitting in an era of cattle rustlers and horse thieves, but not in the 1990s. Douglass later said the same law could allow a home owner to legally shoot kids who were wrapping his house with toilet paper.

Subsequent occurrences concerning the Morris shooting turned even more strange. In May of 1994 Casey's wife Patricia Ann was convicted on misdemeanor charges of perjury for giving a false statement to a homicide detective after the shooting. She said she called 911 immediately after the shooting and again at 6:30 A.M. The Harris County Sheriff's Department was criticized for failing to respond to her initial call. Some speculated a faster response could have saved Morris' life. The department, however, quickly released its phone records which showed only one call was made at 6:39 A.M. Mrs. Casey later admitted she lied and pled guilty to the charge. She served seven days in the Harris County Jail.

Then on October 3, 1994, Jerry Casey committed suicide, shooting himself in the chest with a shotgun. Sheriff's detectives said a suicide note was found near the body. The contents of the note have never been revealed. They said they were unsure whether Casey's suicide may have been the result of personal and marital problems since the shooting. The Caseys were separated at the time of his suicide, with Patricia Casey saying she feared retribution from her husband once he found out she lied about having called the police just after the shooting.

Houston repo men were incredulous about the grand jury's decision not to indict Casey. "I quit repoing the day Casey wasn't indicted," said ex-repo man Dennis Vandergrifft of Freeport. "It's open season on repo men now. That grand jury said it's OK to murder repo men at night if you think they're trying to steal your car. The profession just became lots more dangerous."

Some observers of the repo man profession, however, suggest that the repo business is the sleaziest in town, that repo men are little better than car thieves. A January 1995 article in the *Chronicle* stated that unscrupulous repo companies are taking advantage of a law which has allowed them to seize cars from owners who are tardy on simple repair bills. Apparently some repo men are buying hot auto repair checks, repoing the vehicles, and then demanding large fees for the return of the car.

In the cult classic movie *Repo Man*, one macho fellow who carries a gun and is not afraid to use it tells rookie repo man Emilio Estevez, "The Rodriguez brothers (rival repo men) are not scumbags: they're car thieves just like us." Much of the black comedy concerns Harry Dean Stanton's efforts to educate Estevez in the code of the repo man. It should be noted that different states have different laws on repoing automobiles. Louisiana and Wisconsin require court orders and an accompanying policeman to repo a car. Wreckers are used almost exclusively in Texas, but none were present in the movie set in California. Jim Douglass says the reason there are no repo wreckers in California is that insurance costs for repo wreckers there are astronomical. According to my one source who worked there, repo men in California work with sets of master keys. Big Dave Terry said the best California repo men could hotwire a car in under three minutes.

The 1988 *Repo Man* movie was written and directed by former repo man Alex Cox. Much of the film is repo man lore presented to Estevez by Stanton: "Only an asshole gets killed for a car," Stanton said. "And we work on commission; that's better than being paid. Guys that make it are guys that can get in a car any time, get in at 3 A.M. and get out at 4. I never met a repo man who didn't take speed. It also helps if you dress like a detective. People respect you if it looks like you're carrying a gun."

But Stanton keeps stressing that repo men have an ethical code to live by: "Not many people today live by a code, but repo men do. I have never hotwired a car or broken into a trunk. Always remember, it's illegal to damage a car or its contents."

When Estevez asks Stanton if all repo men live by the code, Stanton says, "Of course you see a lot of damaged cars, but ninety-nine percent of the time it's the customers who tear them up." At one point in the movie Estevez gets beaten up by an auto's owners, and all the employees of the Helping Hands Acceptance Corporation extract revenge on the culprit: "A repo man doesn't run to the man," Stanton said. "He does it alone like John Wayne. If a repo man gets beaten up in the line of duty, the man who did it has got to pay the price."

Big Dave, the California repo man, said his boss told him the proper repo man method was to walk up, knock on the door, and announce our intentions to repo the car, "but we figured it was lots easier to take the car and then announce our intentions. The funniest job we ever went on was in San Diego. When we found the car, the owner had put a 'for sale' sign on it. I pretended to be interested and asked to take it for a test drive. The fellow said OK and gave me the keys. We called him later to report we had repoed his car.

"Our style was to use a two-man team. My partner would go inside to talk to the owner, and I'd use my key ring to steal the car. We used to follow folks to bars. One would go in and shoot pool with the person to occupy his attention, and the other would repo his car. The easiest repo is while the person is at work. We'd park a half block from his house and follow him to work."

Big Dave emphasized that used car dealers are the most unethical repo men around. "Lots of used car dealers will repo a car one day after the payment is due in order to sell the car again. If they can sell the same car five times, they're way ahead. Lots of unethical dealers will even give the car back to the owner for a fat repo fee."

Another of Big Dave's funny stories concerned a repo car with battery problems. "One time in San Diego we were repoing a car, but it wouldn't start because of a dead battery. We asked a next door neighbor if we could borrow a battery. He loaned us one, and we started the car and returned the battery. He said he knew the man next door, so we pretended to be his brother-in-law helping him out. The neighbor was glad to be of assistance. The owner later asked us how we got his car started with a dead battery. I told him we got his neighbor to loan us a battery—but I didn't tell him which neighbor."

Del Robertson of Surfside was a repo man in Houston two years: "Unless you're working for one of the shyster used car lots, most repos are two or three months past due. We got a flat fee of $75 per car unless we had to do a skip trace and extra leg work. Then we'd get $125. The value of the car seldom matters. It's regular work if you can stand the hassle. The money you make is about the same as having a $7 or $8-an-hour job. It's a cutthroat business. People were always trying to steal our accounts. The only way to deal with that is to try and do a good job and not tear up the repo."

"It's true some people in the profession have a macho thrill of danger, kind of like cops, I suspect. People cuss you out and scream, 'You ain't getting my car.' Then it's fun to zap 'em, maybe even honk at 'em on the way out. But I got out of the business because of the danger. My girlfriend got nervous. My boss at Guaranteed Adjusters, Gary Denson, knew Morris. Lots of people get shot at, but he's the first murder victim anyone around Houston can remember. Think about the possibilities of cruising a black complex in the Fifth Ward area late at night. All sorts of bad things can happen to you. Lots of guys go in the daytime, especially if the person has a job. It's safer that way since people usually don't carry a gun to work. Night work is mostly deadbeats who don't have a job."

"My most frightening experience occurred one night in Fifth Ward on Lyons Avenue. We were looking for a Toyota. When we found it and began to tie on, the owner and some of his friends came running out with baseball bats. We dropped the car and took off. That was about 12:30 A.M. But we went back at 3 and dropped pins in the car. That way you don't have to get out of the truck. We hooked on from the rear (the car had front wheel drive) and drug it with the front wheels dragging for about four blocks. They chased us again but we got far enough away to drop it and pick it up right."

"Another time we were after a Ford van, and the couple who owned it knew we were coming. They were sleeping in the van. We got hooked up and they began screaming we were kidnapping them, that the van was their home. We let them out with their personal stuff but repoed the van anyway."

Jim Douglass tried to put the profession in a brighter light. He's been a repo man in Houston since 1978, and his father was a repo man in Detroit. "The job of a repo man used to be fun. You get to work at your own pace, and since no job is ever the same, you're never bored. There are lots of reputable repo men around. Tommy Morris was one of those. Heck, he lived in a $250,000 house."

"Repoing is like fishing; some nights they're biting and some nights they're not. We'll run 12–16 addresses a night. Some nights we can't find anything. The next night at the same addresses we'll strike gold. But the stigma of repo men is getting worse. Nobody respects us. Seven years ago liability insurance on a repo wrecker was $2,400 a year. Now it's $5,000, and there are only three companies in Texas that will write insurance for a repo man. We're a necessary evil; if it weren't for the repo man, auto interest rates would be out of sight."

Like all the others, Douglass has a wealth of funny repo stories: "One time we were in Galveston repoing a Nissan Sentra. The owner was a body man who had wrecked the car and repaired it incorrectly. When I drove off, only the front half of the car came with me. One night in the NASA area I repoed a car with a master key. Just as I was about to start the engine, I felt something cold on my neck. I figured it was a gun barrel. But it turned out to be a dog in the back seat cold nosing me.

"The strangest thing I can remember is our repo of a new Thunderbird. The owner had built a shed around it to keep repo men at bay. I guess he tore it down on Sundays so he could go for a ride. He said we'd have to dismantle the building. He added that his pet baboon was in the shed too and that he would bite. We had to tear out one side of the shed and distract the monkey with a coke in order to repo the car."

Douglass said laws vary from county to county and city to city in Texas: "In Liberty you have to get a court order. In small towns we're in competition with the cops for repo work. In some towns cops will help you repo the car. I have observed that the farther south in Texas you go, the more helpful and considerate the cops are. When you go north, cops hassle you worse."

By far my funniest repo man source was Dennis Vandergrifft of Freeport. My interview with him was supposed to last twenty minutes, but I was there for almost two hours. He would still be telling funny repo stories had I stayed.

"One time after we had hooked up, the wrecker broke down, and we had to call another wrecker to tow us both. Another time we had finished hooking up a pickup and the owner and his girlfriend came running out in their underwear. The girl was in her bra and panties. He had called the police, and the couple refused to move from in front of my truck. When the cops arrived, the couple was told to go in the house and put some clothes on. Naturally at that point off we went.

"I've had preachers pull guns on me. The worst folks to deal with are preachers, cops and government employees. I repoed a TABC (Texas Alcoholic Beverage Commission) man's car off La Brisa's (a Freeport night club) parking lot one night. One preacher told me, 'If you pull out of here, you're going to die.' I didn't believe him and called his bluff, but he pulled his pistol out from under his choir robe, so I dropped his car. But the next Sunday I came back and repoed it while he was preaching his sermon.

"One night I repoed a car which belonged to a Brazoria County Sheriff's Deputy. I was dropping off the car at the bank's parking lot when he raced up with his partner and repoed my repo. I called the police, and they said, 'All he was doing is what you were doing. He hasn't broken the law. You'll have to repo it back.'

"I repoed another cop's car at his station house. He came out and caught me before I could get away and arrested me for auto theft. He was embarrassed in front of his buddies and said he was going to shoot me. But his supervisor stepped in and let me go with my repo.

"One fellow chased me in my wrecker. When I stopped, he reached in his pocket like he was going for his gun. I picked up a crowbar in case it was just a knife. But it was the keys to the car. He threw them and hit me in the chest. I thought he had thrown a knife at me. He said, 'If you're going to take the car, you'll need these.'

"My closest call was in Needville when I was repoing a '91 280Z. My partner had jumped out of the wrecker when the guy came out of the house with his shotgun. I tried to get his wife to get him to put the gun down, but he wouldn't listen. She ran a couple of blocks away to get some money from her daddy. My partner by that time had hooked up the car, and the owner fired at the ground several times. His father-in-law finally showed up with enough money to make the late payments. I made $200 that night, but I was never so scared in my life."

According to Vandergrifft, people often park their cars in a location or position making it impossible to hook up: "It's impossible to get one off Dow Chemical's lot. You can't get on the plant site because of security. I remember one exception. Dow had fired this fellow for drugs, and they knew he was about to leave town in his unpaid-for car. Texas Dow Credit Union actually called me that time and helped me hook up his car. The best repo man is a good talker, since ninety percent of the jobs are on the up and up, but nobody knows the law, what a repo man can and can't do. Most repo men are wreckers doing repo on the side."

Vandergrifft had nothing good to say about Charlie Thomas Used Cars: "They're what's known as three-day jerkers. You miss a payment three days, and they steal your car and resell it. Dealers like that are almost crooks. Hell, they are crooks. I quit repoing the day the grand jury didn't indict Jerry Casey. It's open season on repo men now. People say we're assholes, but repo men aren't bad asses. They're just doing a job. But it's a thankless job. I bet Charlie Thomas didn't even pay for Tommy Morris' funeral. We took up a collection and gave his widow $1600, but that won't bring her husband back."

Donna Morris reports that she is diligently continuing her efforts to get Texas law on repoing automobiles changed so that repo men can't be legally shot in the future. But she says she's not having much luck. "It's hard going in such a law and order state, she said. "And I can understand people wanting to protect their property from thieves. But my husband wasn't a thief."

"If enough people become aware of the problem, maybe we can get some relief," she said.

References

From the *Houston Chronicle*: 2/26/94—First report of the Tommy Morris shooting; 3/23/94—Grand jury probe; 3/26/94—No-billing of Jerry Casey and statements by DA; 4/4/94—Indictment of Casey's wife for perjury; 5/5/94—Casey's wife pleads guilty; 10/4/94—Casey commits suicide; 1/3/95—unscrupulous repo men.

Interviews: Jim Douglass, Houston, Texas, 10/22/94; Del Robertson, Surfside, Texas, 8/13/94; Donna Morris, Houston, Texas, 10/27/94; Dave Terry, Surfside, Texas, 8/27/94; Dennis Vandergrifft, Freeport, Texas, 9/17/94.

Rebecca Cornell

Tex-Mex Dialect or Gidget Goes to Acuna

Speakers of Spanish have inhabited what is now the southwestern United States since the end of the sixteenth century, following the first explorations of Francisco Coronado in 1540 and Juan de Oñate who, in 1598 established the settlement of San Juan de Nuevo México and later Santa Fe in 1610 (Cotton and Sharp). By the middle of the nineteenth century there were perhaps 100,000 Spanish speakers in the northern territories of New Mexico, Colorado, Arizona, Texas and California. Today, there are upwards of six million Spanish speakers in the southwestern United States. However, I shall concentrate only on the link between Texas and Mexico, as it is the longest border. The other states involved also have words and phrases distinctive to their particular area.

Tex-Mex dialect is the language of the folk who inhabit the border between Texas and Mexico. It is passed on orally, although recently studies have been made that explore and set out written definitions. It exists in different versions, particularly in the Spanish contractions, as some just get shorter and shorter, eliminating more and more, leaving only a consonant and a vowel in some cases (Onofre-Madrid). It does, however, tend to become formularized, as almost any Texan or Mexican knows the meaning of a phrase such as *Que pasó?* Most of these phrases are transmitted back and forth across the international border as access is easy and comfortable for a majority of travelers.

One discovers in Texas that anyone who depends solely upon literary Spanish can barely converse with or understand Mexicans of the border and rural areas of Texas because of the many slang expressions and localisms which have made this dialect almost a separate language (Kelly and Kelly). Anyone who speaks, speaks a dialect (Devereux). Therefore, it is extremely difficult to give a definition of dialect that is not also a definition of language. When one mentions dialect, probably the first thing most people think of is regional speech, and that is indeed one of the principal types of variation. In some countries geographical dialects may prove to be a real barrier to communication, and in others, such as Mexico and the United States, they may simply provide local color.

The dialect spoken along the border between Texas and Mexico is called Tex-Mex or Spanglish. Many words of Mexican origin are half-anglicized and have become a part of the daily vocabulary in this area. Other people of both Anglo and Mexican descent speak both languages, and they have also taken many English words and "españolized" them (Treviño 451). English words are taken over into Spanish primarily through the spoken medium. Thus their form and flavor is distinctly "pocho" or these words are called "pochismos" (Galván and Teschner). The regular use of Anglicized words appears to indicate a fairly general acceptance of them. Hence, the flow back and forth of adaptations to and from both English and Spanish create the Tex-Mex dialect.

However, some general rules of language, particularly Spanish, apply in forming some Tex-Mex words and sentences. In a Spanish matrix with English insertions, the word order must be Spanish, with the adjective following the noun, as in: *Me huele a* toast *quemado.* (Translation—I smell burnt toast.) Additionally, an English predicate adjective is oftentimes used for emphasis: *Es muy* wild, or *Está muy* heavy (Hernandez-Chavez et al). There is an entire group of words which are borrowed from English, but are modified to conform to basic patterns of phonology in Spanish. *Por ejemplo: daime, gasolín* (dime, gasoline). Another group contains English words Hispanized beyond immediate recognition: *garejel, quiande, sanamagón.* (Go to hell, candy, son of a gun) (Galván and Teschner). For the creation of words from English to Spanish, one follows the standard form of masculine and feminine nouns with the appropriate modifiers. Car goes to *carro,* and truck goes to *troca. Carro* ends in o, so is a masculine noun, hence *el carro. Troca* ends in a, is a feminine noun, and becomes *la troca* (Devereux). A noticeable trait of Texas Spanish or Tex-Mex is the frequent incidence of non-standard verb forms. Most verb forms use the Anglo word with the Spanish ending, such as *baquear* or *baquiar*—to back the car or truck (Onofre-Madrid). Certain Spanish words are often contracted in Tex-Mex such as *ahora/hora, pues/pos, muchacito/muchito* (Stavans 564). In Texas, we have many Spanish words in everyday use: *patio, norte, bronco, arroyo, mesa, alamo, burro, plaza, frijoles, taco, enchilada.* In San Angelo, we have a number of streets with Spanish names: *Vista del Arroyo, Alta Loma, Montecito, Alta Vista.* Tex-Mex, language or dialect, is created with the substitution of either the English or Spanish word whichever does not come immediately to mind of the bilingual speaker.

In the interest of improving border communication, I now propose a short outing to a baseball game written in Tex-Mex which any native speaker of either English or Spanish along the Texas border should be able to interpret with minimum effort.

Vámanos a fil a ver el juego de béisbal. Diga a mamá a baquear el carro del driveway and put el baisicle in el garage. Vamos a brincar el charco at the brich. Los niños want a balún y pacón with sus daimes. Los hombres con el batero and el fíler will have el doblepley in un cincho. Hey vato—que pasó? Dame cinco. Quiere un aiscrín? Puso el antifrís in la troca? Ay! Mira a la copequeic, la masota with the cabus! You think she va a Dallas? Hey—you bulchitero. Is her name Luisa Morales? No, ella es de Alíz, Tejas. Pero, 'hora, we got a jit and you got a estraique. Que buen esporte for el esprín. Oh, no—un fáubal. El quecha and el réferi are giving a big blofe. Que huiquén! I'm ready a ir de baybay for lonche and have an escoch jaibol a ca de butlega in Igle Pas. Éjele! Perdieron el juego. Pobrecito. I am ready cuitear, pero we have un detur. I want chuingom and cuqui, so I won't be entosequida. Por favor, bring el Doche pícop and vamos al pardi and hear el cruner. Es la hora a colgar el tenis.

Translation:

Let's go out to the field to see the baseball game. Tell Mama to back the car out of the driveway and put up the bicycle in the garage. We're going to cross the Rio Grande at the bridge. The kids want to buy a balloon and popcorn with their dimes. The batter's team will give the fielder a sure double play. Hey man—What's happening? Give me five! Do you want an ice cream? Did you put anti-freeze in the truck? Ay! Look at that doll—she's a red hot mama with a big caboose. You think she'll give us any? Hey—what a bullsh-ter! Is her name "Loose Morals?" No—she's from Alice. But—Now—we got a hit and you have a strike. What a great sport for spring! Oh, no—a foul ball. The catcher and the referee are trying to bluff each other. What a week-end! I'm ready to go bye-bye and have lunch and a scotch highball at the bootlegger's house in Eagle Pass. Éjele! You all lost the game. Poor guy. I'm ready to quit but we have a detour. I want some chewing gum and a cookie so I won't get drunk. Bring the Dodge pick-up please and we'll go to the party and hear the singer. It's time to call it a day.

The following shall hopefully serve as a dictionary for some Tex-Mex classifications and translations (Galván and Teschner):

Spanish Contractions:

A casa de, a cas de, a ca = to the house of
pues, pos = well
ahora, hora = now
también, tamién = also
papá, apá, pá = papa, father, dad
Ejemplos: Voy a casa de papá. Voy a cas de apá. Voy a ca pá.
    Each of which can be translated as "I am going to dad's house."

Other Hispanized and Anglicized Terms:
aiscrín = ice cream
anda, vete, andavete = Get out of here!

babay, bai = bye-bye (*ir de babay* = to take a walk)

baisicle = bicycle

balún = balloon

batero = batter

beibi, bebe = baby

beibisira = baby sitter

beís = base (baseball)

bet = bat (baseball)

blofe, blaf = bluff

boca grande = big mouth, talker

boi escout = boy scout

briche, brich = bridge

butlega = bootlegger

caboí = cowboy

cabús = caboose, big buttocks

cadilaque = cadillac

calofrío = hot flash

dame cinco = give me five

cincho = cinch, sure thing

copequeic = cupcake

crúner = crooner

cuqui = cookie

chuingom = chewing gum

daime = dime

ir a Dallas (darlas) = to give sexual favors

detur = detour

doblepley = double play

Doche = Dodge

Éjele! = interjection used to poke fun

entosequido/a = intoxicated

escoch = scotch; *escoch teip* = scotch tape

esprín = spring

esporte = sport

estraique = strike

fáubol = foul ball

fil = field

hombrazo = he-man, stud

huiquén = week-end

jaibol = high ball

jit = hit

lonche = lunch

Luis / Luisa Morales = loose morals

masota = red hot mama

nochebuena = poinsettia

pacón = popcorn

pardi, pare = party

pícop = pick up truck

pochismo = English influence

pocho = derogatory term for a person who speaks a mixture
of English and Spanish

quecha = catcher

réferi = referee

shirroc = sheet rock

tenis = tennies; *colgar los tenis* = hang up the tennies, to die

Texas Place Names:

Alíz = Alice, Texas

Biure = Buda, Texas

Brómfil = New Braunfels, Texas

Bronsvil = Brownsville, Texas

Cai = Kyle, Texas

Farucas = Falfurrias, Texas

Huimble = Wimberly, Texas

Igle Pas = Eagle Pass, Texas

Lobica = Lubbock, Texas

Menarde, Menarve = Menard, Texas

El Pachuco = El Paso, Texas
San Felipe del Rio = Del Rio, Texas
Yoche = George West, Texas

Verbs:
baquear, baquiar = to back up
batear = to bat
blichar, blichear = to bleach—hair or clothes
brequear = to brake
brincar el charco = to cross the Rio Grande river
bulchitear = to bull s . . t
cabaretear = to go night clubbing
cachar = to catch, to cash check
desfrozar = to defrost
guachar, huachar = to watch, *Huáchalo!* = watch it!
laquiar = to lock shut
totachar = to use a mix of English and Spanish

Although Tex-Mex or Spanglish dialect is a regional folklore phenomena, with irregular forms from both English and Spanish, it serves as the basis of communication between two elements. Hopefully, even if sometimes viewed as less than desirable, it will lead the way in communicating and linking Mexico and Texas together. Any linkage or reaching out to learn and form one another's language can only benefit both the bilingual and monolingual speaker. Additionally, with the onset of a free trade agreement between Mexico and the United States, communication is the key. As Tex-Mex continues to be transmitted among its speakers, with some variation in structure and meaning, one would hope it would reach a higher purpose in serving to connect the peoples of Mexico and Texas. Tex-Mex is joined through language and culture and continues to grow and enhance both Texas and Mexico.

Bibliography/Sources

Cotton, Eleanor Greet, and John M. Sharp. *Spanish in the Americas*, Washington, D.C.: Georgetown University Press, 1988.

Devereux, Neil. Angelo State University, Department of Modern Languages, San Angelo, Texas. (Native Californian who learned Spanish in Northern Mexico.)

Galván, Roberto A., and Richard V. Teschner. *El diccionario del español Chicano*. Silver Spring, Maryland: Institute of Modern Languages, Inc., 1977.

Hernandez-Chavez, Eduardo, Andres Cohen, and Anthony F. Beltramo, Eds. *El Lenguaje de los Chicanos*. Arlington, Virginia: Center for Applied Linguistics, 1975.

Kelly, George W., and Rex R. Kelly. *Farm and Ranch Spanish*. Vanderpool, Texas: Kelly Brothers, 1960.

Onofre-Madrid, Maria. Angelo State University, Department of Modern Languages, San Angelo, Texas. (Native Mexican who learned English in Western Texas.)

Stavans, Ilan. "The sounds of Spanglish." *Commonweal*. 11 October 1991, Vol. 118, No. 17.

Treviño, Roberto R. "Prensa Y Patria: The Spanish language press and the biculturation of the Tejano middle Class, 1920–1940." *The Western Historical Quarterly*. Nov. 1991, Vol. 22, No. 4.

Ernestine Sewell Linck

Punching Sticks, Flannel Wrapped Bricks, and Pink Powder Purgatives:
Spring Rituals

Upward striving middle class best describes my family. My father owned his own business, and he and my mother knew just how important it was to put up a good front. He anglicized his French surname and built the family a large brick house when most houses were still frame. He and my mother attended whatever cultural events occurred in Texarkana, like an evening with opera diva Galli-Curci. He joined the right civic clubs and the right church, and every Sunday found the family in place in its pew.

After church we went for drives. That's what townspeople did. We had a four-door black Packard with two little jump seats to set up in front of the back seat for guests. There were silver (probably plated) vases attached to the sides by the back doors and or-

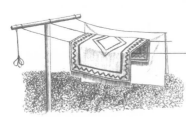

ange artificial flowers stood stiffly in them

My earliest memories of those drives were of stopping by the newsstand for Sunday papers—the *Dallas Morning News*, the *Arkansas Gazette*, the *St. Louis Post-Dispatch*, and the *Denver Post*; of being treated to a package of Life Savers and of being hustled away from the racks of lurid pulps and Westerns back to our places in the car, and we were off to some neighboring small town for a boarding house dinner. I recall particularly a well-known place in Naples.

Back to town, we toured the park, that haunted place where the explorer De Soto was said to have stopped to drink from the refreshing spring and hanged a rebellious soldier. My sister and I wandered around among the pine trees and wondered which tree De Soto had used for his nefarious deed. The pines were so tall! And they had no low limbs! Then we went to Broad Street, cruising (of course, no one called the drive by that name in those days) up and down slowly from one viaduct to the other. The viaducts, one on the Arkansas side of town and the other on the Texas, spanned the railroad yards, for our town was a prosperous railroad center. Daddy always made a quick U-turn at the Texas viaduct. I found out later that vagrants had a shanty town beneath it, and strung along the streets at that end of town were houses where "soiled doves" lived. I remember crossing that viaduct only once in my life. We rarely crossed the Arkansas viaduct either, though it was not really off limits. There were not many brick houses over there. Sometimes if my mother and father saw friends cruising, they would gesture to park in front of one of the big department stores and visit a spell. That's what folks did.

Finally we would go home, after picking up hot tamales from a Mexican who wheeled out his cart just on Sunday for such families as ours. They were good! And we might stop by the ice house for a brick of ice cream that was a third strawberry, a third vanilla, and a third chocolate, so everybody was happy. At home we were given the funny papers to read the Katzenjammer Kids, Barney Google, the Gumps, and Maggie and Jiggs. From the papers we would be told about the mysterious deaths that followed explorers' entry into Tutankhamen's tomb, and the Rosetta Stone, which had been deciphered and placed in the British Museum, whatever election was taking place—particularly at the national level—and the glories of Arizona and its native inhabitants. They were making a special effort to inform us of the world that lay beyond our own sidewalks and paved streets.

The drives took different routes the day I announced at the dinner table that black cows gave black milk. The groceryman had told me so, and he was a respected man, so why the look of astonishment on my parents' faces? From that day on, our Sunday drives became a conscious effort on their parts to enlighten us about life in Texas.

Annually each spring we drove to Index to look with awe at the flood waters of the Mighty Red as they coursed their way downstream. Daddy always timed this drive to coincide with the raising of the drawbridge that spanned the river, a tribute to man's ingenuity. We watched men desperately carrying sand bags to hold the levees. When summer was its hottest, we drove, though not regularly, to Fouke, a frightfully boggy cypress swampland, where cypress knees rose out of Sulphur River, where the forest was so thick the sun could not break through. Few folks lived around here, for it was rumored that monstrous creatures lived in these woods, perhaps mutants from the Big Raft that had made Red River unnavigable years and years ago. We were not told of such things, but we could sense the anxiety of our parents should we wander too far looking for wild flowers. And I distinctly remember my mother faintly uttering the word "bootleggers" to my father. It was a new word to me. But we would learn about bootleggers before many more excursions there. One Sunday, as we were unloading our picnic supplies and spreading the blankets for a pleasant afternoon, some "revenooers" rushed up and told us to leave at once. There was gunfire in the woods and we were in the line of fire.

In the fall we drove to Mandeville on the Red in a northerly direction through plantations where black folks still picked cotton by hand.

Yes, we learned a lot about how other folk lived. Many a time we passed a yard where "nary" a blade of grass raised its head. No bushes, no trees, no flowers. "Mama," I asked, "why is that woman sweeping her yard?" A woman was thrashing her broom about, raising clouds of dust from the hard-packed earth. "She is a God-fearing woman," she answered. "Cleanliness is next to Godliness. She sweeps the yard, just as we sweep our porch. I'm sure her house is clean inside too." Then she added, "Besides, with the yard so clean, she can see snakes and keep them away from her house."

How many times would we hear, "Cleanliness is next to Godliness." I wondered about the swept yards when we went for butter—that was another trip to the rural scene, designed for our education. A little old Welsh lady made butter for us in one-pound bricks with a fancy flower design on it, and we were shown something of the farm. We watched the hired man milk the cows. My quesion about milking the onery-looking black brute penned alone beyond the barn went unanswered. Why didn't they milk it? I wanted to see black milk coming from a black cow! Truly I was a naive child. I was practically grown before I learned about bulls and that "bull" is a perfectly legitimate word.

The Welsh family had given a home to an orphan girl about my age. One of her duties was to sweep the back yard. She laughed when I told her about godliness.

"Do you really want to know why I have to sweep the yard? Well, there ain't nothin' worse than chicken do between your toes. See all them chickens? I have to sweep up behind them because chicken do is squishy, slippery."

That seemed a natural and good reason, as I looked around, though I didn't doubt the virtue of the girl for sweeping up for God's favor.

Another time we stopped by a small house for my mother to deliver some boxes of clothes and toys. Although it was Sunday, the laundry had been laid across fences and hedges and even laid on the ground for drying.

"Mama," I asked, "why do they hang their clothes on the bushes like that?" It looked tacky to me. My mother's answer was, as usual, "Cleanliness is next to Godliness. Clothes dry in the sun that way and bleach out white and fluffy. These people may be too poor to send their clothes to the laundry, but they do have their pride and they will wear clean clothes." I'm sure I heard her mutter to our father, "That good-for-nothing man sitting on the porch chewing tobacco could at least put up some lines for her."

It wasn't rare to see a sewing machine on the front porch.

"Why?"

"The woman is virtuous. She can enjoy being outside and continue to work. And should a neighbor happen to pass by, she can visit a while and not miss a stitch."

That answer was far from satisfactory to me. I thought furniture belonged inside the house, except, of course, for porch swings and the like. Often we would see bed springs leaning against trees and mattresses on saw horses.

"Why?"

"Cleanliness is next to Godliness. Sometimes when company comes, particularly a traveling man, he may leave little black bugs in the bed and those bugs multiply. The woman takes the springs out, douses them with kerosene and sets them afire. That's the only way to get rid of the bugs."

I shuddered, while considering the excitement of seeing those springs blazing.

"Have we ever had bugs? Have you ever burned the springs?"

"Indeed not," she answered indignantly. And nothing more was said.

There was a rich woman in our neighborhood whom the other women sneered at. I heard our next door neighbor say one time, "She may be rich enough to have her poodle's toes manicured at Neiman-Narcus these days, but I remember when she lived on a dirt road and washed her clothes in a washpot, screaming at her kids if her sacred punching stick was lost." I think I saw my mother's lips form the words, "A woman does what she has to do."

Folklore has it that the Northern women are excellent house-keepers and that Southern women are not so excellent, border-ing on the slovenly. That idea is totally wrong and comes from misunderstanding. The roots of such careless talk lies in their plan of attack.

The Northerner never lets her house get dirty all at one time. Every week she cleans one room thoroughly, digging into cor-ners, etc. The Southerner, on the other hand is "laid back," as the saying goes, being brought up to believe that what folks see when they come to visit (and they visit a lot; they come early and stay late, expecting meals of course) is what matters most. I know many a Southern woman who rises early and dresses for the day—she is ready to receive her guests. And they will come. She keeps things neat and clean enough, but springtime is the time for the hard cleaning. The Southern woman is closer to the earth; the rhythms of her life are in harmony with the seasons. Some-one has said poetically that the pulse of the Southern woman responds more readily to the drumming of the earth's heart. So much of the South remained virgin for so long a time that the folk remained tied to the land and dependent upon that land. When the earth threw off the ravages of winter and refreshed itself, the people likewise felt the need for renewing the spirit. For the women, this meant the ordeal of spring cleaning.

My Southern mother was a fashionable woman. Her legs, clad in Realsilk hose, seams straight as arrows, would have made a Dallas cheerleader envious. Her hands were delicate, nails always buffed and polished, hair marcelled softly, with no gray wisps, and she smelled of fine perfume. But there came a day in early spring annually when we were rudely awakened, hustled off to school after oatmeal and given cold lunches to take along.

When we arrived home that afternoon, the house was turned out of doors literally, and my mother had turned into a witch. She wore an apron over a faded shapeless wrapper, run-over felt slippers, hair in aluminum curlers, an old scarf tied around head—and a scowl on her face that warned us of a disposition gone awry. Now that I think of it, it was as if she had bared herself before her god and shed all semblance of graciousness, loveliness and warmth. Certainly she was no longer keeping up that good front. What was left was a woman going about her work frenetically, I should say maniacally.

We were given apples and graham crackers and ordered to stay outside—out of her way. Did she worry that we might be cold on an early spring day? No, she was obsessed totally with her chores. The "cullud" woman who did day work for her was given a paid vacation, and the yard man, George, was brought into the house to help with the really hard tasks like moving the furniture. Day by day and room by room, she and George moved pieces of furniture out on the front porch, even the sewing machine. Mattresses were laid on saw horses in our back yard and turned and turned as the sun moved. Bed springs (we didn't have box springs in those days) were leaned against trees, not to be burned off, but washed down thoroughly. After a good shaking, rugs were laid across the hedges. Boxes of books, stacks of pictures, more boxes of kitchen items, pots and pans, bathroom necessaries, silver, dishes, everything was put temporarily into boxes until all shelves and storage receptacles were cleaned, freshly painted or repapered.

Our clothing was hung on a line out back and folded over the bannisters of the front porch—actually a large veranda. As we lived on a corner, all passersby were alerted that spring house-cleaning was in progress. It was embarrassing to be so exposed.

One neighbor who dared to break the routine to talk across the back fence laughingly said to my mother, "Nell, I won't be surprised to see you go up a ladder to sweep the roof. Have you cleaned your telephone with lysol? Germs might travel through the wires, you know." My mother made no response, just scowled at her and further attempts at conversation lapsed.

Our neighbor across the street came from Dallas and affected citified ways. No Southern earth mother, she. While her hired man and live-in maid put the Persian rugs on the line and beat them with giant rattan swatters, our man George was on his hands and knees scrubbing our hardwood floors, which he afterward waxed and polished with flannel-wrapped bricks to a high mirror-like gloss. To put a footprint on that polished surface was to suffer disgrace. Every morning, to reach the piano for my daily practice, I leaped from scatter rug to scatter rug, knowing full well that I would miss a rug and that God had destined me, the clumsy one, to bring that dreaded look of disgust, disdain, and impatience to my mother's face.

And so it was, while the neighbor's maid took down the brocade drapes for professional cleaning and packing away for the summer, my mother washed, starched, and ironed our ruffled organdy curtains and panels, a chore that took hours. Windows—

we had over-sized French windows—were washed with vinegar water and made to shine with old newspapers. The screens were washed with kerosene—but not burned!

To keep us busy, we were required to stand by as "gofers" and to watch for the ice man to get a new card with its markings 5, 12-1/2, 25, and 50 pounds that would inform him of our order for the day. The old card would bear the grimy marks of many fingers during a year's use.

One day we arrived home from school to find her perspiring—no, sweating—over a big boiler on the stove. She had a punching stick! She was boiling all the linen that the laundry had not bleached white enough to suit her. And, ignominy of ignominies, she carefully spread tea towels and pillow cases and such on the grass so they could benefit from bleaching in the sunshine!

It took two to three weeks, each day set aside for a special chore while the neighbor, evidently satisfied that her spring cleaning was completed once the maid had polished the silver and put it away, would sit at the piano, windows open, shrilly vocalizing the scales. My mother, usually a forbearing woman, was convinced that the neighbor practiced just to remind her that she was emancipated from the slave work. I have known my mother to throw down her broom, sit at the piano and sing at the top of her lungs (she was a trained vocalist) "The Sheik of Araby" (who can remember Rudolph Valentino?), "Louise" (Maurice Chevalier?), "It happened in Monterrey," or "The Lady in Red" to drown out the do-re-mi-fa-so-la-ti-do from across the way.

I realize now that, to her, the ritual was a duty thrust upon woman by an angry god that did not make women equal to men and the ordeal grew out of pent-up frustrations. It was as if she stored up for a year all the loathing she was capable of and expended the poison of it masochistically upon the house that imprisoned her. We stayed outside, playing jacks, jumping rope, making mud houses, or something equally time consuming, guessing how she might reposition the furniture for the year to come. Nothing ever went back where it had been. During the years she went through every floor plan a decorator could have dreamed up.

At length the day came when she appeared satisfied that she had placated her god, that she could hopefully look forward to a new beginning, a new year when she might possibly resume her musical studies or embark upon some program for self-development. Had she not effaced herself sufficiently that her god might smile down on her? Had she not sacrificed herself on the altar of domesticity?

George was back at work in the yard now, preparing for spring planting. She would dress to go downtown with big-brimmed hat, fashionable store-bought dress with lots of color (no black silk faded to a dingy purple for her), spike-heeled shoes, her nails polished, and smelling of rose water, if not one of her perfumes. She marched us to her car, a Nash, and drove to the corner drug store where we were treated to old-fashioned sodas. We sat at the high stools, going round and round, enjoying our chocolate or strawberry concoctions while our mother talked (I think she smiled sadistically) to the pharmacist (I know *he* smiled sadistically) as he compounded pink liver powders. For my mother believed that Cleanliness was next to Godliness for her children, believe me, and spring cleaning meant that the children were cleaned out too. After our treat at the fountain, we were marched back to the car; she drove home, lined us up at the kitchen table where we opened our mouths obediently and swallowed the nasty pink purgative powders which were supposed to dissolve in milk but never did. She would say, "This is not so bad; what if you had to swallow sulphur and molasses?" We never found an answer to that question, thank goodness.

Now at last the complete metamorphosis took place. My mother was like one reborn. She became herself—sweet, kind, affectionate, solicitous. In our weakened condition—the cleaning-out took several days—she could not do enough to please us and assure us of our virtue. I wonder if she thanked ancient wrathful gods and goddesses of the hearth that her children grew up strong and healthy when the daughter of the singing neighbor across the street died of worms?

Rituals seem to disappear but they die a hard death. Even the activity of cleaning out the closet to take to the Salvation Army those things to share with less fortunate folks is a gesture left over from the ritual. It was, for my mother, a religious act, her Easter-time renewal.

J. G. Pinkerton

When Harvey Sadler's Tent Show Came to Town

Harley Sadler ruled supreme in repertoire theatre, or "repper-tore" as it was called, in Texas
and Eastern New Mexico in the 1920s and 30s.
Early last year, I began remembering what fun it
was when Harley's tent show would come to my
hometown of Junction, Texas. This set me off on
a year of research.

I put out a call for memories of "Harley Sadler's
Tent Show" in *The Junction Eagle*, my hometown
newspaper. And, I am still getting responses. The
Museum of Repertoire Americana in Mt. Pleas-
ant, Iowa, sold me a book entitled *Trouping
Through Texas: Harley Sadler and his
Tent Show*, written by Clifford
Ashby and Susanne DePauw May
and published in 1982 by the
Bowling Green University Popu-
lar Press. And much of the follow-

ing material is taken directly from Ashby and May's book.

Ashby and May's book led me to the Southwest Collection at Texas Tech University in Lubbock. There I poured over the articles, news clippings, records, letters, and show scripts that these two authors had collected. Most fun of all was listening to hours of audiotapes that Ashby and May recorded during their interviews of people who knew and loved Harley Sadler. From all these sources, I began to reconstruct how it was when Harley Sadler's Tent Show came to town.

It would all begin a few days in advance of the show, when Harley Sadler's brother, Ferd Sadler, arrived. After settling into a hotel or rooming house, Ferd would howdy and shake hands from one business establishment to another along Main Street, leaving poster cards in each storefront. To make sure merchants welcomed putting a Harley Sadler poster card in their store window, Ferd was always free with the complimentary tickets Harley insisted be handed out.

If there was going to be opposition from the local moving picture man, Ferd Sadler would usually pick up such rumors as he made his rounds. "All a tent show does is take money out of our town," was the common accusation. But, Harley Sadler was too popular for a movie manager to risk direct confrontation with the showman. Besides, he knew that when Sadler's troupe hit town, they would shop in every store, support local events, and even attend church. Harley insisted on it.

One of Ferd's stops as he proceeded through town was the newspaper office where he placed large ads for the following week. He would then call on the president of whatever organization was to sponsor the show's appearance.

Organizations like the American Legion, Shriners, VFW, Lions, or the volunteer fire department, were overjoyed to provide the three "L's" (lot, license, and 'lectricity) for Harley Sadler in exchange for ten percent of the gross ticket sales of the show.

Expensive though the ten percent might be, this system had the virtue of allying Sadler with a reputable local organization.

Along his route through town, the youngest Sadler would pick up several requests for free entertainment. There was usually a noontime Rotary program (Harley was a member with a long record of perfect attendance), a church social, a fund-raiser for the hospital or for new band uniforms, a civic celebration of one sort or another. Ferd accepted all invitations to perform, assuring whoever asked that Harley would have some of his troupe there, and would try to appear himself.

Immediately, people began preparations for play-going. Aside from what to wear, especially for young adults in the courting years, money had to be found for tickets, popcorn, shaved ice, and prize candy. The luckiest people were those with passes for the entire week. All local dignitaries—mayor, town council, police chief, ministers, school superintendents together with their families—were automatically "complimented" when Sadler was in town.

A Sadler show was not to be missed. The twenty-five cents for adults and fifteen cents for children simply had to be found. For weeks afterward, conversations would begin with something like, "Hey, you remember when that quartet sang, with old Harley not knowin' what the words were?" Anyone who didn't remember found himself left out of a lot of conversations.

Once, when Ferd was in a furniture store, he remarked that the town looked a little quiet. "Don't you worry none," the store owner snorted in reply. "Folks around here would sell their furniture to see Harley's show."

The reason Ferd was in the furniture store was to see about borrowing properties for the show. Harley traveled with just the essentials, knowing that he would have his choice of furnishings from several of the town's living rooms and many of the stores. A few passes and a mention of the lender's name during his curtain speech was all that was needed.

On put-up days, a great mass of equipment—bundles of canvas, poles, coiled ropes, stakes, marquee, lights, wardrobe, bleachers, chairs, scenery, ticket booth, stage platforming, and curtains—had to be brought to the show site, unloaded from the trucks, and moved and set in place, all for the opening performance that night.

The first stroll of the actors and actresses through a town was an important social event, one greatly anticipated by the local citizens. Knowing they were "on show," performers chose their most attention-getting outfits for their initial appearance. Harley insisted that his troupe appear neat and clean at all times. The successful ones spent a great deal of time and money on their wardrobes.

For the ladies of the town, the daytime attire of the performers provided as much grist for the conversation mills as the evening's entertainment at the tent. For the local ladies, who sewed their own dresses from cotton prints found on flour sacks, Billie Sadler walking down Main Street was as much of a fashion show as they were ever to witness. What Billie wore influenced the patterns and fabrics ordered from the latest catalog or purchased locally.

Harley collected a crowd wherever he went. After a quick round of handshakes with whoever was on hand for his initial appearance, he would hurry to the show lot to check the positioning of the tent. Harley always believed that proper placement of the marquee and front door greatly influenced attendance. Only Harley could make this decision. No one else could do it.

By the time Harley finished with this self-imposed chore, the area around the show lot would be ringed with small boys desperately hoping for a "Hey you, boy, grab some of them chairs and carry 'em inside." Work meant a pass for the week and the reflected glory of telling Dad at supper that "I helped Harley put up the tent this morning."

While the actors got reacquainted with old friends around the town, the canvas crews were hard at work, intent on raising their stately pleasure dome in time to get a hot supper before the evening performance. The stage had to be erected, bleachers assembled, and dressing rooms set up. The canvas was spread out and sections laced together. Gangs of three or four men rhythmically swung heavy sledge hammers and drove wooden stakes into the soil. Other crews raised the centerpoles and guyed them out. At a signal, everyone turned-to and joined in hoisting the bale-rings to the tops of the poles. During these moments, tension could be felt in the air. Instructions would be shouted back and forth. But no swearing! Harley didn't want any of the small fry learning any new words to carry home. Everywhere Harley went as he strolled through town, he managed to convey the impression that this particular town was one of his very special favorites.

Late on the afternoon of opening show, the members of Harley's all-male parade band would change into their marching uniforms for the concert in the town square. Sadler had long since given up playing the trombone that had first got him a job in tent shows. Instead, he carried an enormous bass drum. This allowed him to call out greetings to the spectators along the line of march. Only, his eager greetings did little for the tempo of the band, which found itself constantly out of step and off beat.

"Harley," said a cornet player one day, "You've got to hire another man for the band, either someone to wave at the people or someone to beat that derned drum. Because you cain't do both!"

Harley Sadler followed the tent show tradition and presented a "ballyhoo," usually in the middle of a busy downtown street intersection, as part of the opening day parade. Harley would unstrap his bass drum and step to the front of his band. From the Repertoire Page of *Billboard* we have the following description of his "ballyhoo":

[Sadler] is a likeable fellow. He has a real man's voice which he uses in a pleasing manner. He talks in a conversational tone, never in the raucous, ponderous style assumed by most spielers. Neither does he assume the patronizing tone nor the broad smile of undue familiarity. He tells them about his show in a quiet, modest, unassuming manner, but with evident sincerity. Then he steps behind his bass drum, they play another tune and the crowd is his from then on.

The band would form again into marching order and parade back to the tent, all the while doing its best to keep step with their ever-erratic drummer. Little boys liked to fall in behind the band and walk with giant steps to match the stride of the band. Hundreds of spectators trailed behind, eager to buy their ticket from Harley's wife, Billie, who ran the box office, and then hurry inside for a good seat. Above the tent show entry, and framed on both sides with fluttering pennants, a large banner proclaimed THE HARLEY SADLER SHOW. Out front of the tent, sandwich boards displayed pictures of the performers. Inside the small lobby there was a popcorn machine and other concessions.

The cheaper, general admission areas were located just inside the main tent. These bleachers were called "blues" because of the circus tradition of painting these seats that color. Locally, however, they were called the "buzzard's roost." Toward the stage, a low wooden fence separated the reserved seats from the rest.

Another ticket-catcher was stationed at an opening in the wooden divider, to collect an additional charge from those who wanted a closer view and a somewhat more comfortable seat. These slip-covered, unpadded chairs were reserved in name only, seating being on a first-come basis. During his heyday, Sadler's tent would seat a total of two thousand people.

Harley's red and blue trim helped lend a festive air to the otherwise dull khaki-colored canvas. The atmosphere was relaxed, neighborly, and welcoming. On warm evenings, men were in shirt sleeves, women in cotton dresses, and they came with babies, grand parents, and the inevitable stray dog. Everyone laughed, talked, sipped soft drinks, munched popcorn, and nibbled snow cones. It was a fun place to be.

The stage floor was raised five feet above the ground. A six-foot no-man's-land separated the stage from the first row. Sometimes this space was used for the orchestra on a large musical production, but more often it was filled with small boys who had managed to slip away from their parents and "sit up front on the ground."

The stage opening was thirty feet in width and was covered by a bluish plush curtain which drew up in a series of folds. Sequins spelled out HARLEY SADLER in a flowing script across the width of the curtain and framed at the sides by glittering masks of comedy and tragedy. Harley always insisted that the front curtain have a heavy pipe in the bottom hem; he knew that applause would be triggered by the loud "thunk" as the pipe hit the floor. The pipe also kept the curtain from billowing when the Texas winds blew. There was no limit to the number of local advertising banners that might appear above and around the stage. Each banner represented additional income for the show's owners and the team that had the banner concession.

Usually, a favored couple on the show handled this advertising concession. The pretty wife would turn on her most dazzling

Harley Sadler as Toby the cowboy, taken in Shawnee, Oklahoma, in 1917 or 1918. *Courtesy Southwest Collection, Texas Tech University, Lubbock*

Harley Herman Sadler (1892–1954), king of the west Texas tent showmen, on stage from 1908 to 1947; wildcatter during the 1940s; from 1942 was in Texas House of Representatives or the State Senate; died from on-stage heart attack. *Courtesy Southwest Collection, Texas Tech University, Lubbock*

smile as she visited the shops of the local merchants and "sold" the advertisements. Back at the tent, the busy husband frantically lettered the butcher-paper signs so the signs would be up and ready on opening night.

The orchestra platform was at the left side of the proscenium arch. It was usually a foot below the level of the stage and large enough to accommodate twelve to fifteen musicians. A sign that read "IF THE BABY CRIES, PLEASE TAKE IT TO THE REAR OF THE TENT" hung over the piano.

Curtain time varied with the setting of the sun, but usually it was no later than 7:45 or 8:00 P.M., since farm families needed to greet the sun's reappearance on the following morning. Ten minutes before show time, the orchestra members dressed in tuxedos and evening gowns and took their places on the left platform. Again, as reported in a 1921 *Billboard*:

(Harley's) orchestra is somewhat better than average— considerably better than some. They do not play a half hour before the show starts, wearing out their welcome and the patience of the audience as well. They go in just ten minutes before the curtain rises and play an overture, just like a theatre orchestra. No long ballyhoo for the candy sale, with the audience growing impatient every time the orchestra renders another tune. When [Harley Sadler's] orchestra comes in it means overture and then the show.

House lights consisted of bare bulbs mounted on iron buggy tires. They dimmed as the orchestra "played the curtain up." The stage was illuminated mainly with footlights and overhead borders, but follow spots were provided for some of the vaudeville acts. The *Billboard* report continues:

Although (Harley Sadler) uses some of the same plays used by other shows they seem different and more satisfying, because they are put on with pep, with attention to details and no stage waits; no loud talking in the dressing rooms, and no stalling by the orchestra. His actors and actresses are not wonders. They are not better than those with other rep shows, but it is the way they work; natural, smoothly—as though they enjoyed it, which indeed they do.

These "rag opries," as they were called, always preferred scripts that could be adapted to local situations. Actors spoke in the dialect of their audience, not in the London East End accent which Broadway actors regarded as the only proper speech for the stage in those days. The unsophisticated audiences of Texas and eastern New Mexico didn't want sophistication. They wanted characters and situations with which they could easily identify. A moral dilemma could be presented only if the neat solution by the final curtain was reached through the generous application of such homely virtues as charity, chastity, forgiveness, conformity, and (above all) Christian love.

The company's repertoire contained a variety of plays. Many of the dramas had contemporary settings concerned with the redemption of a man by the love of a good woman after he had been led astray by a bad one. Comedy was the staple ingredient of all the plays. Even *Ten Nights in a Barroom*, a serious temperance drama, contained some low-comedy drunk scenes and an improbable courtship between Sample Switchel and the town's resident old maid.

"Comedy is my forte," Harley once told a reporter, "but I have always wanted to have a part in a play with dramatic moments." Harley knew a barrel full of laughs seasoned with a sprinkling of tears kept audiences crowding into his tent. This self-taught actor, one who had never had a lesson in his life, played a variety of roles; crooks, politicians, policemen, top-hat sophisticates, and the misunderstood miscreant of *Saintly Hypocrites and Honest Sinners.*

However, Toby, the comedy heart of the tent show, was his best-remembered role. Though these clownish, silly-kid roles had a certain sameness to them, they did have some variations, ranging from Sputters, the stuttering cowboy who could only talk fluently when outlining an imaginary square with his finger, to the hick farm boy in *Toby from Arkansas.*

Mary Roberts, a Sweetwater chum of Sadler's daughter, remembered, "His Toby character was always lovable and funny in his oversized shoes and red wig and overalls with one strap broken. Toby made you laugh at the start of the play but toward the end, when he lost the beautiful girl to the handsome leading man, only a very cold heart would have left the theatre dry-eyed."

Again from an account in *Billboard*:

At night, they come to the show to see what this boy with a man's voice can do on stage. And they see plenty. He comes on a rube kid with freckles, large blue eyes, and eyebrows high up on his forehead. No exaggerated, silly grin, no extremely foolish mannerisms, just a natural country boy with the unsophisticated look of wonderment on his face. A rare, high class comedian is Harley Sadler. Nothing obnoxious, nothing overdone.

In his performance, Sadler tended to avoid stagey, actorish flourishes which might call attention to technique. The rest of the company tended to conform to their star's unassuming naturalness. Within the limits of scripts that were not noted for subtlety or characterization, the actors played sincerely and honestly.

Bob Siler, a multi-talented actor-musician who was with the show for many years, recalls that in *Seventh Heaven*, a drama about a blind girl, "I'd get to crying so hard I couldn't get my lines out."

Three- or four-act plays were presented with vaudeville at each intermission. These vaudeville turns were as important in pleasing the audience as the plays themselves.

Louise Hefner Sorensen particularly remembers a specialty dance team. A woman in a black evening gown and a man in white tie and tails danced slowly and dreamily to "Three o'clock in the Morning," with only their faces illuminated by tight follow spots operated from the back of the reserved section. "To me," she remembers, "it was very sophisticated."

The editor from Albany's *Texas Weekly Astonisher* agreed. "The vaudeville stunts between the acts were worth the price of the show, each act brought the house down, and think of it—not a single vulgar stunt was pulled."

Usually, after the first act, Harley made the bally candy pitch common to all tent shows. Still wearing his show costume, the owner-manager would step around the curtain with a vendor's tray slung around his neck. He frankly admitted, as did most candy pitchmen, that the few pieces of saltwater taffy contained in the boxes of his tray were not particularly valuable or even very edible. However, some of the boxes contained a numbered coupon which would win a prize.

Then, Harley motioned for the curtain to rise and the stage would be covered with prizes which ranged from small, but genuine, diamond rings to rocking chairs, cake dishes, canning kettles, sparkling glassware, and radios. Such items would have been purchased from local merchants as a means of gaining their good will. Harley's candy "pitch" might run something like:

A couple of years ago during our candy sale, a young lady came to the stage with a coupon calling for a man's shaving kit. About the same time a young man came with one calling for a pair of lady's hose. I suggested they trade coupons. They did and became friends. A year later when we were again playing their town and having our candy sale, they came to the stage carrying a beautiful little baby. I tell you folks, you never can tell what you might get out of a box of candy!

Then, while the band played galloping music, people rushed forward and bought five, ten, or even more boxes at a time. There would be shouts and squeals when someone extracted a coupon from a lucky box and ran up on the stage. There, a smiling Billie Sadler handed the lucky person his or her prize.

For West Texans, the "bally candy" (from ballyhoo) sale was as exciting as a good horse race. For Sadler, this bit of gambling (forbidden by law, but not enforced in his case) helped build the excitement of the evening, and provided him with a very valuable supplement to his income. As with everything else, the candy pitch was handled quickly; nothing could be allowed to interfere with the fast pace of the evening's presentation.

Before the last act of the play, usually after a short vaudeville number, Harley would step in front of the curtain for his talk to the audience. If he happened to be playing a Toby that night, he would remove the tousled red wig, emphasizing that he spoke as himself, not as a stage character.

As a necessary part of business, Harley would plug the show for the following evening, telling something of the plot, the actors who would have featured roles and what vaudeville would be presented. Other local events were also publicized, even when they represented competition. He even had a kind word for his bitterest rival, the motion picture show manager. "This man's doing the best he can to bring you good, wholesome entertainment," Harley would say, "and you need to patronize him."

Often he would preach a short sermon, a homily about loving, or forgiving, or helping. By his conclusion, his audience would nod in agreement as he made his points. Then, he would walk to the left side of the curtain, turn, smile shyly, and say the same lines every night: "And so, at the end of the last act, I bid each and every one of you a fond good night."

Members of the orchestra stole silently into place as the final act of the play was winding down to a satisfactory conclusion, so that they were ready to play the "chaser" after the curtain calls were completed. "Good Night, Sweetheart" was one of Harley's favorite concluding tunes. But if this was the first of two shows that night (as so often happened on Friday and Saturday) a quick march was used to hurry the departing spectators from the first show. The entire show, from overture through play, vaudeville, candy pitch, and curtain speech, was completed in a little over two hours.

If the show was the final one for the town, tear-down began while the final concert was in progress. At the front of the tent, the marquee and ticket office were removed; then bleachers were silently taken apart behind the rapt audience. Finally, vacant chairs would be folded and taken to waiting trucks and wagons. Scenery and costumes were packed away as each act finished. The audience never seemed to mind that the show was vanishing around them. By the end of the closing concert, a considerable portion of the show was ready to move.

If the show wasn't moving on the next day, the boss canvasman or some of his workers stayed with the tent all night, partly in case of a sudden wind or downpour, and partly to see that the town boys didn't get up to any mischief.

If Sadler did not perch at the absolute pinnacle of the several thousand shows touring under canvas across the country, he certainly had as legitimate a claim to the honor as any other. According to Rolland Haverstock, who grew up on his family's show while it toured North Texas and Oklahoma, "Harley was what we called the cream of the crop. He was class. The rest of us . . . well, you couldn't tell our shows apart."

In 1929, a *Billboard* reporter, visiting the show, wrote: "In towns, large or small, no ill is spoken of Harley Sadler or his company. Everybody boosts him . . . Harley Sadler knows more people by their first name and is called by his first name by more people than any Governor the State of Texas ever had, in this high, wide, windy West Texas area."

When Harley Sadler's curtain—with the heavy pipe in the bottom hem—had "thunked" down on the final show, the tent show packed up and pulled out. The lot was left clean. The people were left with memories and momentos and things to talk about until Harley Sadler's Tent Show came to town again.

James Ward Lee

Eating Over the Sink and Other Marital Strategies

Men, if you want to drive a woman as crazy as a bessy bug, here are some things to do. First, every time you get half a chance, eat something over the sink. Cut a big old slice of pie and hold it in your hand and lean way over the sink and eat it. The little woman—and for godsakes don't call her that—is almost sure to say to you—sweetly— "Bubba, why don't you get a plate and a fork and sit down and eat that pie like a human being." O. K., at this point you reply—with your mouth full, of course—"Naw, hon, this is how I like to eat pie." Don't snap at her (that's just going to give her leverage); just be offhand. Then turn back and keep on eating your pie.

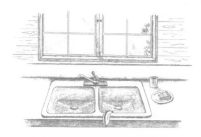

If you do what I tell you, you may never again find pie in the refrigerator or anywhere else. But what the hey? This is about turf—

and mental health and maybe weight loss. Anyway, if the pie supply is cut off, do not give up! Go to plan B. Make a sandwich and eat it over the sink. Time out for a digression: Never make a whole sandwich. Make a fold-over. Even if you know in advance that you want a whole sandwich, make a fold-over. This is important, so pay attention. This is the weight-loss part. Fold-overs contain almost no calories. You can eat four fold-overs and not get any more calories than you would from a Texas Ruby Red grapefruit. Even the *New England Journal of Medicine* admits that. Now, don't get me started on the damned *New England Journal of Medicine*, which is out to confuse and take away what little pleasure I have left in life. I can't open the paper that the *NEJM* hasn't decided that I am digging my grave with my teeth or breathing in noxious fumes or drinking polluted water. What do they want me to do, give up the hamburgers and fries? That'll be the day! They got me this far and I-God they'll take me the rest of the way. And as far as my lungs go, am I supposed to move off to East Jesus for my lungs' sake? Now don't get me started about the lovely village of East Jesus—I drive through it every time I go to Arkansas. And anyway if I moved to East Jesus, the *New England Journal of Medicine* would decide that the best air is somewhere else—probably in Lubbock, which is only a few miles from West Jesus. This digression is not over, so keep on reading.

Where was I? Oh, yeah: the damned Yankee *New England Journal of Medicine*. Well, here's the latest bulletin about that: there *is* no *New England Journal of Medicine*. It is a propaganda hoax started by the broccoli growers. Let me ask you this. Have you ever seen a copy of the *NEJM*? No, I thought not. I rest my case. Just don't get me started on that.

Where was I? Oh, yeah, it was about calories derived from eating over the sink. When you are standing up eating—over the sink or not—calories don't count. You can eat a greasy cheeseburger and large fries and drink a shake for about 200 calories if you do it standing up. Speaking of good things to eat while standing up: here is the best kind of sandwich in the world—next, of course, to a grease-dripping hamburger the size of a DeSoto hubcap—Slice a banana on the bias; lather the bread with mayonnaise; then smear a hefty coating of peanut butter on top of the mayo; then put on the banana. Now you are ready for the *piece de resistance*—or I guess I should say *"pieces" de resistance*. Crumble up a handful of potato chips and pile them on the bread before you fold it. Well, of course you pretty much *have* to eat this over the sink because those chips—even when partly soggy—are going to go everywhere. If you are challenged by your blushing bride when eating a peanut butter/mayo/potato chip/banana sandwich over the old kitchen sink, make out that you are doing this to save her work. So chips won't get all over the floor. There are not many comebacks she can make to that. And if she challenges the PB/M/PC/B sandwich on the basis of health, you can always say, "It worked for Elvis, didn't it?"

Now, about four of these fold-overs need to be washed down with several slugs of milk. Wait! I know the real men in the audience are ahead of me here, but be patient. Don't ever pour milk in a glass. Milk is high in calories and hefty in fat—but only if you pour it in a glass. If you drink it straight out of the carton, you get the same effect as you do when you eat standing up. A pint of milk has no more calories than a kumquat. Now, if the little woman—which, as I said earlier, you *do not* want to call her to her face, at least not with your mouth full of peanut butter, bananas, potato chips, and mayo—but if the little woman catches you drinking from the carton, be contrite. Promise never to do it again. But just as she walks out of the kitchen, take one last furtive gulp. Now trust me on this: she is almost certain to turn back and catch you. Now, you've got her. Really be contrite when she tells you that all those potato chips are falling back into the milk. Say, "Oh, heavens, Hon, I never thought about that. But I was being careful. Then wipe your hand across your mouth—or mustache or beard or whatever you've got on your face as your first line of defense—wipe your hand so that whatever you have on your face will fall into the sink. Then you can say, "See? See how eating over the sink helps you with your housework?"

You people may think I don't know what I am talking about. Well, I do. I am a married man. And not for the first time either. And apparently not for the last if I read the signs right. So I have learned the tricks. And I am hardly started with them, so shut up and pay attention.

Rule two. Never use an implement when you can use your hands. You know about fried chicken, so I won't bore you with how to eat that finger-licking delicacy. But let's take the noble pork chop. It's stupid to take a knife and fork to a pork chop. Pick it up by the handle that God put there for the sole purpose of giving you a way to hold the pesky little devil. Then eat inward toward the bone. This is the only sensible way to eat a chop of any kind, even a mutton chop if you can stomach eating one of Mary's Little Lambs—or venison chops if you favor eating poor Bambi's kinfolks. I hasten to say that I cannot. Of course you should start eating a T-bone steak with knife and fork—that's only polite—but when you get close to the end, you just have to pick that sucker up by the handle to get that sweet meat down next to the bone. And don't just do that at home; do it at the Cattleman's; do it at the Steak and Ale; do it at the Mansion on Turtle Creek if you can afford such luxury. And certainly do it at Joe Allen's Barbecue in Abilene. (Of course, at Joe Allen's everybody there will be doing the same thing, so it won't be noticed.) As Mrs. Patrick Campbell once said about something else, "I don't care where you do it as long as you don't do it in the street and scare the horses."

Want to drive a woman wild? Go in the kitchen where she is cooking and start lifting the pot lids off the pots and staring down in them—maybe pick up a spoon and stir whatever she is cooking. Now hold the pot lid away from your body and back behind you. All the condensation in the lid will drip on the floor and make a wet, greasy spot. My friend Delsie Moore of Mena, Arkansas, claims that her husband Lloyd ruined her new indoor-outdoor carpet in less than six months by holding dripping pot lids out at arm's length. It didn't break up their marriage. Well of course it didn't! And here's why: Delsie and Lloyd got married in 1936 in the front seat of a Model-A Ford Tudor sedan in front of the Polk County Courthouse. She never mentioned what happened in the back seat. And God knows I wouldn't want *her* to get started on that. Besides, I am not sure they did that sort of thing in 1936.

Now here is another thing to copy down and remember. Don't ever eat a casserole. That just encourages a woman. Even if you love casseroles—or "castle rolls" as an old lady of my acquaintance calls them—even if you love casseroles, refuse to eat a bite of one. If you try to be polite to your new princess and take some bites of a tuna fish casserole, you are on the road to culinary slavery. You are going to live a life of rice and broccoli casseroles and tamale pies. And remember what former major league pitcher Gaylord Perry said when, early in his married life, his wife served him a casserole. Gaylord—who was a mean man in other ways—took a look at the tuna or broccoli or eggplant or whatever casserole and said, "Where's supper?" Mrs. G. Perry never strayed again. See what I mean about getting your bluff in on a woman in the first place?

Now here is something about fish. Never eat any fish that is not fried hard as a shoe sole. If you ever start eating poached fish and baked fish and broiled fish, it's over for you, Junior. You are going to find yourself eating a lot of orange roughy floating in watery oleo. Now, what I am about to tell you is the God's truth if I ever told it. Orange roughy is a made-up name. A name made up for the American market. The real name of that fish is New Zealand Slimehead. I swear it! It's just like that damned Kiwi fruit. The real name of that unappetizing little green yuppie lump is "Chinese gooseberry." Next time you go out fancy and see a pile of grapes from Chile, out-of-season watermelon from Mexico, and processed cheese from South Georgia, all lying nestled up to a pile of crosscut Kiwi fruit, remember that its real name is Chinese gooseberry.

But I am getting off the subject here. Let's get back to marital strategies that can sink a marriage like the *Lusitania* going down in the North Atlantic in 19 and 17. Take finger sandwiches. You know the kind where they cut the crust off—well, you don't want to get me started on that! Now, here is my advice when you go to a party and come up on a plate of finger sandwiches: eat all of them. Then say, "What are these little things; a hungry fellow could eat 100 of 'em." Your wife will sink through the floor. If you are not married, this is a good test for a girl friend. If she doesn't blanch, you may have found a keeper—unless, of course, her name is Blanche, which raises a whole 'nother can of worms—or as my late Daddy always said, "Well, that makes the cheese more binding, don't it?"

Now talking about cheese. You know they always serve for-eign-made cheese at the toniest parties. When you see a cheese tray next time you are out for a delightful evening with the Gotrocks family, walk over to the Brie and cut yourself a big old pie-sized slice and eat it out of your hand. Then say in a loud voice, "What kind of pie *is* this? That crust tastes like waxed cardboard." This is guaranteed to divide the ewes from the nannies.

At receptions and dress-up parties, never take one of those little old plates that they put on the table to keep you from eating enough. Just drift around the table and graze. Pick up stuff in your hand and lean way over the table to eat it. Graze like a Red Angus Bull in a bed of crimson clover. Keep circling the table, round and round and round. You will finally get full if the finger food holds out. But then all food is finger food for a real man, right? When the hostess offers you a cup of punch, take it and drink it down! Gulp it down like those athletes on the Gator Aid commercials. Drink it and hold out your cup for more, and keep doing this till you have made a serious dent in the punch bowl. If you are at a Christmas party and the punch is eggnog, all the better. Good eggnog—with lots of nog—will loosen you up so you can turn a rich neighbor's Christmas party into a Delta House food riot.

It's all right to eat quiche if you don't call it that. Call it a scrambled egg pie and eat it over the sink when you can. Women hate to have a Quiche Lorraine called a plate pie. But it is. I say if a thing has a crust like a pie, crumbles like a pie, and eats like a pie, it *is* a pie. I rest my case on that. Speaking of French stuff, you may someday be invited somewhere and be served crepes. Don't call them that. Say to your hostess, "Boy these are good. I didn't know they made a sweet enchilada." If your wife hammers you with her elbow and says it's a crepe, say in a loud voice, "What are you saying—crap or crape?"

Now it is unlikely that you will ever be invited where they have finger bowls. I mean if you live here where the fanciest kind of food is barbecue, I call that prima facie evidence that you are not ever going to be invited to someplace where they have finger bowls. But just in case, here is a guaranteed strategy for marital revenge. As soon as these little bowls are put on the table and before anybody has a chance to dip a digit in one, pick yours up and drink from it. I don't mean sip at it. Pick it up and drain it down; then eat the lemon slice and say in a loud voice to your hostess, "Boy, y'all think of everything. I hope y'all got pie for dessert." You know they won't have. Rich people that use finger bowls don't eat common pie. They eat frappes and glacés and sorbets. But you *know* you do not want to get me started on the subject of pie!

All right, I just have one more thing to help you old boys on your way to single bliss in Man Town. When you finish eating, if you are in a nice place like the Old Warsaw or the French Room of the Adolphus Hotel, lean back and say in a loud and satisfied voice, "I-God, I feel like everybody's eat." I know this works. I mean, I *know.* Years ago, when my children were young, my little family of four took my late, sainted Aunt Rene on a tour of the West. We went to Bandolier, to Mesa Verde, and to the Grand Canyon in a Ford station wagon that used a quart of oil every 300 miles. But, God knows, you don't want to get me started on that! Anyhow, we ate in Denny's after Denny's after Denny's, and it was always the same thing. When she got full, my Aunt Rene—Alabama born and bred and cultured—would *always* say, "I feel like everybody's eat." My impressionable and embarrassable sons would cringe and bend low for fear that someday, somewhere, somebody among these crowds of strangers would pick them out of the crowd and remember that they had a Great Aunt Rene who felt like "everybody had eat." Years passed, my Aunt Rene died, my children grew into middle-aged men, and I forgot about my Aunt Rene's exit line. But once, when a new wife and I were dining—not eating, but dining out—with my younger son and his soon-to-be ex-wife, he suddenly leaned back and said in a voice that chilled the Pyramid Room, "I-God, I feel like everybody's eat." I nearly died laughing. What those two women did won't bear talking about in the presence of senior citizens and widder women. But I can tell you this, if my son had had children, he would still be paying child support.

Oh, I almost forgot another important point: *Never use a napkin* to wipe your mouth with. I know that Frederick the Great or

Alexander the Great or Alfred the Great or Ivan the Terrible or somebody put those brass buttons on military sleeves to break soldiers from wiping their noses on their sleeves. Well, you don't have buttons on the back of your hands, so use them to wipe stuff from off your face. Here's what you do with your napkin: tuck it under your chin like old Al Capone and Don Corleone in the movies did. There is a reason: real men slop stuff. And since neckties cost $3.00 or $4.00 apiece, you can save a lot of money by tucking your napkin under your chin. And women hate it. I mean *they hate it.*

Now, all my bits of advice will put your new lawfully wedded wife to the acid test. And if you do it early enough, you may get out of ever having to pay child support. But, Lord knows, don't get me started on that. I could write a damned book on that.

Contributors

Francis Edward Abernethy is a professor of English at Stephen F. Austin State University, the Executive Secretary and Editor of the Texas Folklore Society since 1971, and a member of the Texas Institute of Letters. His books include *Singin' Texas*, *Legends of Texas' Heroic Age* and two volumes of a history of the Texas Folklore Society, in addition to editing numerous Texas Folklore Society Publications. He plays the bass fiddle in the East Texas String Ensemble of Nacogdoches.

Phyllis Bridges has been a member of the English faculty at Texas Women's University since 1972. She has also served as Dean of the Graduate School, Assistant to the President, and interim Vice President for Academic Affairs. In 1990 she served as chairman of the Southwest American Culture Association and the Australian Literature Section of the South Central Modern Language Association. She has also been a member of the board of the Australian and American Fiction and Film Foundation. Presently she is serving as President of the Southwest American Culture Association and Popular Culture Association

Rebecca E. Cornell is a native Texan who received a B.A. in history from Texas Tech University and a B.A. in Spanish from Angelo State University. She is a docent for the San Angelo Museum of Fine Arts, the past President of the San Angelo Junior League, a member of Sigma Delta Pi-National Spanish Honorary, secretary of the Fort Concho Museum Board, and co-author of *Some of My Best Friends are Green.*

Kenneth W. Davis, Professor Emeritus of English at Texas Tech University, is now the university's Liaison Officer for Retired Faculty and Staff. He continues to write about folklore and literature of the Southwest, participate in conferences, review books, and work as a consultant to university and private presses.

Born in 1951, **Patrick Dearen** grew up in Sterling City, Texas, and earned a journalism degree from the University of Texas at Austin. A former award-winning reporter for two West Texas daily newspapers, and a current member of Western Writers of America, he is the author of eight books. His newest book is *A Cowboy of the Pecos* (Republic of Texas Press, 1997), the story of cowboying on the Pecos River from the earliest trail drive days through the 1920s. His four novels include *The Illegal Man* (1981), and *When Cowboys Die* (1994), a finalist for Western Writers of America's Spur Award for best western novel. He also scripted and co-produced the documentary video *Graveyard of the West: The Pecos River of Texas Where Myth Meets History* (1993). He worked five years with the mentally retarded, and is an avid backpacker, canoeist, and ragtime pianist. He lives in Midland, Texas, with his wife Mary and son Wesley.

Robert J. (Jack) Duncan is a former president of and frequent contributor to the Texas Folklore Society. He is a long-time resident of McKinney, a free-lance writer and a manager at Richmond College in Dallas. Bill Porterfield once called him "a roothog who digs up the damnedest truffles."

Cynthia Fisher of Nacogdoches was born in Afghanistan, lived her early years in the Bahamas and on Indian reservations in Washington State and Oklahoma. She received a Basic Art Certificate from the Art Instruction Schools of Minneapolis, Minnesota, before returning to SFA as an art student. As a full-time single parent and part-time grounds keeper, Cynthia still finds time to draw. Her subject matter ranges from plants to animals, people to buildings. Her finepoint inkwork reflects a keen eye for detail, perspective, and realism.

Chris Goertzen studied ethnomusicology and music history at the University of Illinois and has been exploring topics that mix the two fields since. He has taught in a number of places—just now, he's working at Kenyon College in Ohio—but looks forward to coming home to Texas someday.

Joe S. Graham was born and raised on ranches in the Big Bend of West Texas. He received his bachelor's degree from Texas A&M University at College Station, his master's degree from Brigham Young University, and his Ph.D. from the University of Texas at Austin. He has taught at UTEP, Sul Ross State University, Texas A&M University at College Station, and Texas A&M University at Kingsville. He published nine books, including *El Rancho in South Texas: Continuity and Change from 1750* and edited the TFS Publication, *Hecho en Tejas: Texas-Mexican Folk Arts and Crafts*. His primary interest is Mexican-American folklore, including folk medicine, folk narratives, folk architecture, vaquero equipment, and other elements of traditional culture.

Jim Harris is a poet and teacher who has taught English at New Mexico Junior College in Hobbs, New Mexico, for several years. He is a past president of the Texas Folklore Society and has published several articles in TFS publications on such subjects as cockfighting and oil field humor. In 1989 he was named a New Mexico Eminent Scholar. He is a photographer, operates Hawk Press, and writes a weekly column called "The Southwest" for the *Hobbs News-Sun*. He is the husband of Mary and the father of Hawk.

James Ward Lee has eaten over sinks in Alabama, Tennessee, Arkansas, Texas, the Territory of Hawaii, and the U.S. Trust Territory of the Pacific. A past president of the Texas Folklore Society and the Society's favorite lecturer, Lee has taught English at the University of North Texas for forty years. He is a member of the Texas Institute of Letters. His books include *Texas, My Texas* and *1941: Texas Goes to War*.

John Lightfoot grew up in Comanche, Texas, and has lived in Dublin, Waco, the north end of the Rio Grande Valley, Lubbock, Beaumont, and Brazosport. He studied English at Tarleton State, Baylor, and Texas Tech and has taught at Pan American, Texas Tech, and Brazosport College. He was a newspaper reporter/editor in Beaumont from 1974–77 and the public relations director at Brazosport College from 1977–92.

Ernestine Sewell Linck is a retired professor of English from the University of Texas at Arlington. Her latest books are *The Amazing Etta Booth Mayo, How the Cimarron River Got Its Name and Other Stories about Coffee,* and *Eats: A Folk History of Texas Foods,* winner of the Texas Institute of Letters Carr P. Collins $5000 award for 1990. Forthcoming are "One Woman's Trail of Tears," an update of Larry McMurtry's work for a revised *Literary History of the American West*, entries in *Texas Women's Writers*, and *Laughing Aloud Allowed*. She is speaker for the Northeast Texas Library Association, and member of Western Writers of America, Women Writing the West, Westerners International, Texas historical organizations, and past president of the Texas Folklore Society. Currently she studies music and is "printer's devil" at her husband Charles Linck's Cow Hill Press.

Robert Nieman was born in McLeansboro Illinois, attended the University of Tennessee, and moved to Longview in 1978.

He is owner and president of Trailer Delivery Service Inc., a nationwide trucking company. He is a member of the History Club of East Texas, National Outlaw-Lawman Historical Association, New London Museum, Texas Ranger Association Foundation, and Texas Ranger Heritage Society. He was commissioned by the Texas Ranger Association Foundation to videotape Texas Ranger oral histories, has in excess of thirty-five hours of videotaped oral history on file with survivors of the New London school explosion, and has more than fifteen hours of video tape on the East Texas boom years.

Charlie Oden retired as Chief Train Dispatcher from the Espee (Southern Pacific Railroad) in 1981 after forty-one plus years of service on its four Texas and Louisiana Divisions. He retired from a tax practice in 1993. Presently living in Austin, he is a member of the Houston Folklore Society, the Texas Folklore Society, Story Tellers' Guild, the 36th Infantry (The Texas Division) Association, and the 2nd Infantry (Indianhead) Division Association. He was a contributor to the Texas Folklore Society books *Hoein' the Short Rows* and *Texas Toys and Games.*

Jackson Gershom Pinkerton, who is called "J. G." for short, claims Junction, Texas, as his hometown. He served in the U. S. Navy in World War II, graduated from The University of Texas with a BBA, and worked for Texasgulf, Inc. J. G. discovered the world of storytelling in 1982, when he read an article in an airline's inflight magazine describing the renaissance of storytelling in America. J. G. launched his second career, this time as freelance storyteller, "J. G. 'Paw-Paw' Pinkerton." He travels extensively telling stories and teaching and promoting the art of storytelling. "Paw-Paw's" research on Harley Sadler came about because he was working on a story "about the time I dreamed of running away from home and joining Harley Sadler's Tent Show."

Dennis E. Read has a BA in Library Science with a minor in history. He has a MLS from the University of Oklahoma. He has also done graduate work at Mississippi College and Northern Illiniois University. He is currently Director of Learning Resources at LeTourneau University in Longview. He is a member of the East Texas History Club, Civil War Society, and Texas Oral History Association. He has made several presentations and has written on the subject of the Civil War and oral history.

Joyce Gibson Roach grew up in Jacksboro, Texas, and has never gotten over it, nor is she trying. Her rural roots provide much of the inspiration for her writing in fiction, non-fiction, musical folk-drama and humorous prose. Currently she speaks, writes, and teaches about folklore, Texas, and the Southwest. On the adjunct English faculty at Texas Christian University in Fort Worth, she specializes in western American literature. She writes a folklore column for the *Fort Worth Star Telegram NE*, and is an invited speaker for the Texas Council for the Humanities' "Explorations '97" series. Joyce is a three-time Spur Award winner from Western Writers of America for *The Cowgirls*, non-fiction book (UNT Press); "A High Toned Woman," short non-fiction (*Hoein' the Short Rows*, UNT Press); "Just As I Am," short fiction (*Women of the West*, Doubleday). She and co-author, Ernestine Sewell Linck, shared the Carr P. Collins non-fiction book prize from the Texas Institute of Letters for *Eats: A Folk History of Texas Foods* (TCU Press). She is a member of the Texas Institute of Letters, Fellow of Texas State Historical Association and Fellow of the Clements Center for Southwest Studies.

Jan Roush is an associate professor of English at Utah State University where she teaches folklore and writing. She has a doctorate in composition and rhetoric from Texas A&M, Commerce. Formerly the director of the Writing Center and Computer Lab, she now serves as the technology liaison for faculty. Her research interests focus on the use of stories in establishing a community's identity.

Rhett Rushing, currently a graduate student in folklore at Indiana University, received his BA from Texas A&M University and his MA in Folklore from Western Kentucky University. Rhett has been a junior high and high school teacher, a frequent contributor to the Society's meetings, and plans to frame his dissertation by first teaching a community of retirees how to collect and preserve their own family folklore and history. His interests in community outreach and service learning ("give before taking") have clearly shaped the way he undertakes folklore fieldwork.

Richard Stewart lives in Beaumont where he is chief of the *Houston Chronicle*'s East Texas Bureau. An amateur historian, he makes his living traveling the state in search of the new and unusual. He's witnessed oxen clear ground for a new mobile home in East Texas, interviewed robbers and royalty, and proudly flaunts his prized possession—a key to the cemetery in which outlaw Clyde Barrow is buried.

Allan Turner, a veteran newspaper editor and reporter, is a Houston-based roving state reporter for the *Houston Chronicle*. A student of the South, he has for decades documented on film and tape the ethnic music and oral history of Texas and Louisiana. His work has been in the archives of the Center for American History, University of Texas, Austin.

Ken Untiedt has undergraduate degrees in criminal justice and English, and he is completing a Master's degree in American literature at Texas Tech University. He lives with his wife and three children in Lubbock, where he is employed as a City of Lubbock police officer. He is interested in all aspects of folklore associated with law enforcement, especially lore about legendary peace officers depicted in fiction about the American West.

James W. Winfrey graduated in mechanical engineering at The University of Texas, where he was an English literature student of J. Frank Dobie during 1926–27. Mr. Dobie influenced him to join the Texas Folklore Society in 1934. He contributed "Oil Patch Talk" to TFS Publication No. XIX, *From Hell to Breakfast* in 1944, and to *Texas Toys and Games*, Publication XLVIII, in 1989. He is a registered Professional Engineer and worked as a Petroleum Production Engineer for forty years, living in oil field camps for fourteen years.

Index